Data Analytics with Hadoop
An Introduction for Data Scientists

Benjamin Bengfort and Jenny Kim

Beijing · Boston · Farnham · Sebastopol · Tokyo

Data Analytics with Hadoop

by Benjamin Bengfort and Jenny Kim

Published by O'Reilly Media, Inc., 1005 Gravenstein Highway North, Sebastopol, CA 95472.

O'Reilly books may be purchased for educational, business, or sales promotional use. Online editions are also available for most titles (*http://safaribooksonline.com*). For more information, contact our corporate/institutional sales department: 800-998-9938 or *corporate@oreilly.com*.

Editor: Nicole Tache	**Indexer:** WordCo Indexing Services
Production Editor: Melanie Yarbrough	**Interior Designer:** David Futato
Copyeditor: Colleen Toporek	**Cover Designer:** Randy Comer
Proofreader: Jasmine Kwityn	**Illustrator:** Rebecca Demarest

June 2016:   First Edition

Revision History for the First Edition

2016-05-25:   First Release

See *http://oreilly.com/catalog/errata.csp?isbn=9781491913703* for release details.

978-1-491-91370-3

[LSI]

Table of Contents

Part II.   Workflows and Tools for Big Data Science

Preface

The term *big data* has come into vogue for an exciting new set of tools and techniques for modern, data-powered applications that are changing the way the world is computing in novel ways. Much to the statistician's chagrin, this ubiquitous term seems to be liberally applied to include the application of well-known statistical techniques on large datasets for predictive purposes. Although big data is now officially a buzzword, the fact is that modern, distributed computation techniques are enabling analyses of datasets far larger than those typically examined in the past, with stunning results.

Distributed computing alone, however, does not directly lead to data science. Through the combination of rapidly increasing datasets generated from the Internet and the observation that these data sets are able to power predictive models ("more data is better than better algorithms"[1]), data products have become a new economic paradigm. Stunning successes of data modeling across large heterogeneous datasets—for example, Nate Silver's seemingly magical ability to predict the 2008 election using big data techniques—has led to a general acknowledgment of the value of data science, and has brought a wide variety of practitioners to the field.

Hadoop has evolved from a cluster-computing abstraction to an operating system for big data by providing a framework for distributed data storage and parallel computation. Spark has built upon those ideas and made cluster computing more accessible to data scientists. However, data scientists and analysts new to distributed computing may feel that these tools are *programmer* oriented rather than *analytically* oriented. This is because a fundamental shift needs to occur in thinking about how we manage and compute upon data in a *parallel* fashion instead of a sequential one.

This book is intended to prepare data scientists for that shift in thinking by providing an overview of cluster computing and analytics in a *readable*, straightforward fashion.

---

1 Anand Rajaraman, *"More data usually beats better algorithms"* (*http://anand.typepad.com/datawocky/2008/03/ more-data-usual.html*), Datawocky, March 24, 2008.

We will introduce most of the concepts, tools, and techniques involved with distributed computing for data analysis and provide a path for deeper dives into specific topics areas.

What to Expect from This Book

This book is not an exhaustive compendium on Hadoop (see Tom White's excellent *Hadoop: The Definitive Guide* for that) or an introduction to Spark (we instead point you to Holden Karau et al.'s *Learning Spark*), and is certainly not meant to teach the operational aspects of distributed computing. Instead, we offer a survey of the Hadoop ecosystem and distributed computation intended to arm data scientists, statisticians, programmers, and folks who are interested in Hadoop (but whose current knowledge of it is just enough to make them dangerous). We hope that you will use this book as a guide as you dip your toes into the world of Hadoop and find the tools and techniques that interest you the most, be it Spark, Hive, machine learning, ETL (extract, transform, and load) operations, relational databases, or one of the other many topics related to cluster computing.

Who This Book Is For

Data science is often erroneously conflated with big data, and while many machine learning model families do require large datasets in order to be widely generalizable, even small datasets can provide a pattern recognition punch. For that reason, most of the focus of data science software literature is on corpora or datasets that are easily analyzable on a single machine (especially machines with many gigabytes of memory). Although big data and data science are well suited to work in concert with each other, computing literature has separated them up until now.

This book intends to fill in the gap by writing to an audience of data scientists. It will introduce you to the world of clustered computing and analytics with Hadoop, from a data science perspective. The focus will not be on deployment, operations, or software development, but rather on common analyses, data warehousing techniques, and higher-order data workflows.

So who are data scientists? We expect that a data scientist is a software developer with strong statistical skills or a statistician with strong software development skills. Typically, our data teams are composed of three types of data scientists: data engineers, data analysts, and domain experts.

Data engineers are programmers or computer scientists who can build or utilize advanced computing systems. They typically program in Python, Java, or Scala and are familiar with Linux, servers, networking, databases, and application deployment. For those data engineers reading this book, we expect that you're accustomed to the difficulties of programming multi-process code as well as the challenges of data wrangling and numeric computation. We hope that after reading this book you'll have a better understanding of deploying your programs across a cluster and handling much larger datasets than can be processed by a single computer in a sufficient amount of time.

Data analysts focus primarily on the statistical modeling and exploration of data. They typically use R, Python, or Julia in their day-to-day work, and should be familiar with data mining and machine learning techniques, including regressions, clustering, and classification problems. Data analysts have probably dealt with larger datasets through sampling. We hope that in this book we can show statistical techniques that take advantage of much larger populations of data than were accessible before— allowing the construction of models that have depth as well as breadth in their predictive ability.

Finally, *domain experts* are those influential, business-oriented members of a team that understand deeply the types of data and problems that are encountered. They understand the specific challenges of their data and are looking for better ways to make the data productive to solve new challenges. We hope that our book will give them an idea about how to make business decisions that add flexibility to current data workflows as well as to understand how general computation frameworks might be leveraged to specific domain challenges.

How to Read This Book

Hadoop is now over 10 years old, a very long time in technology terms. Moore's law has still not yet slowed down, and whereas 10 years ago the use of an economic cluster of machines was far simpler in data center terms than programming for super computers, those same economic servers are now approximately 32 times more powerful, and the cost of in-memory computing has gone way down. Hadoop has become an operating system for big data, allowing a variety of computational frameworks from graph processing to SQL-like querying to streaming. This presents a significant challenge to those who are interested in learning about Hadoop—where to start?

We set a very low page limit on this book for a reason: to cover a lot of ground as briefly as possible. We hope that you will read this book in two ways: either as a short, cover-to-cover read that will serve as a broad introduction to Hadoop and distributed data analytics, or by selecting chapters of interest as a preliminary step to doing a deep dive. The purpose of this book is to be *accessible*. We chose simple examples to expose ideas in code, not necessarily for the reader to implement and run themselves. This book should be a guidebook to the world of Hadoop and Spark, particularly for analytics.

Overview of Chapters

This book is intended to be a guided walk through of the Hadoop ecosystem, and as such we've laid out the book in two broad parts split across the halves of the book. Part I (Chapters 1–5) introduces distributed computing at a very high level, discussing *how* to run computations on a cluster. Part II (Chapters 6–10) focuses more specifically on tools and techniques that should be recognizable to data scientists, and intends to provide a *motivation* for a variety of analytics and large-scale data management. (Chapter 5 serves as a transition from the broad discussion of distributed computing to more specific tools and an implementation of the big data science pipeline.) The chapter break down is as follows:

Chapter 1, The Age of the Data Product
> We begin the book with an introduction to the types of applications that big data and data science produce together: data products. This chapter discusses the workflow behind creating data products and specifies how the sequential model of data analysis fits into the distributed computing realm.

Chapter 2, An Operating System for Big Data
> Here we provide an overview of the core concepts behind Hadoop and what makes cluster computing both beneficial and difficult. The Hadoop architecture is discussed in detail with a focus on both YARN and HDFS. Finally, this chapter discusses interacting with the distributed storage system in preparation for performing analytics on large datasets.

Chapter 3, A Framework for Python and Hadoop Streaming
> This chapter covers the fundamental programming abstraction for distributed computing: MapReduce. However, the MapReduce API is written in Java, a programming language that is not popular for data scientists. Therefore, this chapter focuses on how to write MapReduce jobs in Python with Hadoop Streaming.

Chapter 4, In-Memory Computing with Spark
> While understanding MapReduce is essential to understanding distributed computing and writing high-performance batch jobs such as ETL, day-to-day interaction and analysis on a Hadoop cluster is usually done with Spark. Here we introduce Spark and how to program Python Spark applications to run on YARN either in an interactive fashion using PySpark or in cluster mode.

Chapter 5, Distributed Analysis and Patterns
> In this chapter, we take a practical look at how to write distributed data analysis jobs through the presentation of design patterns and parallel analytical algorithms. Coming into this chapter you should understand the mechanics of writing Spark and MapReduce jobs and coming out of the chapter, you should feel comfortable actually implementing them.

Chapter 6, Data Mining and Warehousing

Here we present an introduction to data management, mining, and warehousing in a distributed context, particularly in relation to traditional database systems. This chapter will focus on Hadoop's most popular SQL-based querying engine, Hive, as well as its most popular NoSQL database, HBase. Data wrangling is the second step in the data science pipeline, but data needs somewhere to be ingested to—and this chapter explores how to manage very large datasets.

Chapter 7, Data Ingestion

Getting data into a distributed system for computation may actually be one of the biggest challenges given the magnitude of both the volume and velocity of data. This chapter explores ingestion techniques from relational databases using Sqoop as a bulk loading tool, as well as the more flexible Apache Flume for ingesting logs and other unstructured data from network sources.

Chapter 8, Analytics with Higher-Level APIs

Here we offer a review of higher-order tools for programming complex Hadoop and Spark applications, in particular with Apache Pig and Spark's DataFrames API. In Part I, we discussed the implementation of MapReduce and Spark for executing distributed jobs, and how to think of algorithms and data pipelines as data flows. Pig allows you to more easily describe the data flows without actually implementing the low-level details in MapReduce. Spark provides integrated modules that provide the ability to seamlessly mix procedural processing with relational queries and open the door to powerful analytic customizations.

Chapter 9, Machine Learning

Most of the benefits of big data are realized in a machine learning context: a greater variety of features and wider input space mean that pattern recognition techniques are much more effective and personalized. This chapter introduces classification, clustering, and collaborative filtering. Rather than discuss modeling in detail, we will instead get you started on scalable learning techniques using Spark's MLlib.

Chapter 10, Summary: Doing Distributed Data Science

To conclude, we present a summary of doing distributed data science as a complete view: integrating the tools and techniques that were discussed in isolation in the previous chapters. Data science is not a single activity but rather a lifecycle that involves data ingestion, wrangling, modeling, computation, and operationalization. This chapter discusses architectures and workflows for doing distributed data science at a 20,000-foot view.

Appendix A, Creating a Hadoop Pseudo-Distributed Development Environment

This appendix serves as a guide to setting up a development environment on your local machine in order to program distributed jobs. If you don't have a cluster available to you, this guide is essential in order to prepare to run the examples provided in the book.

Appendix B, Installing Hadoop Ecosystem Products
An extension to the guide found in Appendix A, this appendix offers instructions for installing the many ecosystem tools and products that we discuss in the book. Although a common methodology for installing services is proposed in Appendix A, this appendix specifically looks at gotchas and caveats for installing the services to run the examples you will find as you read.

As you can see, this is a lot of topics to cover in such a short book! We hope that we have said enough to leave you intrigued and to follow on for more!

Programming and Code Examples

As the distributed computing aspects of Hadoop have become more mature and better integrated, there has been a shift from the computer science aspects of parallelism toward providing a richer analytical experience. For example, the newest member of the big data ecosystem, Spark, exposes programming APIs in four languages to allow easier adoption by data scientists who are used to tools such as data frames, interactive notebooks, and interpreted languages. Hive and SparkSQL provide another familiar domain-specific language (DSL) in the form of a SQL syntax specifically for querying data on a distributed cluster.

Because our audience is a wide array of data scientists, we have chosen to implement as many of our examples as possible in Python. Python is a general-purpose programming language that has found a home in the data science community due to rich analytical packages such as Pandas and Scikit-Learn. Unfortunately, the primary Hadoop APIs are usually in Java, and we've had to jump through some hoops to provide Python examples, but for the most part we've been able to expose the ideas in a practical fashion. Therefore, code in this book will either be MapReduce using Python and Hadoop Streaming, Spark with the PySpark API, or SQL when discussing Hive or Spark SQL. We hope that this will mean a more concise and accessible read for a more general audience.

GitHub Repository

The code examples found in this book can be found as complete, executable examples on our GitHub repository (*https://github.com/bbengfort/hadoop-fundamentals*). This repository also contains code from our video tutorial on Hadoop, *Hadoop Fundamentals for Data Scientists* (O'Reilly).

Due to the fact that examples are printed, we may have taken shortcuts or omitted details from the code presented in the book in order to provide a clearer explanation of what is going on. For example, generally speaking, import statements are omitted.

This means that simple copy and paste may not work. However, by going to the examples in the repository complete, working code is provided with comments that discuss what is happening.

Also note that the repository is kept up to date; check the *README* to find code and other changes that have occurred. You can of course fork the repository and modify the code for execution in your own environment—we strongly encourage you to do so!

Executing Distributed Jobs

Hadoop developers often use a "single node cluster" in "pseudo-distributed mode" to perform development tasks. This is usually a virtual machine running a virtual server environment, which runs the various Hadoop daemons. Access to this VM can be accomplished with SSH from your main development box, just like you'd access a Hadoop cluster. In order to create a virtual environment, you need some sort of virtualization software, such as VirtualBox (*https://www.virtualbox.org*), VMWare (*http://www.vmware.com/products/desktop-virtualization*), or Parallels (*http://www.parallels.com*).

Appendix A discusses how to set up an Ubuntu x64 virtual machine with Hadoop, Hive, and Spark in pseudo-distributed mode. Alternatively, distributions of Hadoop such as Cloudera or Hortonworks will also provide a preconfigured virtual environment for you to use. If you have a target environment that you want to use, then we recommend downloading that virtual machine environment. Otherwise, if you're attempting to learn more about Hadoop operations, configure it yourself!

We should also note that because Hadoop clusters run on open source software, familiarity with Linux and the command line are required. The virtual machines discussed here are all usually accessed from the command line, and many of the examples in this book describe interactions with Hadoop, Spark, Hive, and other tools from the command line. This is one of the primary reasons that analysts avoid using these tools—however, learning the command line is a skill that will serve you well; it's not too scary, and we suggest you do it!

Permissions and Citation

This book is here to help you get your job done. In general, if example code is offered with this book, you may use it in your programs and documentation. You do not need to contact us for permission unless you're reproducing a significant portion of the code. For example, writing a program that uses several chunks of code from this book does not require permission. Selling or distributing a CD-ROM of examples from O'Reilly books does require permission. Answering a question by citing this book and quoting example code does not require permission. Incorporating a significant amount of example code from this book into your product's documentation does require permission.

We appreciate, but do not require, attribution. An attribution usually includes the title, author, publisher, and ISBN. For example: "*Data Analytics with Hadoop* by Benjamin Bengfort and Jenny Kim (O'Reilly). Copyright 2016 Benjamin Bengfort and Jenny Kim, 978-1-491-91370-3."

If you feel your use of code examples falls outside fair use or the permission given above, feel free to contact us at *permissions@oreilly.com*.

Feedback and How to Contact Us

To comment or ask technical questions about this book, send email to *bookquestions@oreilly.com*.

We recognize that tools and technologies change rapidly, particularly in the big data domain. Unfortunately, it is difficult to keep a book (especially a print version) at pace. We hope that this book will continue to serve you well into the future, however, if you've noticed a change that breaks an example or an issue in the code, get in touch with us to let us know!

The best method to get in contact with us about code or examples is to leave a note in the form of an issue at Hadoop Fundamentals Issues on GitHub (*https://github.com/bbengfort/hadoop-fundamentals/issues/*). Alternatively, feel free to send us an email at *hadoopfundamentals@gmail.com*. We'll respond as soon as we can, and we really appreciate positive, constructive feedback!

Safari® Books Online

 *Safari Books Online* is an on-demand digital library that delivers expert content in both book and video form from the world's leading authors in technology and business.

Technology professionals, software developers, web designers, and business and creative professionals use Safari Books Online as their primary resource for research, problem solving, learning, and certification training.

Safari Books Online offers a range of plans and pricing for enterprise, government, education, and individuals.

Members have access to thousands of books, training videos, and prepublication manuscripts in one fully searchable database from publishers like O'Reilly Media, Prentice Hall Professional, Addison-Wesley Professional, Microsoft Press, Sams, Que, Peachpit Press, Focal Press, Cisco Press, John Wiley & Sons, Syngress, Morgan Kaufmann, IBM Redbooks, Packt, Adobe Press, FT Press, Apress, Manning, New Riders, McGraw-Hill, Jones & Bartlett, Course Technology, and hundreds more. For more information about Safari Books Online, please visit us online.

How to Contact Us

Please address comments and questions concerning this book to the publisher:

O'Reilly Media, Inc.
1005 Gravenstein Highway North
Sebastopol, CA 95472
800-998-9938 (in the United States or Canada)
707-829-0515 (international or local)
707-829-0104 (fax)

We have a web page for this book, where we list errata, examples, and any additional information. You can access this page at *http://bit.ly/data-analytics-with-hadoop*.

To comment or ask technical questions about this book, send email to *bookquestions@oreilly.com*.

For more information about our books, courses, conferences, and news, see our website at *http://www.oreilly.com*.

Find us on Facebook: *http://facebook.com/oreilly*

Follow us on Twitter: *http://twitter.com/oreillymedia*

Watch us on YouTube: *http://www.youtube.com/oreillymedia*

Acknowledgments

We would like to thank the reviewers who tirelessly offered constructive feedback and criticism on the book throughout the rather long process of development. Thanks to Marck Vaisman, who read the book from the perspective of teaching Hadoop to data scientists. A very special thanks to Konstantinos Xirogiannopoulos, who—despite his busy research schedule—volunteered his time to provide clear, helpful, and above all, positive comments that were a delight to receive.

We would also like to thank our patient, persistent, and tireless editors at O'Reilly. We started the project with Meghan Blanchette who guided us through a series of misstarts on the project. She stuck with us, but unfortunately our project outlasted her time at O'Reilly and she moved on to bigger and better things. We were especially glad, therefore, when Nicole Tache stepped into her shoes and managed to shepherd us back on track. Nicole took us to the end, and without her, this book would not have happened; she has a special knack for sending welcome emails at critical points that get the job done. Everyone at O'Reilly was wonderful to work with, and we'd also like to mention Marie Beaugureau, Amy Jollymore, Ben Lorica, and Mike Loukides, who gave advice and encouragement.

Here in DC, we were supported in an offline fashion by the crew at District Data Labs, who deserve a special shout out, especially Tony Ojeda, Rebecca Bilbro, Allen Leis, and Selma Gomez Orr. They supported our book in a variety of ways, including being the first to purchase the early release, offering feedback, reviewing code, and generally wondering when it would be done, encouraging us to get back to writing!

This book would not have been possible without the contributions of the amazing people in the Hadoop community, many of whom Jenny has the incredible privilege of working alongside every day at Cloudera. Special thanks to the Hue team; the dedication and passion they bring to providing the best Hadoop user experience around is truly extraordinary and inspiring.

To our families and especially our parents, Randy and Lily Bengfort and Wung and Namoak Kim, thank you for your endless encouragement, love, and support. Our parents have instilled in us a mutual zeal for learning and exploration, which has sent us down more than a few rabbit holes, but they also cultivated in us a shared tenacity and perseverance to always find our way to the other end.

Finally, to our spouses—thanks, Patrick and Jacquelyn, for sticking with us. One of us may have said at some point "my marriage wouldn't survive another book." Certainly, in the final stages of the writing process, neither of them was thrilled to hear we were still plugging away. Nonetheless, it wouldn't have gotten done without them (our book wouldn't have survived without our marriages). Patrick and Jacquelyn offered friendly winks and waves as we were on video calls working out details and doing rewrites. They even read portions, offered advice, and were generally helpful in all ways. Neither of us were book authors before this, and we weren't sure what we were getting into. Now that we know, we're so glad they stuck by us.

## PART I

Introduction to Distributed Computing

The first part of *Data Analytics with Hadoop* introduces distributed computing for big data using Hadoop. Chapter 1 motivates the need for distributed computing in order to build data products and discusses the primary workflow and opportunity for using Hadoop for data science. Chapter 2 then dives into the technical details of the requirements for distributed storage and computation and explains how Hadoop is an operating system for big data. Chapters 3 and 4 introduce distributed programming using the MapReduce and Spark frameworks, respectively. Finally, Chapter 5 explores typical computations and patterns in both MapReduce and Spark from the perspective of a data scientist doing analytics on large datasets.

CHAPTER 1

The Age of the Data Product

We are living through an information revolution. Like any economic revolution, it has had a transformative effect on society, academia, and business. The present revolution, driven as it is by networked communication systems and the Internet, is unique in that it has created a surplus of a valuable new material—data—and transformed us all into both consumers and producers. The sheer amount of data being generated is tremendous. Data increasingly affects every aspect of our lives, from the food we eat, to our social interactions, to the way we work and play. In turn, we have developed a reasonable expectation for products and services that are highly personalized and finely tuned to our bodies, our lives, and our businesses, creating a market for a new information technology—*the data product*.

The rapid and agile combination of surplus datasets with machine learning algorithms has changed the way that people interact with everyday things and one another because they so often lead to immediate and novel results. Indeed, the buzzword trends surrounding "big data" are related to the seemingly inexhaustible innovation that is available due to the large number of models and data sources.

Data products are created with data science workflows, specifically through the application of models, usually predictive or inferential, to a domain-specific dataset. While the potential for innovation is great, the scientific or experimental mindset that is required to discover data sources and correctly model or mine patterns is not typically taught to programmers or analysts. Indeed, it is for this reason that it's cool to hire PhDs again—they have the required analytical and experimental training that, when coupled with programming foo, leads almost immediately to data science expertise. Of course, we can't all be PhDs. Instead, this book presents a pedagogical model for doing data science at scale with Hadoop, and serves as a foundation for architecting applications that are, or can become, data products.

What Is a Data Product?

The traditional answer to this question is usually "any application that combines data and algorithms."[1] But frankly, if you're writing software and you're not combining data with algorithms, then what are you doing? After all, data is the currency of programming! More specifically, we might say that a data product is the combination of data with statistical algorithms that are used for inference or prediction. Many data scientists are also statisticians, and statistical methodologies are central to data science.

Armed with this definition, you could cite Amazon recommendations as an example of a data product. Amazon examines items you've purchased, and based on similar purchase behavior of other users, makes recommendations. In this case, order history data is combined with recommendation algorithms to make predictions about what you might purchase in the future. You might also cite Facebook's "People You May Know" feature because this product "shows you people based on mutual friends, work and education information ... [and] many other factors"—essentially using the combination of social network data with graph algorithms to infer members of communities.

These examples are certainly revolutionary in their own domains of retail and social networking, but they don't necessarily seem different from other web applications. Indeed, defining data products as simply the combination of data with statistical algorithms seems to limit data products to single software instances (e.g., a web application), which hardly seems a revolutionary economic force. Although we might point to Google or others as large-scale economic forces, the combination of a web crawler gathering a massive HTML corpus with the PageRank algorithm alone does not create a data economy. We know what an important role search plays in economic activity, so something must be missing from this first definition.

Mike Loukides argues that a data product is not simply another name for a "data-driven app." Although blogs, ecommerce platforms, and most web and mobile apps rely on a database and data services such as RESTful APIs, they are merely using data. That alone does not make a data product. Instead, he defines a data product as follows:[2]

> A data application acquires its value from the data itself, and creates more data as a result. It's not just an application with data; it's a data product.

This is the revolution. A data product is an economic engine. It derives value from data and then produces more data, more value, in return. The data that it creates may

---

1 Hillary Mason and Chris Wiggins, "A Taxonomy of Data Science" (*http://bit.ly/taxonomy-of-data-science*), Dataists, September 25, 2010.

2 Mike Loukides, "What is Data Science?" (*http://oreil.ly/1Tl3h5S*), O'Reilly Radar, June 2, 2010.

fuel the generating product (we have finally achieved perpetual motion!) or it might lead to the creation of other data products that derive their value from that generated data. This is precisely what has led to the surplus of information and the resulting information revolution. More importantly, it is the *generative* effect that allows us to achieve better living through data, because more data products mean more data, which means even more data products, and so forth.

Armed with this more specific definition, we can go further to describe data products as systems that *learn from data*, are *self-adapting*, and are *broadly applicable*. Under this definition, the Nest thermostat is a data product. It derives its value from sensor data, adapts how it schedules heating and cooling, and causes new sensor observations to be collected that validate the adaptation. Autonomous vehicles such as those being produced by Stanford's Autonomous Driving Team also fall into this category. The team's machine vision and pilot behavior simulation are the result of algorithms, so when the vehicle is in motion, it produces more data in the form of navigation and sensor data that can be used to improve the driving platform. The advent of "quantified self," initiated by companies like Fitbit, Withings, and many others means that data affects human behavior; the smart grid means that data affects your utilities.

Data products are self-adapting, broadly applicable economic engines that derive their value from data and generate more data by influencing human behavior or by making inferences or predictions upon new data. Data products are not merely web applications and are rapidly becoming an essential component of almost every single domain of economic activity of the modern world. Because they are able to discover individual patterns in human activity, they drive decisions, whose resulting actions and influences are also recorded as new data.

Building Data Products at Scale with Hadoop

An oft-quoted tweet[3] by Josh Wills provides us with the following definition:

> Data Scientist (n.): Person who is better at statistics than any software engineer and better at software engineering than any statistician.

Certainly this fits in well with the idea that a data product is simply the combination of data with statistical algorithms. Both software engineering and statistical knowledge are essential to data science. However, in an economy that demands products that derive their value from data and generate new data in return, we should say instead that as data scientists, it is our job to build data products.

---

3 Available at *http://bit.ly/data-scientist-tweet*.

Harlan Harris provides more detail about the incarnation of data products:[4] they are built at the intersection of data, domain knowledge, software engineering, and analytics. Because data products are systems, they require an engineering skill set, usually in software, in order to build them. They are powered by data, so having data is a necessary requirement. Domain knowledge and analytics are the tools used to build the data engine, usually via experimentation, hence the "science" part of data science.

Because of the experimental methodology required, most data scientists will point to this typical analytical workflow: ingestion→wrangling→modeling→reporting and visualization. Yet this so-called *data science pipeline* is completely human-powered, augmented by the use of scripting languages like R and Python. Human knowledge and analytical skill are required at every step of the pipeline, which is intended to produce unique, non-generalizable results. Although this pipeline is a good starting place as a statistical and analytical framework, it does not meet the requirements of building data products, especially when the data from which value is being derived is too big for humans to deal with on a single laptop. As data becomes bigger, faster, and more variable, tools for automatically deriving insights without human intervention become far more important.

Leveraging Large Datasets

Intuitively, we recognize that more observations, meaning more data, are both a blessing and a curse. Humans have an excellent ability to see large-scale patterns—the metaphorical forests and clearings though the trees. The cognitive process of making sense of data involves high-level overviews of data, zooming into specified levels of detail, and moving back out again. Details in this process are anecdotal because fine granularity hampers our ability to understand—the metaphorical leaves, branches, or individual trees. More data can be both tightly tuned patterns and signals just as much as it can be noise and distractions.

Statistical methodologies give us the means to deal with simultaneously noisy and meaningful data, either by describing the data through aggregations and indices or inferentially by directly modeling the data. These techniques help us understand data at the cost of computational granularity—for example, rare events that might be interesting signals tend to be smoothed out of our models. Statistical techniques that attempt to take into account rare events leverage a computer's power to track multiple data points simultaneously, but require more computing resources. As such, statistical methods have traditionally taken a sampling approach to much larger datasets, wherein a smaller subset of the data is used as an estimated stand-in for the entire population. The larger the sample, the more likely that rare events are captured and included in the model.

---

4 Harlan Harris, "What Is a Data Product?" (*http://bit.ly/1EjYZog*), Analytics 2014 Blog, March 31, 2014.

As our ability to collect data has grown, so has the need for wider generalization. The past decade has seen the unprecedented rise of data science, fueled by the seemingly limitless combination of data and machine learning algorithms to produce truly novel results. Smart grids, quantified self, mobile technology, sensors, and connected homes require the application of personalized statistical inference. Scale comes not just from the amount of data, but from the number of facets that exploration requires —a forest view for individual trees.

Hadoop, an open source implementation of two papers written at Google that describe a complete distributed computing system, caused the age of big data. However, distributed computing and distributed database systems are not a new topic. Data warehouse systems as computationally powerful as Hadoop predate those papers in both industry and academia. What makes Hadoop different is partly the economics of data processing and partly the fact that Hadoop is a platform. However, what really makes Hadoop special is its timing—it was released right at the moment when technology needed a solution to do data analytics at scale, not just for population-level statistics, but also for individual generalizability and insight.

Hadoop for Data Products

Hadoop comes from big companies with big data challenges like Google, Facebook, and Yahoo; however, the reason Hadoop is important and the reason that you have picked up this book is because data challenges are no longer experienced only by the tech giants. Commercial and governmental entities from large to small: enterprises to startups, federal agencies to cities, and even individuals. Computing resources are also becoming ubiquitous and cheap—like the days of the PC when garage hackers innovated using available electronics, now small clusters of 10–20 nodes are being put together by startups to innovate in data exploration. Cloud computing resources such as Amazon EC2 and Google Compute Engine mean that data scientists have unprecedented on-demand, instant access to large-scale clusters for relatively little money and no data center management. Hadoop has made big data computing democratic and accessible, as illustrated by the following examples.

In 2011, Lady Gaga released her album *Born This Way*, an event that was broadcast by approximately 1.3 trillion social media impressions from "likes" to tweets to images and videos. Troy Carter, Lady Gaga's manager, immediately saw an opportunity to bring fans together, and in a massive data mining effort, managed to aggregate the millions of followers on Twitter and Facebook to a smaller, Lady Gaga–specific social network, LittleMonsters.com. The success of the site led to the foundation of Backplane (now Place), a tool for the generation and management of smaller, community-driven social networks.

More recently, in 2015, the New York City Police Department installed a $1.5 million dollar acoustic sensor network called ShotSpotter. The system is able to detect impulsive sounds that are related to explosions or gunfire, enabling rapid response by emergency responders to incidents in the Bronx. Importantly, this system is also smart enough to predict if there will be subsequent gunfire, and the approximate location of fire. Since 2009, the ShotSpotter system has discovered that over 75% of gunfire isn't reported to the police.

The quantified self movement has grown in popularity, and companies have been striving to make technological wearables, personal data collection, and even genetic sequencing widely available to consumers. As of 2012, the Affordable Care Act mandates that health plans implement standardized secure and confidential electronic exchange of health records. Connected homes and mobile devices, along with other personal sensors, are generating huge amounts of individual data, which among other things sparks concern about privacy. In 2015, researchers in the United Kingdom created the *Hub of All Things (HAT)*—a personalized data collection that deals with the question "who owns your data?" and provides a technical solution to the aggregation of personal data.

Large-scale, individual data analytics have traditionally been the realm of social networks like Facebook and Twitter, but thanks to Place, large social networks are now the provenance of individual brands or artists. Cities deal with unique data challenges, but whereas the generalization of a typical city could suffice for many analytics, new data challenges are arising that must be explored on a per-city basis (what is the affect of industry, shipping, or weather on the performance of an acoustic sensor network?). How do technologies provide value to consumers utilizing their personal health records without aggregation to others because of privacy issues? Can we make personal data mining for medical diagnosis secure?

In order to answer these questions on a routine and meaningful (individual) basis, a data product is required. Applications like Place, ShotSpotter, quantified self products, and HAT derive their value from data and generate new data by providing an application platform and decision-making resources for people to act upon. The value they provide is clear, but traditional software development workflows are not up to the challenges of dealing with massive datasets that are generated from trillions of likes and millions of microphones, or the avalanche of personal data that we generate on a daily basis. Big data workflows and Hadoop have made these applications possible and personalized.

The Data Science Pipeline and the Hadoop Ecosystem

The data science pipeline is a pedagogical model for teaching the workflow required for thorough statistical analyses of data, as shown in Figure 1-1. In each phase, an analyst transforms an initial dataset, augmenting or ingesting it from a variety of data sources, wrangling it into a normal form that can be computed upon, either with descriptive or inferential statistical methods, before producing a result via visualization or reporting mechanisms. These analytical procedures are usually designed to answer specific questions, or to investigate the relationship of data to some business practice for validation or decision making.

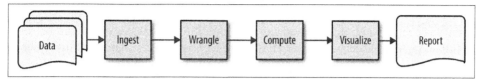

Figure 1-1. The data science pipeline

This original workflow model has driven most early data science thought. Although it may come as a surprise, original discussions about the application of data science revolved around the creation of meaningful information visualization, primarily because this workflow is intended to produce something that allows humans to make decisions. By aggregating, describing, and modeling large datasets, humans are better able to make judgments based on patterns rather than individual data points. Data visualizations are nascent data products—they generate their value from data, then allow humans to take action based on what they learn, creating new data from those actions.

However, this human-powered model is not a scalable solution in the face of exponential growth in the volume and velocity of data that many organizations are now grappling with. It is predicted that by 2020 the data we create and copy annually will reach 44 zettabytes, or 44 trillion gigabytes.[5] At even a small fraction of this scale, manual methods of data preparation and mining are simply unable to deliver meaningful insights in a timely manner.

In addition to the limitations of scale, the human-centric and one-way design of this workflow precludes the ability to efficiently design self-adapting systems that are able to learn. Machine learning algorithms have become widely available beyond academia, and fit the definition of data products very well. These types of algorithms derive their value from data as models are fit to existing datasets, then generate new data in return by making predictions about new observations.

To create a framework that allows the construction of scalable, automated solutions to interpret data and generate insights, we must revise the data science pipeline into a framework that incorporates a feedback loop for machine learning methods.

---

5 EMC Digital Universe with Research & Analysis by IDC, "The Digital Universe of Opportunities" (*http://bit.ly/1PgS7yy*), April 2014.

Big Data Workflows

With the goals of scalability and automation in mind, we can refactor the human-driven data science pipeline into an iterative model with four primary phases: *ingestion*, *staging*, *computation*, and *workflow management* (illustrated in Figure 1-2). Like the data science pipeline, this model in its simplest form takes raw data and converts it into insights. The crucial distinction, however, is that the data product pipeline builds in the step to operationalize and automate the workflow. By converting the ingestion, staging, and computation steps into an automated workflow, this step ultimately produces a reusable data product as the output. The workflow management step also introduces a feedback flow mechanism, where the output from one job execution can be automatically fed in as the data input for the next iteration, and thus provides the necessary self-adapting framework for machine learning applications.

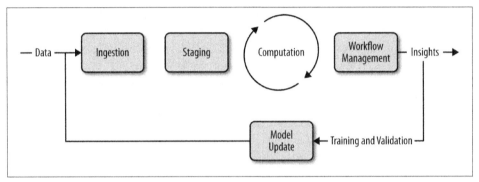

Figure 1-2. The big data pipeline

The *ingestion* phase is both the initialization of a model as well as an application interaction between users and the model. During initialization, users specify locations for data sources or annotate data (another form of ingestion). During interaction, users consume the predictions of the model and provide feedback that is used to reinforce the model.

The *staging* phase is where transformations are applied to data to make it consumable and stored so that it can be made available for processing. Staging is responsible for normalization and standardization of data, as well as data management in some computational data store.

The *computation* phase is the heavy-lifting phase with the primary responsibility of mining the data for insights, performing aggregations or reports, or building machine learning models for recommendations, clustering, or classification.

The *workflow management* phase performs abstraction, orchestration, and automation tasks that enable the workflow steps to be operationalized for production. The end result of this step should be an application, job, or script that can be run on-demand in an automated fashion.

Hadoop has specifically evolved into an ecosystem of tools that operationalize some part of this pipeline. For example, Sqoop and Kafka are designed for ingestion, allowing the import of relational databases into Hadoop or distributed message queues for on-demand processing. In Hadoop, data warehouses such as Hive and HBase provide data management opportunities at scale. Libraries such as Spark's GraphX and MLlib or Mahout provide analytical packages for large-scale computation as well as validation. Throughout the book, we'll explore many different components of the Hadoop ecosystem and see how they fit into the overall big data pipeline.

Conclusion

The conversation regarding what data science is has changed over the course of the past decade, moving from the purely analytical toward more visualization-related methods, and now to the creation of data products. Data products are *trained from data*, *self-adapting*, and *broadly applicable* economic engines that derive their value from data and generate new data in return. Data products have engaged a new information economy revolution that has changed the way that small businesses, technology startups, larger organizations, and government entities view their data.

In this chapter, we've described a revision to the original pedagogical model of the data science pipeline, and proposed a data product pipeline. The data product pipeline is iterative, with two phases: the building phase and the operational phase (which is comprised of four stages: interaction, data, storage, and computation). It serves as an architecture for performing large-scale data analyses in a methodical fashion that preserves experimentation and human interaction with data products, but also enables parts of the process to become automated as larger applications are built around them. We hope that this pipeline can be used as a general framework for understanding the data product lifecycle, but also as a stepping stone so that more innovative projects may be explored.

Throughout this book, we explore distributed computing and Hadoop from the perspective of a data scientist—and therefore with the idea that the purpose of Hadoop is to take data from many disparate sources, in a variety of forms, with a large number of instances, events, and classes, and transform it into something of value: a data product.

## CHAPTER 2

An Operating System for Big Data

Data teams are usually structured as small teams of five to seven members who employ a *hypothesis-driven* workflow using agile methodologies. Although data scientists typically see themselves as jack-of-all-trades generalists with a wide array of data-oriented skills,[1] they tend to specialize in either software, statistics, or domain expertise. Data teams therefore are composed of members who fit into three broad categories: *data engineers* are responsible for the practical aspects of the wiring and mechanics of data, usually relating to software and computing resources; *data modelers* focus on the exploration and explanation of data and creating inferential or predictive data products; and finally, *subject matter experts* provide domain knowledge to problem solving both in terms of process and application.

Data teams that utilize Hadoop tend to place a primary emphasis on the data engineering aspects of data science due to the technical nature of distributed computing. Big datasets lend themselves to aggregation-based approaches (over instance-based approaches) and a large toolset for distributed machine learning and statistical analyses exists already. For this reason, most literature about Hadoop is targeted at software developers, who usually specialize in Java—the software language the Hadoop API is written in. Moreover, those training materials tend to focus on the architectural aspects of Hadoop as those aspects demonstrate the fundamental innovations that have made Hadoop so successful at tasks like large-scale machine learning.

In this book, the focus is on the analytical employment of Hadoop, rather than the operational one. However, a basic understanding of how distributed computation and storage works is essential to a more complete understanding of how to work with Hadoop and build algorithms and workflows for data processing. In this chapter, we

---

1 Harris, Harlan, Sean Murphy, and Marck Vaisman, *Analyzing the Analyzers* (*http://oreil.ly/1PxPrNg*) (O'Reilly, 2013).

present Hadoop as an *operating system for big data*. We discuss the high-level concepts of how the operating system works via its two primary components: the distributed file system, HDFS ("Hadoop Distributed File System"), and workload and resource manager, YARN ("Yet Another Resource Negotiator"). We will also demonstrate how to interact with HDFS on the command line, as well as execute an example MapReduce job. At the end of this chapter, you should be comfortable interacting with a cluster and ready to execute the examples in the rest of this book.

Basic Concepts

In order to perform computation at scale, Hadoop distributes an analytical computation that involves a massive dataset to many machines that each simultaneously operate on their own individual chunk of data. Distributed computing is not new, but it is a technical challenge, requiring distributed algorithms to be developed, machines in the cluster to be managed, and networking and architecture details to be solved. More specifically, a distributed system must meet the following requirements:

Fault tolerance
> If a component fails, it should not result in the failure of the entire system. The system should gracefully degrade into a lower performing state. If a failed component recovers, it should be able to rejoin the system.

Recoverability
> In the event of failure, no data should be lost.

Consistency
> The failure of one job or task should not affect the final result.

Scalability
> Adding load (more data, more computation) leads to a decline in performance, not failure; increasing resources should result in a proportional increase in capacity.

Hadoop addresses these requirements through several abstract concepts, as defined in the following list (when implemented correctly, these concepts define how a cluster should manage data storage and distributed computation; moreover, an understanding of why these concepts are the basic premise for Hadoop's architecture informs other topics such as data pipelines and data flows for analysis):

- Data is distributed immediately when added to the cluster and stored on multiple nodes. Nodes prefer to process data that is stored locally in order to minimize traffic across the network.

- Data is stored in blocks of a fixed size (usually 128 MB) and each block is duplicated multiple times across the system to provide redundancy and data safety.

- A computation is usually referred to as a job; jobs are broken into tasks where each individual node performs the task on a single block of data.

- Jobs are written at a high level without concern for network programming, time, or low-level infrastructure, allowing developers to focus on the data and computation rather than distributed programming details.

- The amount of network traffic between nodes should be minimized transparently by the system. Each task should be independent and nodes should not have to communicate with each other during processing to ensure that there are no interprocess dependencies that could lead to deadlock.

- Jobs are fault tolerant usually through task redundancy, such that if a single node or task fails, the final computation is not incorrect or incomplete.

- Master programs allocate work to worker nodes such that many worker nodes can operate in parallel, each on their own portion of the larger dataset.

These basic concepts, while implemented slightly differently for various Hadoop systems, drive the core architecture and together ensure that the requirements for *fault tolerance*, *recoverability*, *consistency*, and *scalability* are met. These requirements also ensure that Hadoop is a data management system that behaves as expected for analytical data processing, which has traditionally been performed in relational databases or scientific data warehouses. Unlike data warehouses, however, Hadoop is able to run on more economical, commercial off-the-shelf hardware. As such, Hadoop has been leveraged primarily to store and compute upon large, heterogeneous datasets stored in "lakes" rather than warehouses, and relied upon for rapid analysis and prototyping of data products.

Hadoop Architecture

Hadoop is composed of two primary components that implement the basic concepts of distributed storage and computation as discussed in the previous section: HDFS and YARN. HDFS (sometimes shortened to DFS) is the Hadoop Distributed File System, responsible for managing data stored on disks across the cluster. YARN acts as a cluster resource manager, allocating computational assets (processing availability and memory on worker nodes) to applications that wish to perform a distributed computation. The architectural stack is shown in Figure 2-1. Of note, the original MapReduce application is now implemented on top of YARN as well as other new distributed computation applications like the graph processing engine Apache Giraph (*http://giraph.apache.org*), and the in-memory computing platform Apache Spark (*http://spark.apache.org*).

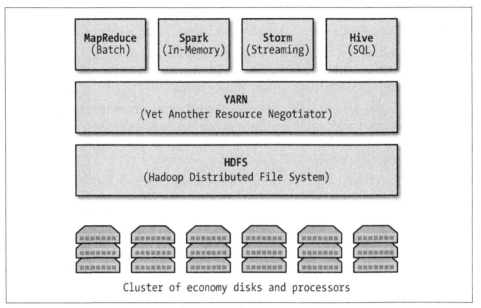

Figure 2-1. Hadoop is made up of HDFS and YARN

HDFS and YARN work in concert to minimize the amount of network traffic in the cluster primarily by ensuring that data is local to the required computation. Duplication of both data and tasks ensures fault tolerance, recoverability, and consistency. Moreover, the cluster is centrally managed to provide scalability and to abstract low-level clustering programming details. Together, HDFS and YARN are a platform upon which big data applications are built; perhaps more than just a platform, they provide an operating system for big data.

Like any good operating system, HDFS and YARN are flexible. Other data storage systems aside from HDFS can be integrated into the Hadoop framework such as Amazon S3 or Cassandra. Alternatively, data storage systems can be built directly on top of HDFS to provide more features than a simple file system. For example, HBase is a columnar data store built on top of HDFS and is one the most advanced analytical applications that leverage distributed storage. In earlier versions of Hadoop, applications that wanted to leverage distributed computing on a Hadoop cluster had to translate user-level implementations into MapReduce jobs. However, YARN now allows richer abstractions of the cluster utility, making new data processing applications for machine learning, graph analysis, SQL-like querying of data, or even streaming data services faster and more easily implemented. As a result, a rich ecosystem of tools and technologies has been built up around Hadoop, specifically on top of YARN and HDFS.

A Hadoop Cluster

At this point, it is useful to ask ourselves the question—*what is a cluster?* So far we've been discussing Hadoop as a cluster of machines that operate in a coordinated fashion; however, Hadoop is not hardware that you have to purchase or maintain. Hadoop is actually the name of the software that runs on a cluster—namely, the distributed file system, HDFS, and the cluster resource manager, YARN, which are collectively composed of six types of background services running on a group of machines.

Let's break that down a bit. HDFS and YARN expose an application programming interface (API) that abstracts developers from low-level cluster administration details. A set of machines that is running HDFS and YARN is known as a cluster, and the individual machines are called nodes. A cluster can have a single node, or many thousands of nodes, but all clusters scale horizontally, meaning as you add more nodes, the cluster increases in both capacity and performance in a linear fashion.

YARN and HDFS are implemented by several daemon processes—that is, software that runs in the background and does not require user input. Hadoop processes are services, meaning they run all the time on a cluster node and accept input and deliver output through the network, similar to how an HTTP server works. Each of these processes runs inside of its own Java Virtual Machine (JVM) so each daemon has its own system resource allocation and is managed independently by the operating system. Each node in the cluster is identified by the type of process or processes that it runs:

Master nodes
> These nodes run coordinating services for Hadoop workers and are usually the entry points for user access to the cluster. Without masters, coordination would fall apart, and distributed storage or computation would not be possible.

Worker nodes
> These nodes are the majority of the computers in the cluster. Worker nodes run services that accept tasks from master nodes—either to store or retrieve data or to run a particular application. A distributed computation is run by parallelizing the analysis across worker nodes.

Both HDFS and YARN have multiple master services responsible for coordinating worker services that run on each worker node. Worker nodes implement both the HDFS and YARN worker services. For HDFS, the master and worker services are as follows:

NameNode (Master)
> Stores the directory tree of the file system, file metadata, and the locations of each file in the cluster. Clients wanting to access HDFS must first locate the appropriate storage nodes by requesting information from the NameNode.

Secondary NameNode (Master)

Performs housekeeping tasks and checkpointing on behalf of the NameNode. Despite its name, it is not a backup NameNode.

DataNode (Worker)

Stores and manages HDFS blocks on the local disk. Reports health and status of individual data stores back to the NameNode.

At a high level, when data is accessed from HDFS, a client application must first make a request to the NameNode to locate the data on disk. The NameNode will reply with a list of DataNodes that store the data, and the client must then directly request each block of data from the DataNode. Note that the NameNode does not store data, nor does it pass data from DataNode to client, instead acting like a traffic cop, pointing clients to the correct DataNodes.

Similarly, YARN has multiple master services and a worker service as follows:

ResourceManager (Master)

Allocates and monitors available cluster resources (e.g., physical assets like memory and processor cores) to applications as well as handling scheduling of jobs on the cluster.

ApplicationMaster (Master)

Coordinates a particular application being run on the cluster as scheduled by the ResourceManager.

NodeManager (Worker)

Runs and manages processing tasks on an individual node as well as reports the health and status of tasks as they're running.

Similar to how HDFS works, clients that wish to execute a job must first request resources from the ResourceManager, which assigns an application-specific ApplicationMaster for the duration of the job. The ApplicationMaster tracks the execution of the job, while the ResourceManager tracks the status of the nodes, and each individual NodeManager creates containers and executes tasks within them. Note that there may be other processes running on the Hadoop cluster as well—for example, JobHis tory servers or ZooKeeper coordinators, but these services are the primary software running in a Hadoop cluster.

Master processes are so important that they usually are run on their own node so they don't compete for resources and present a bottleneck. However, in smaller clusters, the master daemons may all run on a single node. An example deployment of a small Hadoop cluster with six nodes, two master and four worker, is shown in Figure 2-2. Note that in larger clusters the NameNode and the Secondary NameNode will reside on separate machines so they do not compete for resources. The size of the cluster should be relative to the size of the expected computation or data storage because clusters scale horizontally. Typically a cluster of 20–30 worker nodes and a single master is sufficient to run several jobs simultaneously on datasets in the tens of tera-bytes. For more significant deployments of hundreds of nodes, each master requires its own machine; and in even larger clusters of thousands of nodes, multiple masters are utilized for coordination.

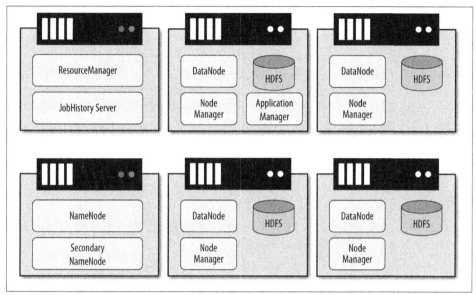

Figure 2-2. A small Hadoop cluster with two master nodes and four workers nodes that implements all six primary Hadoop services

 Developing MapReduce jobs is not necessarily done on a cluster. Instead, most Hadoop developers use a "pseudo-distributed" development environment, usually in a virtual machine. Development can take place on a small sample of data, rather than the entire dataset. For instructions on how to set up a pseudo-distributed development environment, see Appendix A.

Finally, one other type of cluster is important to note: a single node cluster. In "pseudo-distributed mode" a single machine runs all Hadoop daemons as though it were part of a cluster, but network traffic occurs through the local loopback network interface. In this mode, the benefits of a distributed architecture aren't realized, but it is the perfect setup to develop on without having to worry about administering several machines. Hadoop developers typically work in a pseudo-distributed environment, usually inside of a virtual machine to which they connect via SSH. Cloudera, Hortonworks, and other popular distributions of Hadoop provide pre-built virtual machine images that you can download and get started with right away. If you're interested in configuring your own pseudo-distributed node, refer to Appendix A.

HDFS

HDFS provides redundant storage for big data by storing that data across a cluster of cheap, unreliable computers, thus extending the amount of available storage capacity that a single machine alone might have. However, because of the networked nature of a distributed file system, HDFS is more complex than traditional file systems. In order to minimize that complexity, HDFS is based off of the centralized storage architecture.[2]

In principle, HDFS is a software layer on top of a native file system such as ext4 or xfs, and in fact Hadoop generalizes the storage layer and can interact with local file systems and other storage types like Amazon S3. However, HDFS is the flagship distributed file system, and for most programming purposes it will be the primary file system you'll be interacting with. HDFS is designed for storing very large files with streaming data access, and as such, it comes with a few caveats:

- HDFS performs best with a modest number of very large files—for example, millions of large files (100 MB or more) rather than billions of smaller files that might occupy the same volume.

- HDFS implements the WORM pattern—write once, read many. No random writes or appends to files are allowed.

- HDFS is optimized for large, streaming reading of files, not random reading or selection.

Therefore, HDFS is best suited for storing raw input data to computation, intermediary results between computational stages, and final results for the entire job. It is not a good fit as a data backend for applications that require updates in real-time, interactive data analysis, or record-based transactional support. Instead, by writing data only once and reading many times, HDFS users tend to create large stores of heterogeneous data to aid in a variety of different computations and analytics. These stores are sometimes called "data lakes" because they simply hold all data about a known problem in a recoverable and fault-tolerant manner. However, there are workarounds to these limitations, as we'll see later in the book.

Blocks

HDFS files are split into blocks, usually of either 64 MB or 128 MB, although this is configurable at runtime and high-performance systems typically select block sizes of 256 MB. The block size is the minimum amount of data that can be read or written to in HDFS, similar to the block size on a single disk file system. However, unlike blocks

---

2 This was first described in the 2003 paper by Ghemawat, Gobioff, and Leung, "The Google File System" (*http://bit.ly/google-filesystem*).

on a single disk, files that are smaller than the block size do not occupy the full blocks' worth of space on the actual file system. This means, to achieve the best performance, Hadoop prefers big files that are broken up into smaller chunks, if only through the combination of many smaller files into a bigger file format. However, if many small files are stored on HDFS, it will not reduce the total available disk space by 128 MB per file.

Blocks allow very large files to be split across and distributed to many machines at run time. Different blocks from the same file will be stored on different machines to provide for more efficient distributed processing. In fact, there is a one-to-one connection between a task and a block of data.

Additionally, blocks will be replicated across the DataNodes. By default, the replication is three-fold, but this is also configurable at runtime. Therefore, each block exists on three different machines and three different disks, and if even two nodes fail, the data will not be lost. Note this means that your potential data storage capacity in the cluster is only a third of the available disk space. However, because disk storage is typically very cost effective, this hasn't been a problem in most data applications.

Data management

The master NameNode keeps track of what blocks make up a file and where those blocks are located. The NameNode communicates with the DataNodes, the processes that actually hold the blocks in the cluster. Metadata associated with each file is stored in the memory of the NameNode master for quick lookups, and if the NameNode stops or fails, the entire cluster will become inaccessible!

The Secondary NameNode is not a backup to the NameNode, but instead performs housekeeping tasks on behalf of the NameNode, including (and especially) periodically merging a snapshot of the current data space with the edit log to ensure that the edit log doesn't get too large. The edit log is used to ensure data consistency and prevent data loss; if the NameNode fails, this merged record can be used to reconstruct the state of the DataNodes.

When a client application wants access to read a file, it first requests the metadata from the NameNode to locate the blocks that make up the file, as well as the locations of the DataNodes that store the blocks. The application then communicates directly with the DataNodes to read the data. Therefore, the NameNode simply acts like a journal or a lookup table and is not a bottleneck to simultaneous reads.

YARN

While the original version of Hadoop (Hadoop 1) popularized MapReduce and made large-scale distributed processing accessible to the masses, it only offered MapReduce on HDFS. This was due to the fact that in Hadoop 1, the MapReduce job/workload management functions were highly coupled to the cluster/resource management functions. As such, there was no way for other processing models or applications to utilize the cluster infrastructure for other distributed workloads.

MapReduce can be very efficient for large-scale batch workloads, but it's also quite I/O intensive, and due to the batch-oriented nature of HDFS and MapReduce, faces significant limitations in support for interactive analysis, graph processing, machine learning, and other memory-intensive algorithms. While other distributed processing engines have been developed for these particular use cases, the MapReduce-specific nature of Hadoop 1 made it impossible to repurpose the same cluster for these other distributed workloads.

Hadoop 2 addresses these limitations by introducing YARN, which decouples workload management from resource management so that multiple applications can share a centralized, common resource management service. By providing generalized job and resource management capabilities in YARN, Hadoop is no longer a singularly focused MapReduce framework but a full-fledged multi-application, big data operating system.

Working with a Distributed File System

When working with HDFS, keep in mind that the file system is in fact a distributed, remote file system. It is easy to become misled by the similarity to the POSIX file system, particularly because all requests for file system lookups are sent to the Name-Node, which responds very quickly with lookup-type requests. Once you start accessing files, things can slow down quickly, as the various blocks that make up the requested file must be transferred over the network to the client. Also keep in mind that because blocks are replicated on HDFS, you'll actually have less disk space available in HDFS than is available from the hardware.

 In the examples that follow, we present commands and environment variables that may vary depending on the Hadoop distribution or system you're on. For the most part, these should be easily understandable, but in particular we are assuming a setup for a pseudo-distributed node as described in Appendix A.

For the most part, interaction with HDFS is performed through a command-line interface that will be familiar to those who have used POSIX interfaces on Unix or Linux. Additionally, there is an HTTP interface to HDFS, as well as a programmatic interface written in Java. However, because the command-line interface is most familiar to developers, this is where we will start.

In this section, we'll go over basic interactions with the distributed file system via the command line. It is assumed that these commands are performed on a client that can connect to a remote Hadoop cluster, or which is running a pseudo-distributed cluster on the localhost. It is also assumed that the `hadoop` command and other utilities from *$HADOOP_HOME/bin* are on the system path and can be found by the operating system.

Basic File System Operations

All of the usual file system operations are available to the user, such as creating directories; moving, removing, and copying files; listing directories; and modifying permissions of files on the cluster. To see the available commands in the fs shell, type:

```
hostname $ hadoop fs -help
Usage: hadoop fs [generic options]
...
```

As you can see, many of the familiar commands for interacting with the file system are there, specified as arguments to the `hadoop fs` command as flag arguments in the Java style—that is, as a single dash (-) supplied to the command. Secondary flags or options to the command are specified with additional Java style arguments delimited by spaces following the initial command. Be aware that order can matter when specifying such options.

To get started, let's copy some data from the local file system to the remote (distributed) file system. To do this, use either the `put` or `copyFromLocal` commands. These commands are identical and write files to the distributed file system without removing the local copy. The `moveFromLocal` command is similar, but the local copy is deleted after a successful transfer to the distributed file system.

In the */data* directory of the GitHub repository for this book's code and resources (*http://bit.ly/hadoop-fundamentals*), there is a *shakespeare.txt* file containing the complete works of William Shakespeare. Download this file to your local working directory. After download, move the file to the distributed file system as follows:

```
hostname $ hadoop fs -copyFromLocal shakespeare.txt shakespeare.txt
```

This example invokes the Hadoop shell command `copyFromLocal` with two arguments, `<src>` and `<dst>`, both of which are specified as relative paths to a file called *shakespeare.txt*. To be explicit about what's happening, the command searches your current working directory for the *shakespeare.txt* file and copies it to the */user/ analyst/shakespeare.txt* path on HDFS by first requesting information about that path from the NameNode, then directly communicating with the DataNodes to transfer the file. Because Shakespeare's complete works are less than 64 MB, it is not broken up into blocks. Note, however, that on both your local machine, as well as the remote HDFS system, relative and absolute paths must be taken into account. The preceding command is shorthand for:

```
hostname $ hadoop fs -put /home/analyst/shakespeare.txt \
          hdfs://localhost/user/analyst/shakespeare.txt
```

You'll note that there exists a home directory on HDFS that is similar to the home directory on POSIX systems; this is what the */user/analyst/* directory is—the home directory of the analyst user. Relative paths in reference to the remote file system treat the user's HDFS home directory as the current working directory. In fact, HDFS has a permissions model for files and directories that are very similar to POSIX. In order to better manage the HDFS file system, create a hierarchical tree of directories just as you would on your local file system:

```
hostname $ hadoop fs -mkdir corpora
```

To list the contents of the remote home directory, use the ls command:

```
hostname $ hadoop fs -ls .
drwxr-xr-x  -  analyst analyst       0 2015-05-04 17:58 corpora
-rw-r--r--  3  analyst analyst 8877968 2015-05-04 17:52 shakespeare.txt
```

The HDFS file listing command is similar to the Unix ls -l command with some HDFS-specific features. Specified without any arguments, this command provides a listing of the user's HDFS home directory. The first column shows the permissions mode of the file. The second column is the replication of the file; by default, the replication is 3. Note that directories are not replicated, so this column is a dash (-) in that case. The user and group follow, then the size of the file in bytes (zero for directories). The last modified date and time is up next, with the name of the file appearing last.

Other basic file operations like mv, cp, and rm will all work as expected on the remote file system. There is, however, no rmdir command; instead, use rm -R to recursively remove a directory with all files in it.

Reading and moving files from the distributed file system to the local file system should be attempted with care, as the distributed file system is maintaining files that are extremely large. However, there are cases when files need to be inspected in detail by the user, particularly output files that are produced as the result of MapReduce jobs. Typically these are not read to the standard output stream but are piped to other programs like less or more.

To read the contents of a file, use the cat command, then pipe the output to less in order view the contents of the remote file:

```
hostname $ hadoop fs -cat shakespeare.txt | less
```

When using less: use the arrow keys to navigate the file and type q in order to quit and exit back to the terminal.

Alternatively, you can use the `tail` command to inspect only the last kilobyte of the file:

```
hostname $ hadoop fs -tail shakespeare.txt | less
```

There is no similar `hadoop fs -head` command to inspect the first kilobyte of the file. Instead, it is efficient to `hadoop fs -cat` the file and pipe it to the local shell's `head`, as the `head` command terminates the remote stream before the entire file is read. However, using the shell's `tail` in this manner would be less efficient, as all of the data would have to be streamed from the remote file system to your local file system before the output could be computed. Instead the, `hadoop fs -tail` command seeks to the correct position in the remote file and returns only the required data over the network.

To transfer entire files from the distributed file system to the local file system, use `get` or `copyToLocal`, which are identical commands. Similarly, use the `moveToLocal` command, which also removes the file from the distributed file system. Finally, the `get merge` command merges all files that match a given pattern or directory are copied and merged into a single file on the localhost. If files on the remote system are large, you may want to pipe them to a compression utility:

```
hostname $ hadoop fs -get shakespeare.txt ./shakespeare.from-remote.txt
```

Comparing the original *shakespeare.txt* file should prove that it is identical to the *shakespeare.from-remote.txt* file. Hopefully we have demonstrated that the `hadoop fs` command is a fully featured command-line interface to HDFS and is used routinely when developing analytical jobs. Table 2-1 demonstrates other useful commands that are provided by `hadoop fs`.

Table 2-1. Other useful utilities

Command	Output
`hadoop fs -help <cmd>`	Provides information and flags specifically about the *<cmd>* in question.
`hadoop fs -test <path>`	Answer various questions about *<path>* (e.g., exists, is directory, is file, etc.)
`hadoop fs -count <path>`	Count the number of directories, files, and bytes under the paths that match the specified file pattern.
`hadoop fs -du -h <path>`	Show the amount of space, in bytes, used by the files that match the specified file pattern.
`hadoop fs -stat <path>`	Print statistics about the file/directory at *<path>*.
`hadoop fs -text <path>`	Takes a source file and outputs the file in text format. Currently Zip, TextRecordInputStream, and Avro sources are supported.

File Permissions in HDFS

As mentioned earlier, HDFS has POSIX-like file permissions. There are three types of permissions: read (r), write (w), and execute (x). These permissions define the access levels for the owner, the group, and any other system users. For directories, the execute permission allows access to the contents of the directory; however, execute permissions are ignored on HDFS for files. Read and write permissions in the context of HDFS specify who can access the data and who can append to the file.

Permissions are expressed during the directory listing command ls. Each mode has 10 slots. The first slot is a d for directories, otherwise a - for files. Each of the following groups of three indicates the rwx permissions for the owner, group, and other users, respectively. There are several HDFS shell commands that will allow you to manage the permissions of files and directories, namely the familiar chmod, chgrp, and chown commands:

```
hostname $ hadoop fs -chmod 664 shakespeare.txt
```

This command changes the permissions of *shakespeare.txt* to -rw-rw-r--. The 664 is an octal representation of the flags to set for the permission triple. Consider 6 in binary, 110—this means set the read and write flags but not the execute flag. Completely permissible is 7, 111 in binary and read-only is 4, 100 in binary. The chgrp and chown commands change the group and owner of the files on the distributed file system.

A caveat with file permissions on HDFS: the identity of the client is determined by the username and groups of the process operating across HDFS, which means remote clients can create arbitrary users on the system. These permissions, therefore, should only be used to prevent accidental data loss and to share file system resources between known users, not as a security mechanism.

Other HDFS Interfaces

Programmatic access to HDFS is made available to software developers through a Java API, and any serious data ingestion into a Hadoop cluster should consider utilizing that API. There are also other tools for integrating HDFS with other file systems or network protocols—for example, FTP or Amazon S3. In Chapter 6, we'll focus more on data management issues and how to acquire and store data from a variety of sources into HDFS.

There are also HTTP interfaces to HDFS, which can be used for routine administration of the cluster file system and programmatic access to HDFS with Python. HTTP access to HDFS comes in two primary interfaces: direct access through the HDFS daemons that serve HTTP requests, or via proxy servers that expose an HTTP interface then directly access HDFS on the client's behalf using the Java API. Examples of proxies include HttpFS, Hoop, and WebHDFS, each of which allow RESTful network access to the Hadoop cluster, which is easily programmed against using Python.

The NameNode also supplies direct, read-only access to HDFS over HTTP through an HTTP server that runs on port 50070. If running in pseudo-distributed mode, simply open a browser and navigate to *http://127.0.0.1:50070*; otherwise, use the host name of the NameNode on your cluster. The NameNode Web UI provides a high-level overview of the cluster status, including the amount of storage available and used, the number of alive and dead DataNodes, and warning information about under-replicated blocks.

The NameNode also allows users to browse the file system using a search and navigation utility that is found under the Utilities drop-down tab. File meta information is listed similar to the command-line interface, and specific files may even be made available for download. DataNodes themselves can be directly browsed for information, accessing the DataNode host on port 50075; all active DataNodes are listed on the NameNode HTTP site.

By default, the direct HTTP interface is read-only. In order to provide write access to an HDFS cluster, a proxy such as WebHDFS must be used. WebHDFS secures the cluster via authentication with Kerberos. Accessing secure resources on Hadoop depends primarily on the specific configuration of the cluster, and if any third-party management tools are being used. Hadoop was designed to run on completely managed internal clusters without exposure to the outside world, and as a result security in Hadoop is not as mature as the platform itself—although this is one of the prime considerations of Hadoop development moving forward.

Working with Distributed Computation

At this point, you should be comfortable interacting with a cluster (even a pseudo-distributed one) via the command line. For most data scientists and software developers, the file system commands presented in the previous section should be familiar. Aside from a few differences related to the management of large datasets and networking across a cluster, HDFS should be easily integrated to your current operational workflows. For the rest of the book, our primary concern will be related to the management and computation of data that resides on HDFS, and to do that we need to make sure we have a fundamental understanding of distributed computing and its requirements.

While YARN has enabled Hadoop to become a general distributed computing platform, MapReduce (often abbreviated to MR) was the first computational framework for Hadoop. YARN allows for non-MapReduce frameworks such as Spark, Tez, and Storm (to name a few) to run alongside the original MapReduce application on a Hadoop cluster. However, for most Hadoop users, MapReduce is still the primary framework for many applications and analytics. Moreover, a general understanding of how MapReduce works allows us to think more deeply about distributed analytics and inform discussions of how other platforms work, as the theoretical underpinnings of MapReduce are shared with those other frameworks.

In this section, we'll explore the basic principles of the MapReduce programming paradigm and discuss why these functional programming constructs are ideal for distributed systems. We will demonstrate how MapReduce works via two simple analytics that are routinely used to demonstrate computation in a distributed environment: word counting and shared friendships. Finally, we will describe how MapReduce applications are implemented on a Hadoop cluster and show how to submit and manage a sample MapReduce job, fetching the output via the Hadoop command-line interface.

MapReduce: A Functional Programming Model

When people refer to MapReduce, they're usually referring to the distributed programming model.[3] MapReduce is a simple but very powerful computational framework specifically designed to enable fault-tolerant distributed computation across a cluster of centrally managed machines. It does this by employing a "functional" programming style that is inherently parallelizable—by allowing multiple independent tasks to execute a function on local chunks of data and aggregating the results after processing.

Functional programming is a style of programming that ensures unit computations are evaluated in a stateless manner. This means functions depend only on their inputs, and they are closed and do not share state. Data is transferred between functions by sending the output of one function as the input to another, wholly independent function. These traits make functional programming a great fit for distributed, big data computational systems, because it allows us to move the computation to any node that has the data input and guarantee that we will still get the same result. Because functions are stateless and depend solely on their input, many functions on many machines can work independently on smaller chunks of the dataset. By strategically chaining the outputs of functions to the inputs of other functions, we can guarantee that we will reach a final computation across the entire dataset.

It shouldn't be a surprise that the two functions that distribute work and aggregate results are called map and reduce, respectively. Furthermore, the data that is operated upon as input and output in these functions are not simple lists or collections of values; instead, MapReduce utilizes "key/value" pairs to coordinate computation. Pseudocode for map and reduce functions in Python would therefore look as follows:

```python
def map(key, value):
    # Perform processing
    return (intermed_key, intermed_value)
```

---

[3] The distributed programming model was devised and later described by Google in the paper by Jeffrey Dean and Sanjay Ghemawat, "MapReduce: Simplified Data Processing on Large Clusters". (*http://bit.ly/google-mapreduce-paper*)

```
def reduce(intermed_key, values):
    # Perform processing
    return (key, output)
```

A map function takes as input a series of key/value pairs and operates singly on each individual pair. In the preceding pseudocode, we've expressed this as it is represented in the MapReduce Java API: a function that takes two arguments, a key and a value. After performing some analysis or transformation on the input data, the map function may then output zero or more resulting key/value pairs, represented as a single tuple in the preceding pseudocode. This is generally described as shown in Figure 2-3, where a map function is applied to an input list to create a new output list.

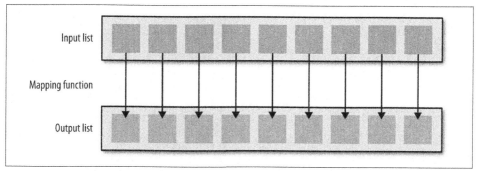

Figure 2-3. A map function takes as input a list of key/value pairs and operates singly upon each individual element in the list, outputting zero or more key/value pairs

Typically, the map operation is where the core analysis or processing takes place, as this is the function that sees each individual element in the dataset. Consider how filters are implemented in a map context: each key/value pair is tested to determine whether it belongs in the final dataset, and is emitted if it does or ignored if not. After the map phase, any emitted key/value pairs will then be grouped by key and those key/value groups are applied as input to reduce functions on a per-key basis. As shown in Figure 2-4, a reduce function is applied to an input list to output a single, aggregated value.

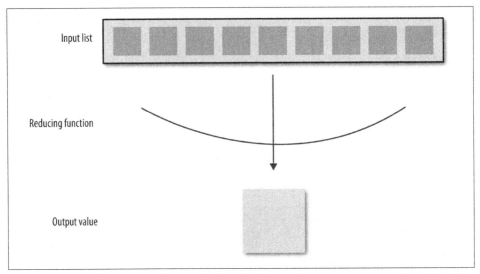

Input list

Reducing function

Output value

Figure 2-4. A reducer takes a key and a list of values as input, operates on the values list as a whole, usually through aggregation operations, and outputs zero or more key/value pairs

As shown in the pseudocode, which is similar to the MapReduce Java API, the definition of a reduce function is one that takes two arguments: a key (`intermed` in the pseudocode), and an iterator or list of values (`values`) associated with that key. The reducer performs final processing on the list of values, usually combination or aggregation, then outputs zero or more key/value pairs. The reducer is intended to aggregate the many values that are output from the map phase in order to transform a large volume of data into a smaller, more manageable set of summary data, but has many other uses as well.

MapReduce: Implemented on a Cluster

Because mappers apply the same function to each element of any arbitrary list of items, they are well suited to distribution across nodes on a cluster. Each node gets a copy of the mapper operation, and applies the mapper to the key/value pairs that are stored in the blocks of data of the local HDFS data nodes. There can be any number of mappers working independently on as much data as possible, really only limited by the number of processors available on the cluster. Because they are stateless, no network communication between processes is required (or possible). Because mappers are deterministic, their output is not dependent on anything but the incoming values, and therefore failed mappers can be reattempted on another node.

Reducers require as input the output of the mappers on a per-key basis; therefore, reducer computation can also be distributed such that there can be as many reduce operations as there are keys available from the mapper output. You should correctly expect that each reducer sees *all* values for a single, unique key. In order to meet this requirement, a shuffle and sort operation is required to coordinate the map and reduce phases, such that reducer input is grouped and sorted by key. Shuffle and sort partitions the keyspace from the map phase in order to allocate a specific keyspace to specific reducers. Therefore, in broad strokes, the phases of MapReduce are shown in Figure 2-5.

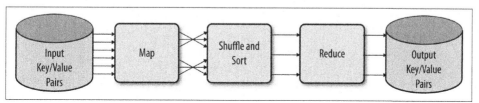

Figure 2-5. Broadly, MapReduce is implemented as a staged framework where a map phase is coordinated to a reduce phase via an intermediate shuffle and sort

The phases shown in Figure 2-5 are as follows:

Phase 1

Local data is loaded into a mapping process as key/value pairs from HDFS.

Phase 2

Mappers output zero or more key/value pairs, mapping computed values to a particular key.

Phase 3

These pairs are then sorted and shuffled based on the key and are then passed to a reducer such that all values for a key are available to it.

Phase 4

Reducers then must output zero or more final key/value pairs, which are the output (reducing the results of the map).

For the most part, data engineers really only have to worry about this broad description of MapReduce in order to implement analytical applications. However, there are a few more details that are required when executing MapReduce on a cluster. For example, consider how the key/value pairs are defined, and what is required in order to do correct partitioning of the keyspace. Enhancements and optimizations like combiners and other intermediate stages may also be required such that simple jobs can be completed with fewer computational resources. Although beyond the scope of this book, the details of data flow in a MapReduce pipeline executed on a cluster of a few nodes are outlined in Figure 2-6.

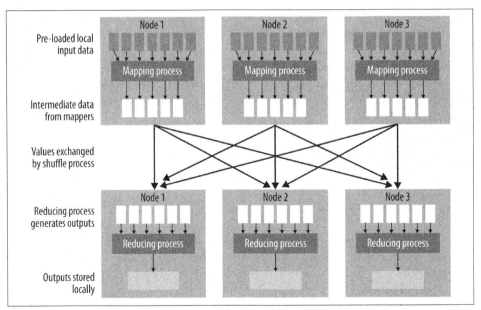

Figure 2-6. Data flow of a MapReduce job being executed on a cluster of a few nodes

In a cluster execution context, a map task is assigned to one or more nodes in the cluster, which contains local blocks of data specified as input to the map operation. Blocks are stored in HDFS and and are split into smaller chunks by an `InputFormat` class, which defines how data is presented to the map applications. For example, given text data, the key might be the file identifier and line number and the value might be the string of the line content. `RecordReader` presents each individual key/ value pair to the map operation supplied by the user, which then outputs one or more intermediate key/value pairs. A common optimization at this point is to apply a combiner—a process that aggregates map output for a single mapper, similar to how a reducer works, but without full knowledge of the keyspace. This prework leads to less work for the reducers and therefore better reducer performance.

The intermediate keys are pulled from the map processes to a partitioner. The partitioner decides how to allocate the keys to the reducers. Typically, a uniformly distributed keyspace is assumed, and therefore a hash function is used to evenly divide keys among the reducers. The partitioner also sorts the key/value pairs such that the full "shuffle and sort" phase is implemented. Finally, the reducers start work, pulling an iterator of data for each key and performing a reduce operation such as an aggregation. Their output key/value pairs are then written back to HDFS using an `Output Format` class.

There are many other tools associated with the management of large-scale jobs inside of a MapReduce cluster execution context as well. To name a few, `Counter` and

`Reporter` objects are used for job tracking and evaluation and caches are used to supply ancillary data during processing. These tools are accessible by developers and are typically implemented in higher-order frameworks such as Pig or Hive. However, in Chapter 3, we will see how to implement many of these features using Python and Hadoop Streaming.

MapReduce examples

In order to demonstrate how data flows through a map and reduce computational pipeline, we will present two concrete examples: *word counting* and *shared friendships*. Both of these applications, while simple, demonstrate how data flows through a distributed system. Word count in particular is used so commonly to demonstrate distributed computing tasks that it is often referred to as the "Hello, World" of big data. Because word counting and shared friends are ``embarrassingly parallel," it not only helps us understand MapReduce, but also signals if there are fundamental flaws in the design of an application.

The word-counting application takes as input one or more text files and produces a list of words and their frequencies as output. More specifically, because Hadoop utilizes key/value pairs—the input key is a file ID and line number and the input value is a string, while the output key is a word and the output value is an integer. Right off the bat, we can see that this can be parallelized in a number of ways. First, each mapper can work on a single document; or if the documents are very large, mappers can work on chunks of single documents—the map operation doesn't care about the context of the words, just that it can count the words it is given as input. Similarly, we can have multiple reducers working on different keys simultaneously because the output key is a word. The following Python pseudocode shows how this algorithm is implemented:

```
# emit is a function that performs Hadoop I/O ❶

def map(dockey, line):
    for word in value.split():
        emit(word, 1)

def reduce(word, values):
    count = sum(value for value in values)
    emit(word, count)
```

❶ Consider for the sake of argument that `emit` is a function that performs Hadoop I/O—that is, it sends its arguments to the next phase of the MapReduce pipeline, similar to how `yield` works in a Python function.

In the diagram in Figure 2-7, we see there are two documents containing two simple sentences. The `map` function will receive some unique ID for the text, and a string of the contents of that document. Its job is to split the value by space and punctuation (getting all the words) and to emit each word as the intermediate key, and the value 1 —because the mapper has seen one instance of this word. The data for each mapper is shown here:

```
# Input to WordCount mappers

(27183, "The fast cat wears no hat.")
(31416, "The cat in the hat ran fast.")

# Mapper 1 output

("The", 1), ("fast", 1), ("cat", 1), ("wears", 1),
("no", 1), ("hat", 1),(".", 1)

# Mapper 2 output

("The", 1), ("cat", 1), ("in", 1), ("the", 1),
("hat", 1), ("ran", 1),("fast", 1),(".", 1)
```

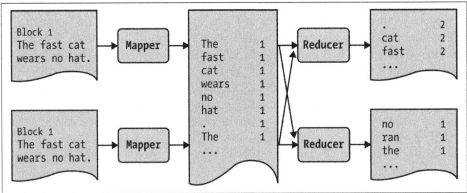

Figure 2-7. Data flow of the word count job being executed on a cluster with two mappers and two reducers

This data is passed to the shuffle and sort phase where the keys (words) are grouped together and sorted and sent to the appropriate reducer. Each reducer receives as input the word as the key and a list of ones as the values. In order to get the counts, it simply sums the ones and emits the word as the key and the count as the value. The data to the input and the output from our example is shown here:

```
# Input to WordCount reducers
# This data was computed by shuffle and sort

(".", [1, 1])
("cat", [1, 1])
("fast", [1, 1])
("hat", [1, 1])
("in", [1])
("no", [1])
```

```
("ran", [1])
("the", [1])
("wears", [1])
("The", [1, 1])

# Output by all WordCount reducers

(".", 2)
("cat", 2)
("fast", 2)
("hat", 2)
("in", 1)
("no", 1)
("ran", 1)
("the", 1)
("wears", 1)
("The", 2)
```

Although a seemingly simple algorithm, only slightly more complex implementations of this algorithm are used routinely in text processing. Consider trying to compute the most common words used in the *New York Times* or in the Google Books corpus; this would certainly require some big data technique. Using *n*-gram language models, it's possible to count co-located words to see if there is a statistical significance between two words appearing together like "white house" or "baseball bat". Additionally, the exercise of being able to imagine how data flows from input source through map operations to reduce operations and out to output is critical to being able to develop analytical processes and data engineering tasks in a distributed environment.

Let's consider a slightly more complex example to make sure that MapReduce makes sense. In the shared friendship task, the goal is to analyze a social network to see which friend relationships users have in common. This is both the first step to downstream analytics like "you might know" recommendations, but also a critical part of social networks that might only want to allow you to share with friends and friends-of-friends. Given an input data source where the key is the name of a user and the value is a comma-separated list of friends, the following Python pseudocode demonstrates how to perform this computation:

```python
def map(person, friends):
    for friend in friends.split(","):
        pair = sort([person, friend])
        emit(pair, friends)

def reduce(pair, friends):
    shared = set(friends[0])
    shared = shared.intersection(friends[1])
    emit(pair, shared)
```

The mapper creates an intermediate keyspace of all of the possible (friend, friend) tuples that exist from the initial dataset. This allows us to analyze the dataset on a per-relationship basis as the value is the list of associated friends. Note also that the pair is sorted, which ensures that the input (`"Mike"`, `"Linda"`) and (`"Linda"`, `"Mike"`) end up being the same key during aggregation in the reducer. The input and mapper output are as follows:

```
# Input (key → value)
Allen → Betty, Chris, David
Betty → Allen, Chris, David, Ellen
Chris → Allen, Betty, David, Ellen
David → Allen, Betty, Chris, Ellen
Ellen → Betty, Chris, David

# Mapper 1 output
(Allen, Betty) → (Betty, Chris, David)
(Allen, Chris) → (Betty, Chris, David)
(Allen, David) → (Betty, Chris, David)

# Mapper 2 output
(Allen, Betty) → (Allen, Chris, David, Ellen)
(Betty, Chris) → (Allen, Chris, David, Ellen)
(Betty, David) → (Allen, Chris, David, Ellen)
(Betty, Ellen) → (Allen, Chris, David, Ellen)

# Mapper 3 output
(Allen, David) → (Allen, Chris, David, Ellen)
(Betty, David) → (Allen, Chris, David, Ellen)
(Chris, David) → (Allen, Chris, David, Ellen)
(David, Ellen) → (Allen, Chris, David, Ellen)

# Mapper 4 output
(Betty, Ellen) → (Betty, Chris, David)
(Chris, Ellen) → (Betty, Chris, David)
(David, Ellen) → (Betty, Chris, David)
```

The reducer is guaranteed to see two friends list values for every friend relationship that exists in the dataset, one for each user in the key. Therefore, in order to perform its final aggregation, it simply transforms those lists into sets and takes the intersection of the two, the shared friendships. It then emits the intersection with the alphabetized relationship tuple and the associated friends. Note that it could have just as easily emitted a result for each person in the relationship, which may be beneficial to data loading downstream for other applications. The data flow to the reducer is as follows:

```
# After shuffle and sort, reducer input:

(Allen, Betty) → (A C D E) (B C D)
(Allen, Chris) → (A B D E) (B C D)
(Allen, David) → (A B C E) (B C D)
(Betty, Chris) → (A B D E) (A C D E)
(Betty, David) → (A B C E) (A C D E)
(Betty, Ellen) → (A C D E) (B C D)
```

```
(Chris, David) → (A B C E) (A B D E)
(Chris, Ellen) → (A B D E) (B C D)
(David, Ellen) → (A B C E) (B C D)

# After reduction:

(Allen, Betty) → (Chris, David)
(Allen, Chris) → (Betty, David)
(Allen, David) → (Betty, Chris)
(Betty, Chris) → (Allen, David, Ellen)
(Betty, David) → (Allen, Chris, Ellen)
(Betty, Ellen) → (Chris, David)
(Chris, David) → (Allen, Betty, Ellen)
(Chris, Ellen) → (Betty, David)
(David, Ellen) → (Betty, Chris)
```

The concrete examples presented in this section, word count and shared friendships, should demonstrate how data flows through a single MapReduce job and give insight into how these jobs need to be developed. Envisioning data flowing through the map and reduce phases is a good start. Determining the keys that are required as output, and those that are input, also helps guide what each stage of the pipeline should do.

Beyond a Map and Reduce: Job Chaining

Many algorithms or data processing tasks can easily be implemented in MapReduce with a simple shift in normal problem-solving workflows to account for the stateless operation and interaction of the map and reduce functions. However, more complex algorithms and analyses cannot be distilled to a single MapReduce job. For example, many machine learning or predictive analysis techniques require optimization, an iterative process where error is minimized. MapReduce does not support native iteration through a single map or reduce.

This leads us to a necessary discussion of terminology. In MapReduce, a job actually refers to the full application (program), and therefore the complete execution of map and reduce functions across all the input data. Jobs for complex analyses are generally comprised of many internal tasks, where a task is the execution of a single map or reduce operation on a block of data. Because there are many workers simultaneously performing similar tasks, some data processing workflows can take advantage of that fact and run "map-only" or "reduce-only" jobs. For example, a binning methodology can take advantage of the built-in partitioner to group similar data together. Binned data can then be used downstream in other MapReduce jobs to perform frequency analysis or compute probability distributions.

In fact, the use of multiple MapReduce jobs to perform a single computation is how more complex applications are constructed, through a process called "job chaining." By creating data flows through a system of intermediate MapReduce jobs, as shown in Figure 2-8, we can create a pipeline of analytical steps that lead us to our end result.

As analysts and developers, our job is to devise algorithms that implement map and reduce in order to come to a single analytical conclusion, a topic that we will explore in detail in Chapter 3.

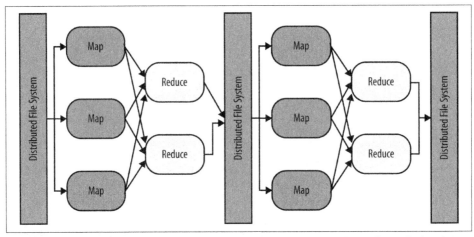

Figure 2-8. Complex algorithms or applications are actually made up through the chaining of MapReduce jobs where the input of a downstream MapReduce job is the output of a more recent one

Throughout the book, we explore how to transform our computational frameworks away from more traditional iterative analytics to "data flows" for large-scale computation. Data flows are directed acyclic graphs of jobs or operations that are applied to a large dataset toward some end computation. In the end, the primary data engineering effort of a big data application is to filter and aggregate the larger datasets toward last-mile computing—potentially to the space where the data can fit into memory and be evaluated. It is easy to see how chained jobs fit this data processing model, although it will also be relevant in other data processing systems such as Storm and Spark.

Submitting a MapReduce Job to YARN

The MapReduce API is written in Java, and therefore MapReduce jobs submitted to the cluster are going to be compiled Java Archive (JAR) files. Hadoop will transmit the JAR files across the network to each node that will run a task (either a mapper or reducer) and the individual tasks of the MapReduce job are executed.

 In this book, we explore several methods for writing analytical jobs for Hadoop, but will primarily write our programs in Python, either using MapReduce Streaming or Spark. In some cases, we will also use Hive and Pig to demonstrate other methods to perform data analysis on a cluster.

The word count example demonstrates the power of distributed computing, as well as how to compute against unstructured data. From the Hadoop Fundamentals repository (*https://github.com/bbengfort/hadoop-fundamentals*), download the example WordCount Java program, *WordCount.zip*. This folder contains the following files:

WordCount.java
    MapReduce driver class to execute the job

WordMapper.java
    A mapper class to emit words

SumReducer.java
    A reducer class to count the words

Compile the Hadoop job into a JAR using the following command:

```
hostname $ hadoop com.sun.tools.javac.Main WordCount.java
hostname $ jar cf wc.jar WordCount*.class
```

This should create a *wc.jar* file in your current working directory. Note that this presumes that several environment variables are configured correctly, including JAVA_HOME and HADOOP_CLASSPATH. See Appendix A for details on these environment variables.

In order to submit the job to the cluster and count the number of words in the complete works of William Shakespeare_, utilize the hadoop jar command, which connects to the ResourceManager and sends the *wc.jar* file to be executed on all nodes of the cluster. The command expects the path to the job archive file, as well as the name of the class whose main method should be invoked. Any other command-line arguments are then passed to the job itself. Our simple program requires the input path of data to analyze, as well as the output path to write the results to. Both the input and output paths are HDFS paths, and the output path cannot exist on the distributed file system, otherwise an error will be raised (to prevent overwriting or deleting data on the cluster). The job is submitted as follows:

```
hostname $ hadoop jar wc.jar WordCount shakespeare.txt wordcounts
```

The job will execute and output the status of mappers and reducers, and when completed will report statistics for the completion of the job. Once complete, the results of the job will be written to the *wordcounts* directory, which can be viewed as follows:

```
hostname $ hadoop fs -ls wordcounts
```

There are several output files named similarly to *part-00000*, and in fact, there should be one part file for each reducer that was used in the computation. There should also be a *_SUCCESS* file as well as a *_logs* directory that store information about the job. In order to read the result of the job, cat the part file from the remote file system and pipe it to less:

```
hostname $ hadoop fs -cat wordcounts/part-00000 | less
```

If something goes wrong in your MapReduce job, you'll need to be able to stop it (consider if you've accidentally added an infinite loop or some memory-intensive process to your mapper or reducer!). However, typing Ctrl-C (issuing a keyboard interrupt on Unix) will only kill the process displaying the progress—it won't actually stop the job! The `hadoop job` command allows you to manage jobs currently running on the cluster. List all running jobs with the `-list` command:

```
hostname $ hadoop job -list
```

Use the output to identify the job ID of the job you'd like to terminate, then kill the job issuing the `-kill` command:

```
hostname $ hadoop job -kill $JOBID
```

Similar to the NameNode web interface, the ResourceManager also exposes a web interface to view the status of jobs and their logfiles. The ResourceManager web UI can be accessed via port 8088 of the machine hosting the ResourceManager service. This web UI displays all currently running jobs as well as the status of the NodeManagers across the cluster. The ResourceManager does not track a historical record of jobs, however—instead, use the `JobHistory` server, which can be accessed on port 19888 of the machine hosting the `JobHistory` server.

Conclusion

This chapter presented a lot of detail about the architecture of a Hadoop cluster and briefly touched on many points about the requirements and implementation of a large-scale distributed computation system. However, we do not claim that we covered everything, simply enough to contextualize the concepts in this book. Our goal in covering the conceptual details of MapReduce in the manner that we did was to present the foundation of algorithm development in a distributed context. We will leverage this foundation to discuss more complex analytical algorithms later in the book for the purpose of understanding how they work; however, we will leave more in-depth discussions of their specific implementations for other resources.

Because the goal of this book is to serve as an introduction to distributed computing with Hadoop, we do not focus on the setup, configuration, or maintenance of an Hadoop cluster, but rather on the analyst's interaction with it. To that end, in the next chapter we will look at writing simple distributed jobs with MapReduce in Python by using a framework called Hadoop Streaming. However, in the next chapter, we will take a specific look at how to write MapReduce jobs in Python using Hadoop Streaming.

## CHAPTER 3

A Framework for Python and Hadoop Streaming

The current version of Hadoop MapReduce is a software framework for composing jobs that process large amounts of data in parallel on a cluster, and is the native distributed processing framework that ships with Hadoop. The framework exposes a Java API that allows developers to specify input and output locations on HDFS, `map` and `reduce` functions, and other job parameters as a *job configuration*. Jobs are compiled and packaged into a JAR, which is submitted to the `ResourceManager` by the *job client*—usually via the command line. The `ResourceManager` then schedules tasks, monitors them, and provides status back to the client.

Typically, a MapReduce application is composed of three Java classes: a `Job`, a `Mapper`, and a `Reducer`. Mappers and reducers handle the details of computation on key/value pairs and are connected through a shuffle and sort phase. The Job configures the input and output data format by specifying the `InputFormat` and `OutputFormat` classes of data being serialized to and from HDFS. All of these classes must extend abstract base classes or implement MapReduce interfaces. Needless to say, developing a Java MapReduce application is verbose.

However, Java is not the only option to use the MapReduce framework! For example, C++ developers can use *Hadoop Pipes*, which provides an API for using both HDFS and MapReduce. But what is of most interest to data scientists is *Hadoop Streaming*, a utility written in Java that allows the specification of any executable as the mapper and reducer. With Hadoop Streaming shell utilities, R, or Python, scripts can all be used to compose MapReduce jobs. This allows data scientists to easily integrate Map-Reduce into their workflows—particularly for routine data management tasks that don't require extensive software development.

It may seem that Hadoop Streaming is not a first-class member of the Hadoop ecosystem, and in fact, most Hadoop users probably use higher-level tools such as Pig and Hive even before directly using Hadoop MapReduce. While the Streaming community is small, there are a number of frameworks that build upon it, and Streaming is natively available in many cloud computing Map-Reduce resources, such as Amazon's Elastic MapReduce. Agile data science leverages the rapid development of scripting languages and Hadoop Streaming to quickly build data analyses and even large-scale computational jobs, including machine learning tasks.

In this chapter, we explore the details of how to use Hadoop Streaming, as well as work through the creation of a small framework that will allow us to quickly write MapReduce jobs using Python. At the end of this chapter, we will extend the simple WordCount program that we worked on in Chapter 2 to actually use third-party libraries in Python for natural language processing (NLP), and write a MapReduce job that identifies the frequencies of significant bigrams in text. Finally we will look at some advanced MapReduce topics that are essential to understanding Hadoop, and how to apply these topics to Streaming jobs written in Python.

Hadoop Streaming

Hadoop Streaming is a utility, packaged as a JAR file that comes with the Hadoop MapReduce distribution. Streaming is used as a normal Hadoop job passed to the cluster via the job client, but allows you to also specify arguments such as the input and output HDFS paths, along with the mapper and reducer executable. The job is then run as a normal MapReduce job, managed and monitored by the `ResourceMan ager` and the `MRAppMaster` as usual until the job completes.

In order to perform a MapReduce job, Streaming utilizes the standard Unix streams for input and output, hence the name *Streaming*. Input to both mappers and reducers is read from `stdin`, which a Python process can access via the `sys` module. Hadoop expects the Python mappers and reducers to write their output key/value pairs to `stdout`. Figure 3-1 demonstrates this process in a MapReduce context. Although Python Hadoop developers don't necessarily get access to the full MapReduce API through this technique (features like partitioners or input and output formats must be written in Java), this is enough to express many powerful jobs and tasks that are typical in the workflow of a data scientist.

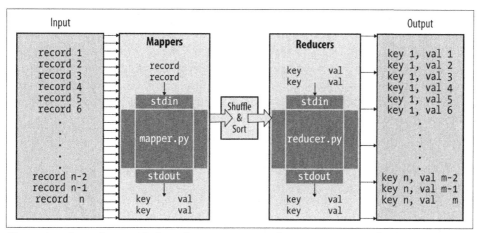

Figure 3-1. Data flow in Hadoop Streaming via Python mapper.py and reducer.py scripts

 Hadoop Streaming is not to be confused with Spark Streaming or other real-time computation frameworks that utilize "unbounded streams of data," such as Apache Storm. Streams in Hadoop Streaming refer to the standard Unix streams: stdin, stdout, and stderr. Spark Streaming and Storm do real-time analytics on an incoming stream of data by batching the data into time windows. They are very different things! The use of "Streaming" specifically refers to Hadoop Streaming in this chapter.

When Streaming executes a job, each mapper task will launch the supplied executable inside of its own process. The mapper then converts the input data into lines of text and pipes it to the stdin of the external process while simultaneously collecting output from stdout. The input conversion is usually a straightforward serialization of the value because data is being read from HDFS, where each line is a new value. The mapper expects output to be in a string key/value format, where the key is separated from the value by some separator character, tab (\t) by default. If there is no separator, then the mapper considers the output to only be a key with a null value. The separator can be customized by passing arguments to the Hadoop Streaming job.

The reducer is also launched as its own executable after the output from the mappers is shuffled and sorted to ensure that each key is sent to the same reducer. The key/value output strings from the mapper are streamed to the reducer as input via stdin, matching the data output from the mapper, and guaranteed to be grouped by key. The output the reducer emits to stdout is expected to have the same key, separator, and value format as the mapper.

Therefore, in order to write Hadoop jobs using Python, we need to create two Python files, *mapper.py* and a *reducer.py*. Inside each of those files we simply need to import the `sys` module to get access to `stdin` and `stdout`. The code itself will need to deal with our input as a string, parsing and converting for each number or complex data type, and we need to serialize our output as a string as well. To demonstrate how this works, we will implement the WordCount example discussed in Chapter 2 in the most simple and Pythonic method as possible.

First, we create our executable mapper in a file called *mapper.py*:

```python
#!/usr/bin/env python

import sys

if __name__ == "__main__":
    for line in sys.stdin:
        for word in line.split():
            sys.stdout.write("{}\t1\n".format(word))
```

The mapper simply reads each line from `sys.stdin`, splits on space, then writes each word and a 1 separated by a tab, line-by-line to `sys.stdout`. The reducer is a bit more complex because we have to track which key we're on at every line of input, and only emit a completed sum when we see a new key. This is because, unlike the native API, individual data values are aggregated to the streaming process during shuffle and sort rather than exposed as a list or iterator. Keep in mind that each reducer task is guaranteed to see all values for the same key, but may also see multiple keys. In a file called *reducer.py*, we implement the reducer executable as follows:

```python
#!/usr/bin/env python

import sys

if __name__ == '__main__':
    curkey = None
    total  = 0
    for line in sys.stdin:
        key, val = line.split("\t")
        val = int(val)

        if key == curkey:
            total += val
        else:
            if curkey is not None:
                sys.stdout.write("{}\t{}\n".format(curkey, total))

            curkey = key
            total  = val
```

As the reducer iterates over each line in the input from `stdin`, it splits the line on the separator character and converts the value to an integer. It then performs a check to ensure that we're still computing the count for the same key; otherwise, it writes the output to stdout and restarts the count for the new key. Both the mapper and reducer are executed in an "ifmain" block, discussed later in the chapter.

 If you've studied MapReduce programming in Java, you might expect a single record passed to stdin at a time, which is what the MapReduce API provides. However, with Streaming, the mapper has access to every line of the block and can treat the entire dataset as a single item. Correspondingly, the reducer does not receive accumulated values as in the Java API, but rather a sorted line-by-line input from the mapper. We will use groupby to simulate the accumulation, but it is not native.

Each Python module will be executed inside its own process—so it will have as many computing resources in terms of processing and memory as are available at the time of execution. It's important to note, however, that because each mapper and reducer is treated as *executable* by Hadoop Streaming, every Python file should start with #!/usr/bin/env python, which alerts the shell that the code should be interpreted using Python rather than bash.

Now that we have a good understanding of how Hadoop Streaming works, let's move beyond this simple code and begin to consider high-quality Python code that might be reused for different streaming jobs, and take a look at how to specifically use Hadoop Streaming to parse CSV data.

Computing on CSV Data with Streaming

Although all a Python script has to do to be used with Hadoop Streaming is read from stdin and write to stdout, there are many improvements we can make on the code from the earlier section. In particular, we can use modules in the Python standard library for fast iteration, string handling, and more. In this section, we'll begin to put together a small, reusable framework with which we can quickly deploy Hadoop jobs for our large data-processing needs. To start on our framework, let's consider a particular example for reading CSV data.

String-typed input and output from our mappers and reducers means that we should carefully consider the datatypes that we're putting into the system, and how much parsing work we want our Python script to do. For example, we could use the built-in ast.literal_eval to parse simple data types (e.g., numbers, tuples, lists, dicts, or booleans); or we could input and output complex data structures with a structured serialization (e.g., JSON or even XML). Because Streaming serializes on a line-by-line basis, Python streaming jobs are perfect for dealing with CSV files and other plain-text file formats, many of which are readily found in our datasets and other semi-structured data stores. Later, we will consider other types, such as Avro or other binary serialization formats that can be used.

In this example, we'll consider a dataset of the on-time performance of domestic flights in the United States. This dataset is provided by the US Department of Transportation, Bureau of Transportation Statistics, and can be downloaded from the its website (*http://bit.ly/rita-transtats*) (a wrangled version of the dataset also exists in the GitHub repository for this book). BTS makes a CSV of every domestic US flight and relevant transportation statistics such as arrival or departure delays available for analysis. In our case, after wrangling the dataset, we have CSV data that is as follows, where each row contains the flight date; the airline ID; a flight number; the origin and destination airport; the departure time and delay in minutes; the arrival time and delay in minutes; and finally, the amount of time in the air as well as the distance in miles:

```
2014-04-01,19805,1,JFK,LAX,0854,-6.00,1217,2.00,355.00,2475.00
2014-04-01,19805,2,LAX,JFK,0944,14.00,1736,-29.00,269.00,2475.00
```

We'll start our example of writing structured MapReduce Python code by computing the average departure delay for each airport. First, let's take a look at the mapper. Write the following code into a file called *mapper.py*:

```python
#!/usr/bin/env python

import sys
import csv

SEP = "\t"


class Mapper(object):

    def __init__(self, stream, sep=SEP):
        self.stream = stream
        self.sep    = sep

    def emit(self, key, value):
        sys.stdout.write("{}{}{}\n".format(key, self.sep, value))

    def map(self):
        for row in self:
            self.emit(row[3], row[6])

    def __iter__(self):
        reader = csv.reader(self.stream)
        for row in reader:
            yield row


if __name__ == '__main__':
```

```
mapper = Mapper(sys.stdin)
mapper.map()
```

Let's step through this piece of code line by line. The first line with the #! (pronounced shebang) tells Linux (or more specifically, bash) what program to use to execute this script—in this case, whatever Python is in the default environment. This simple line helps us create executable scripts and lets Hadoop Streaming know what to do with our file.

In the subsequent lines, we import two modules from the Python standard library: the sys module, which we will use to access stdin and stdout, and the csv module, which we will use to quickly parse CSV data. Note that because these modules are both in the standard lib, they should be available in every node in the cluster. Third-party packages and custom code have to be dealt with specially, which we will talk about in a following section.

Instead of creating a procedural script for dealing with our input, we write all of our code inside of a Mapper class. While Python implements functional programming techniques, it is also a fully object-oriented (OO) programming language. Because Python is an interpreted language, we can write everything from quick scripts to do systems administration to large-scale software libraries and code bases that use OO design to create loosely coupled systems. The use of classes in our code allows us to create an extensible API that we can use for all of our MapReduce tasks. The code here is intended to be reusable and production grade—in "A Framework for Map-Reduce with Python" on page 52, we will combine what we've learned in this example into a full microframework for deploying Hadoop Streaming code with Python.

The Mapper class for our average flight delay example takes two arguments on instantiation, both of which have defaults, namely the infile and the separator. The infile refers to the location that data will be received from, which by default is stdin, as expected with Hadoop. However, this code can be made into a general framework that could analyze standalone files by itself, allowing us to have DRY (don't repeat yourself) type code that scales from smaller analyses to much larger ones. Hadoop computes with key/value pairs, so the second argument is used to determine what part of the input/output strings are the key and which are the values. By default, the separator is the tab character (\t); a module-level "constant" allows us to quickly redefine the separator if needed.

The next thing to note is the use of the built-in __iter__ method on the mapper class. The double underscore usually means that this is a special method or function in Python. In particular, implementing the __iter__ function allows the class to be used as an iterable, and this function should return a generator (usually constructed with the yield statement), another iterable, or if it simply returns self, it must also implement a next or __next__ method that raises StopIteration when the iteration is complete. This class can now be used in for statements as in:

```
for item in Mapper():
    print item
```

When this line of code is executed, Python looks into the __iter__ method to determine exactly how to iterate through an instance of the mapper class—in this case, by parsing each line of stdin using a csv.reader and yielding each row. Our class will use itself as an iterator in the map method, in which we expect to loop through every line in self, which in return simply loops through every line of the infile. It then yields the departure airport (position 3) as the key and the departure delay (position 6) as the value, which is emitted using the emit method—simply writing the key and value as a single line to stdout, separated by the sep character.

The last part of this code is the if __name__=="__main__" block, also called the "ifmain". In Python, this condition will only fire if the script is being run as the main entry point to the program, and will not run if the script is being imported. Python developers use this to test their code if it is in a library or to ensure that any executed code happens at the bottom of their Python scripts for easy debugging. Using this statement, we can ensure that this block will be executed when directly passed as a mapper to Hadoop Streaming and will not be executed if we import the code in order to subclass the mapper (e.g., for our microframework). Now let's take a look at the reducer. Write the following code in a new file called *reducer.py*:

```
#!/usr/bin/env python

import sys

from itertools import groupby
from operator import itemgetter

SEP = "\t"


class Reducer(object):

    def __init__(self, stream, sep=SEP):
        self.stream = stream
        self.sep    = sep

    def emit(self, key, value):
        sys.stdout.write("{}{}{}\n".format(key, self.sep, value))

    def reduce(self):
        for current, group in groupby(self, itemgetter(0)):
            total = 0
            count = 0

            for item in group:
                total += item[1]
                count += 1
```

```
            self.emit(current, float(total) / float(count))

    def __iter__(self):
        for line in self.stream:
            try:
                parts = line.split(self.sep)
                yield parts[0], float(parts[1])
            except:
                continue


if __name__ == '__main__':
    reducer = Reducer(sys.stdin)
    reducer.reduce()
```

The Reducer class is very similar to the mapper class; however, we introduce a couple of new items in this code, namely a memory-safe iterator helper groupby and an operator itemgetter. In the reduce function, as in the mapper, we loop through the entire dataset using an iterable that splits the key and value apart. In this case, the key and the value are split apart using the separator. The key is the first item that is split by the separator, and using Python slices, the value is everything else that followed the first instance of the separator. This matches with the default Hadoop Streaming behavior when dealing with the output of the map task, which is to treat everything up to the first tab character as the key, and everything else as the value. In this case, because we're doing float division to compute the average, we will simply parse the string value as a float.

 It is extremely important to consider the error handling in our Python code. In particular, the float parsing of the value is extremely susceptible to ValueError exceptions if the input is mangled, not a float, or not parseable. Be aware that when working with big data–sized datasets, exception handling is crucial. A common strategy is to just skip any line that raises an exception, as there is such a large volume of data to compute upon anyway.

Because the data is coming to the reducer sorted alphabetically by token due to the shuffle and sort phase of the Hadoop pipeline, we want to automatically group the keys and their values together. The groupby method does just that in a memory-safe manner, allowing you to access the key and access the list of values as though it were one list. The memory safety comes from the fact that groupby returns an iterator rather than a list that is held in memory, and only reads one line at a time (thus ensuring that big datasets do not overwhelm the resource capacity of our worker nodes). The itemgetter operator simply specifies by which value of each tuple being yielded that should be grouped on—in this case, the first element of the tuple.

After memory-efficiently grouping our values together, we simply sum the delays, divide by the number of flights, and emit the airport as the key and the mean as the value as output. Although our code has become more verbose, hopefully it is clear how we can move forward to creating a microframework that eliminates the duplication in much of this code and makes it reusable.

Executing Streaming Jobs

Before we get into how to execute a Streaming job on a Hadoop cluster by submitting the job to the job client, we'll first take a look at a useful way to test your scripts without Hadoop overhead. Because Streaming makes use of the Unix standard pipes, you can simulate the Hadoop MapReduce pipeline using Linux pipes and the sort command.

To test your code, make sure your *mapper.py* and *reducer.py* are executable. Simply use the chmod command in your terminal as follows:

```
hostname $ chmod +x mapper.py
hostname $ chmod +x reducer.py
```

To test your mapper and reducer using a CSV file as input, use the cat command to output the contents of the file, piping the output from stdout to the stdin of the *mapper.py*, which pipes to sort and then to *reducer.py* and finally prints the result to the screen. To test the average delay per airport mapper and reducer from the previous section, execute the following in a terminal where *mapper.py*, *reducer.py*, and *flights.csv* are all in your current working directory:

```
hostname $ cat flights.csv | ./mapper.py | sort | ./reducer.py
ABE     -3.57142857143
ABI     55.375
ABQ     3.83333333333
ABR     -4.0
ABY     -1.33333333333
ACT     -8.2
ACV     109.142857143
ACY     -8.0
ADQ     -14.0
AEX     -6.55555555556
AGS     31.4
ALB     -1.5
ALO     -8.5
AMA     0.8
...
TWF     -7.0
TXK     -4.66666666667
TYR     -6.71428571429
TYS     12.9583333333
VEL     -7.5
VLD     -5.0
```

```
VPS      5.06666666667
WRG      -3.75
XNA      14.2580645161
YAK      -17.5
YUM      -0.222222222222
```

Unix pipes are a simple and effective way to test Hadoop Streaming mappers and reducers, and effectively illustrate how your mapper and reducer code will be used on the cluster. This methodology is very good for quick tests as you're writing your scripts, without the overhead of waiting for the Hadoop Streaming job to complete and having to parse a Java traceback. If you're doing test-driven development, a natural complement to agile data science, you can emulate pipes using Popen to create integration tests.

> In the examples that follow, we use environment variables such as $HADOOP_HOME to specify specific paths or configurations. Often, these environment variables are installed along with the particular Hadoop distribution, although their names can vary. Our examples assume that you are working on the pseudo-distributed node setup, as described in Appendix A.

In order to deploy the code to the cluster, we need to submit the Hadoop Streaming JAR to the job client, passing in our custom operators as arguments. The location of the Hadoop Streaming job depends on how you've set up and configured Hadoop. For now, we'll assume that you have an environment variable, $HADOOP_HOME, that specifies the location of the install and that $HADOOP_HOME/bin is in your $PATH. If so, execute the Streaming job against the cluster as follows:

```
$ hadoop jar $HADOOP_HOME/share/hadoop/tools/lib/hadoop-streaming-*.jar \
    -input flights.csv \
    -output average_delay \
    -mapper mapper.py \
    -reducer reducer.py \
    -file mapper.py \
    -file reducer.py
```

Note the use of the -file option, which causes the Streaming job to send the scripts across the cluster (otherwise, they would be expected to be on the nodes already). Executing this command will cause the job to be started on the Hadoop cluster. The *mapper.py* and *reducer.py* scripts will be sent to each node in the cluster before processing and will be used in each phase of the pipeline.

If there are additional files that should be sent along with the job—for example, a lookup table for the airline IDs—they can also be packaged with the job using the -file option. Any third-party dependencies that you would like to use in your code should also be submitted along with the job, usually packaged in Python ZIP files. For larger dependencies (e.g., NLTK) or dependencies that require compilation using Cython (e.g., Numpy or SciPy), every node will need to have the dependency installed in the system path before the job is launched.

Hadoop Streaming has many other settings, allowing users to specify classes in the Hadoop library for partitioners, input and output formats, and so on. However, Hadoop Streaming can also make use of a Python script as a combiner, which can be especially important in large data analyses. Simply specify the combiner using the -combiner option to Streaming. An alternative is to update the mapper to a pipeline using the same shell script with sort and our reducer as we did in testing our script locally; however, it is usually more effective to simply specify another Python script as the combiner, especially because most combiners are usually the exact same or very similar to the reducer.

A Framework for MapReduce with Python

Slightly more advanced usage of Hadoop Streaming takes advantage of standard error (stderr) to update the Hadoop status as well as Hadoop counters. This technique essentially allows Streaming jobs to access the Reporter object, a part of the Map-Reduce Java API that tracks the global status of a job. By writing specially formatted strings to stderr, both mappers and reducers can update the global job status to report their progress and indicate they're alive. For jobs that take a significant amount of time (especially tasks involving the loading of a large model from a pickle file that is passed with the job), this is critical to ensuring that the framework doesn't assume a task has timed out.

Counters are globally aggregated across the MapReduce framework or application to save a key/value accounting of a numerical value. This is extremely useful in many tasks, and gives analysts and developers a sense of what is going on in the system during data analyses. Counters can be accumulated using associative operations, essentially increment or increase. Hadoop natively implements a number of counters, counting the number of records and bytes processed, but custom counters are an easy way to track metrics within a job, or to provide an associated channel for side computation.

For example, we could implement counters in our simple WordCount program to keep track of the global word count as well as to count our *vocabulary*—that is, the number of unique words. This allows a final computation of *lexical diversity* that is the ratio of the word count to the vocabulary, which expresses the average frequency of any individual token in our text. Metrics such as these are essential to understanding how changing corpora might affect some natural language–processing applications. Side along metrics, particularly counters, that are tracked alongside the main Hadoop job, can be used as output, but do not influence the primary computation.

They can also be used to compute mean squared error or classification metrics when evaluating machine learning models across the dataset.

To use the `Counter` and `Status` features of the `Reporter`, augment the `Mapper` and `Reducer` classes from the last section with the following methods:

```
def status(self, message):
    sys.stderr.write("reporter:status:{}\n".format(message))

def counter(self, counter, amount=1, group="ApplicationCounter"):
    sys.stderr.write(
        "reporter:counter:{},{},{}\n".format(group, counter, amount)
    )
```

The `counter` method allows both the `map` and `reduce` functions to update the count of any named counter by any amount necessary (defaults to incrementing by one). The group can be set to any name, and typically the name of the application is the default. Similarly, the `status` method allows the MapReduce application to send any arbitrary message to the framework, and make them visible either in logs or in the web user interfaces.

In order to extend our average flight delay application to provide a count of early and delayed flights and to send status updates on start and finish, update the `map` function as follows:

```
def map(self):
    self.status("mapping started")
    def map(self):
        for row in self:
            if row[6] < 0:
                self.counter("early departure")
            else:
                self.counter("late departure")

            self.emit(row[3], row[6])

    self.status("mapping complete")
```

This simple addition gives us greater insight into what is happening with average delays without a lengthy Hadoop job simply to count early and late flights. In the reducer, we may want to compute the number of airports that we have flight data for. Because the reducer will see every unique airport in our dataset, we can update our `reduce` function as follows:

```
def reduce(self):
    for current, group in groupby(self, itemgetter(0)):
        self.status("reducing airport {}".format(current))
        ...

        self.counter("airports")
        self.emit(current, float(total) / float(count))
```

As our analytical applications grow, these techniques to implement the full functionality of Hadoop Streaming will become vitally important. Considering natural language processing again, in order to do part-of-speech tagging or named-entity recognition, the application necessarily will have to load pickled models into memory. This process can take a few seconds up to a few minutes—using the status mechanism to alert the framework that the task is still running properly will ensure that speculative execution doesn't bog down the cluster. Counters help analyze large datasets even while running other jobs, and give applications a global scope with which to work off.

Speaking of global scope, there is one last tool that helps augment Streaming applications written in Python: Job Configuration variables (JobConf variables for short). The Hadoop Streaming application will automatically add the configuration variables of the job to the environment, renaming the configuration variable by replacing dots (.) with underscores (_). For example, to access the number of mappers in the job, you would request the `"mapred.map.tasks"` configuration variable. Although this particular example isn't necessarily useful, user-defined configuration values can be submitted to Hadoop Streaming with the `-D` argument in dot notation, and could contain important information like the URL to a shared resource. To access this in Python code, add the following function:

```
import os

def get_job_conf(name):
    name = name.replace(".", "_").upper()
    return os.environ.get(name)
```

At this point, it is clear that Python development for Hadoop Streaming would benefit from a miniature, reusable framework. The framework will have a base class that takes care of the Streaming details for both mappers and reducers, as well as abstract base classes `Mapper` and `Reducer` that should be extended in custom MapReduce Streaming jobs. Consider the following framework:

```
import os
import sys

from itertools import groupby
from operator import itemgetter

SEPARATOR = "\t"


class Streaming(object):

    @staticmethod
    def get_job_conf(name):
        name = name.replace(".", "_").upper()
        return os.environ.get(name)
```

```python
    def __init__(self, infile=sys.stdin, separator=SEPARATOR):
        self.infile = infile
        self.sep    = separator

    def status(self, message):
        sys.stderr.write("reporter:status:{}\n".format(message))

    def counter(self, counter, amount=1, group="Python Streaming"):
        msg = "reporter:counter:{},{},{}\n".format(group, counter, amount)
        sys.stderr.write(msg)

    def emit(self, key, value):
        sys.stdout.write("{}{}{}\n".format(key, self.sep, value))

    def read(self):
        for line in self.infile:
            yield line.rstrip()

    def __iter__(self):
        for line in self.read():
            yield line


class Mapper(Streaming):

    def map(self):
        raise NotImplementedError("Mappers must implement a map method")


class Reducer(Streaming):

    def reduce(self):
        raise NotImplementedError("Reducers must implement a reduce method")

    def __iter__(self):
        generator = (line.split(self.sep, 1) for line in self.read())
        for item in groupby(generator, itemgetter(0)):
            yield item
```

In order to write mappers and reducers to pass to Hadoop Streaming, we simply have to include this file along with the Streaming job and import the appropriate class from the framework. After extending the class, we just implement either the map or the reduce functions in our code. The following section describes a specific example in which this framework is used in conjunction with the Natural Language Toolkit (NLTK) to perform more precise word counting.

Counting Bigrams

The "Hello, World" of Hadoop programs has traditionally been implementing a word count program. Having Python code to perform word counts on files is a good example of distributed computing, but with Hadoop Streaming we can simply use the Linux wc command because this command also takes input from stdin and outputs to stdout. By using mappers and reducers, Python allows us to scale the job from a single aggregation of data on a reducer, and distributes work over extremely large datasets. Furthermore, word counting is the basis of statistical methodologies for language processing and we can use advanced text-processing techniques that are available to us in Python to do more advanced lexical analyses such as bigram counts or more advanced indexing using lemmatization.

Hadoop Streaming is extremely well suited for text processing, not only because it gives us access to libraries such as TextBlob and NLTK, but because Hadoop Streaming natively uses string sequences in a line-by-line fashion. Hadoop Streaming by default expects tab-delimited text values to be passed through the standard input and standard output of the Streaming job—and although it is expected that you still treat data as key/value pairs, it is not necessary.

 NLTK and TextBlob are third-party dependencies, meaning they are not packaged with Python by default. To install these packages, you would use the Python package manager, pip; and *every* node in the cluster must have these dependencies installed. For the purposes of this exercise, we assume that all extra libraries have been installed on the cluster, though cluster administration is beyond the scope of this book. If you are using a pseudo-distributed setup, then executing pip install nltk should do the trick.

Let's use the Python micro-framework to write a MapReduce application that does word counting, but with a few improvements. First, we will normalize our tokens to be all lowercase, so words like "Apple" will be the same as "apple". This isn't the right thing for all language-processing applications—capitalization in English (and many languages) is an important part of grammar, indicating the start of a sentence or a proper name (e.g., Apple Paltrow or Apple, Inc.). However, normalization in the context of vocabulary assessment is probably OK, and whether Apple is used at the beginning of the sentence or as a proper noun does not matter here.

Furthermore, we are going to eliminate punctuation and stopwords from our token counting. Stopwords are words that are used functionally in a language—for example, articles ("a" or "an"), determiners ("the", "this", "my"), pronouns ("his", "they") and prepositions ("over", "on", "for"). Because of their functional use, stopwords are extremely common and make up the bulk of any corpus. For some information retrieval applications, stopwords are said to be the most frequent words given some distribution of vocabulary and are automatically removed to improve performance; in this case, common verbs such as "want" or "has" might find themselves excluded. Either way, the removal of stopwords with punctuation and normalization of text dramatically decreases the vocabulary density and might help give a sense of what the most important words to a particular corpus are.

Finally, we'll use our normalized corpus to count *bigrams*—that is, words that tend to appear together often (e.g., are written consecutively twice in a row while ignoring stopwords). Bigram analysis allows statisticians to capture words that typically belong together, or that might have some significance—for example, "lawn chair" or "vetoed bill". Bigrams are the start of *n*-Gram language models, a technique for building models that can predict the next word given a context.

Using our framework from before, the Mapper does the bulk of the work:

```python
#!/usr/bin/env python

import sys
import nltk
import string

from framework import Mapper


class BigramMapper(Mapper):

    def __init__(self, infile=sys.stdin, separator='\t'):
        super(BigramMapper, self).__init__(infile, separator)

        self.stopwords   = nltk.corpus.stopwords.words("english")
        self.punctuation = string.punctuation

    def exclude(self, token):
        return token in self.punctuation or token in self.stopwords

    def normalize(self, token):
        return token.lower()

    def tokenize(self, value):
        for token in nltk.wordpunct_tokenize(value):
            token = self.normalize(token)
            if not self.exclude(token):
                yield token

    def map(self):
        for value in self:
            for bigram in nltk.bigrams(self.tokenize(value)):
                self.counter("words")  # Count the total number of bigrams
                self.emit(bigram, 1)

if __name__ == "__main__":
    mapper = BigramMapper()
    mapper.map()
```

The map method is pretty straightforward. It loops through the entire input and uses the nltk.wordpunct_tokenizer to tokenize the value, which will be a line of text from our dataset. This tokenizer ensures that not only are the words, including contractions, split apart but that punctuation is also split away as well. The tokenizer also ignores punctuation and stopwords by including the built-in stopwords corpus from nltk. Note that it would not be hard to augment this code to have a custom stopword list packaged with job using the -file argument.

In order to perform our bigram counting, we need to emit the token as the key, along with the value 1. We've created a simple emit helper function, which simply writes the key/value pair, joined by the separator string to the output (in this case, stdout). Bigrams are collected using the built-in nltk.bigrams function.

The reducer implements a very common MapReduce pattern, the SumReducer. This reducer is used so often that you might want to add it to your microframework as a standard class, along with an IdentityMapper and other standard patterns you'll find in Chapter 5. The code for the SumReducer is as follows:

```
#!/usr/bin/env python

from framework import Reducer


class SumReducer(Reducer):

    def reduce(self):
        for key, values in self:
            total = sum(int(count) for count in values)
            self.emit(key, total)


if __name__ == '__main__':
    reducer = SumReducer()
    reducer.reduce()
```

Note that this reducer ignores the key, which is simply a text string representation of the bigram tuple, because it is just counting the occurrences of that tuple. However, consider the case where you need to deal with the compound key, either for keyspace change (e.g., filtering bigrams based on the first word) or in a mapper in a chained MapReduce job; you can use Python's literal eval to convert the string into a tuple:

```
import ast

key = ast.literal_eval(key)
```

In order to submit this job to the cluster via Hadoop Streaming, use the same command as demonstrated earlier, but make sure to also include the *framework.py* file to be packaged and sent with the job. The job submission command is as follows:

```
$ hadoop jar $HADOOP_HOME/share/hadoop/tools/lib/hadoop-streaming-*.jar \
    -input corpus \
    -output bigrams \
    -mapper mapper.py \
    -reducer reducer.py \
    -file mapper.py \
    -file reducer.py \
    -file framework.py
```

Note that in this case, we'll assume that the third-party dependency `nltk` is simply installed on every node in the cluster, which is possible if you have administrative access to the cluster, or are launching the cluster from a specific AMI. If not, `nltk` will need to be bundled into a ZIP file and also passed with the `-file` argument.

Other Frameworks

Although we have already created a small framework from which we can write Map-Reduce jobs, it is important to note that there are several other frameworks that will allow you to write MapReduce jobs with Python. The two most popular frameworks at the time of this writing are Yelp's mrjob (*http://bit.ly/1NqmsvA*) and dumbo on Git-Hub (*http://bit.ly/1UQx8G3*), which wrap Hadoop Streaming and add more functionality. Other frameworks include pydoop (*http://bit.ly/1LizcVD*), which wraps Hadoop Pipes (a C++ API for Hadoop) and hadoopy (*http://bit.ly/1TQugXl*), which wraps Streaming with Cython.

These frameworks attempt to give Python developers a leg up when it comes to writing Hadoop jobs, but they come with a performance penalty. They provide a simpler API and programming interface as well as standard tools in Python, and many also provide a methodology of running and launching jobs that allows the developer to focus on Python development instead of Hadoop integration. More advanced frameworks include the use of `TypedBytes`, a binary serialization format in Hadoop that allows Python objects to be serialized as input and output and improves the performance of these frameworks significantly.

The mrjob library is notable because it is in active development by Yelp, whose platform is entirely within the Amazon Web Services ecosystem. Because of this, mrjob is uniquely suited to quickly deploying and running jobs on Amazon's Elastic Map-Reduce framework via the boto Python library. Jobs written with mrjob are usually single files containing the complete MapReduce code and can be executed directly against the local file system, EMR, or a normal Hadoop cluster. Moreover, jobs can be configured and specified by a simple configuration file.

The dumbo library was one of the first Python Hadoop Streaming frameworks, and although it is not very actively maintained, it enjoys wide usage and was mentioned as a framework of choice in *Hadoop: The Definitive Guide* by Tom White (O'Reilly). The dumbo framework completely wraps Hadoop Streaming and uses `TypedBytes` to improve performance; it can be used to write complex, chained MapReduce jobs efficiently and comes with a command-line script that manages and executes jobs as well as providing interaction with HDFS.

In the end, simple usage of Hadoop Streaming will be by far the most performant solution as it does not rely on the added dependencies of third-party libraries, and because it is lightweight enough to deploy in a variety of analytical scenarios. Throughout the book, examples in MapReduce will make use of the Streaming mechanism described in this chapter. For larger, more complex analyses, developers may want to review these frameworks to make them part of their workflow.

Advanced MapReduce

In this final section, we include some advanced topics that concern MapReduce in particular. The purpose here is to introduce concepts that have played a large role in MapReduce algorithms and optimizations, primarily because you will encounter these terms as you read more about how to implement different analyses. Rather than introducing how to use these tools, we approach this section from a *conceptual* level so that when you explore MapReduce in more detail they are not unfamiliar.

To put it differently, these tools are difficult to implement without the Java API, so they don't fit into a chapter about Hadoop Streaming, but neglecting to mention them would be an egregious omission from a discussion about MapReduce. In particular, we will discuss combiners (the primary MapReduce optimization technique), partitioners (a technique for ensuring there is no bottleneck in the reduce step), and job chaining (a technique for putting together larger algorithms and data flows).

Combiners

Mappers produce a lot of intermediate data that must be sent over the network to be shuffled, sorted, and reduced. Because networking is a physical resource, large amounts of transmitted data can lead to job delays and memory bottlenecks (e.g., there is too much data for the reducer to hold into memory). Combiners are the primary mechanism to solve this problem, and are essentially intermediate reducers that are associated with the mapper output. Combiners reduce network traffic by performing a mapper-local reduction of the data before forwarding it on to the appropriate reducer. Consider the following output from two mappers and a simple sum reduction.

Mapper 1 output:

```
(IAD, 14.4), (SFO, 3.9), (JFK, 3.9), (IAD, 12.2), (JFK, 5.8)
```

Mapper 2 output:

```
(SFO, 4.7), (IAD, 2.3), (SFO, 4.4), (IAD, 1.2)
```

Intended sum reduce output:

```
(IAD, 29.1), (JFK, 9.7), (SFO, 13.0)
```

Each mapper is emitting extra work for the reducer, namely in the duplication of the different keys coming from each mapper. A combiner that precomputes the sums for each key will reduce the number of key/value pairs being generated, and therefore the amount of network traffic. Moreover, because there are fewer duplicate keys, the shuffle and sort operation also becomes faster.

It is extremely common for the combiner and the reducer to be identical, which is possible if the operation is commutative and associative, but this is not always the case. So long as the combiner takes as input the type of data that the mapper is exporting and produces the same data as output, the combiner can perform any partial reduction. It is common, therefore to see algorithms expressed both with a mapper, a reducer, and a combiner if the combiner has a different operation than the reducer. To specify a combiner in Hadoop Streaming, use the -combiner option, similar to specifying a mapper and reducer:

```
$ hadoop jar $HADOOP_HOME/share/hadoop/tools/lib/hadoop-streaming-*.jar \
    -input input_data \
    -output output_data \
    -mapper mapper.py \
    -combiner combiner.py \
    -reducer reducer.py \
    -file mapper.py \
    -file reducer.py \
    -file combiner.py
```

If the combiner matches the reducer, then you would simply specify the *reducer.py* file as the combiner, and not add an extra third combiner file. In the microframework that we have created, a combiner class would simply subclass the Reducer.

Partitioners

Partitioners control how keys and their values get sent to individual reducers by dividing up the keyspace. The default behavior is the HashPartitioner, which is often all that is needed. This partitioner allocates keys evenly to each reducer by computing the hash of the key and assigning the key to a keyspace determined by the number of reducers. Given a uniformly distributed keyspace, each reducer will get a relatively equal workload.

The issue arises when there is a key imbalance, such that a large number of values are associated with one key, and other keys are less likely. In this case, a significant portion of the reducers are underworked, and much of the benefit of reduction parallelism is lost. A custom partitioner can ease this problem by dividing the keyspace according to some other semantic structure besides hashing (which is usually domain specific). Custom partitioners can also be required for some types of MapReduce algorithms, most notably to implement a left outer join. Finally, because every reducer writes output to its own *part-** file, the use of a custom partitioner also allows for clearer data organization, allowing you to write sectioned output to each file based on the partitioning criteria—for example, writing per-year output data.

Unfortunately, custom partitioners can only be created with the Java API. However, Hadoop Streaming users can still specify a partitioner Java class either from the Hadoop library, or by writing their own Java partitioner and submitting it with their streaming job.

Job Chaining

Most complex algorithms cannot be described as a simple `map` and `reduce`, so in order to implement more complex analytics, a technique called *job chaining* is required. If a complex algorithm can be decomposed into several smaller MapReduce tasks, then these tasks can be chained together to produce a complete output. Consider a computation to compute the pairwise Pearson correlation coefficient for a number of variables in a dataset. The Pearson correlation requires a computation of the mean and standard deviation of each variable. Because this cannot be easily accomplished in a single MapReduce, we might employ the following strategy:

1. Compute the mean and standard deviation of each (X, Y) pair.

2. Use the output of the first job to compute the covariance and Pearson correlation coefficient.

The mean and standard deviation can be computed in the initial job by mapping the total, the sum, and the sum of squares to a reducer that computes the mean and standard deviation. The second job takes the mean and standard deviation and computes the covariance by mapping the difference of the value and the mean, and their product for each pair, then reducing by appropriately summing and taking a square root. As you can see in Figure 3-2, the second job is dependent on the first.

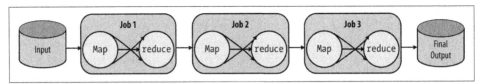

Figure 3-2. Linear job chaining produces complete computations by sending the output of one or more MapReduce jobs as the input to another

Job chaining is therefore the combination of many smaller jobs into a complete computation by sending the output of one or more previous jobs into the input of another. In order to implement algorithms like this, the developer must think about how each individual step of a computation can be reduced to intermediary values, not just between mappers and reducers but also between jobs. As shown in Figure 3-2, many jobs are typically thought of as *linear job chaining*. A linear dependency means that each MapReduce job is dependent only upon a single previous job. However, this is a simplification of the more general form of job chaining, which is expressed as a *data flow* where jobs are dependent on one or more previous jobs. Complex jobs are represented as directed acyclic graphs (DAGs) that describe how data flows from an input source through each job (the directed part) to the next job (never repeating a step, the acyclic part) and finally as final output (see Figure 3-3).

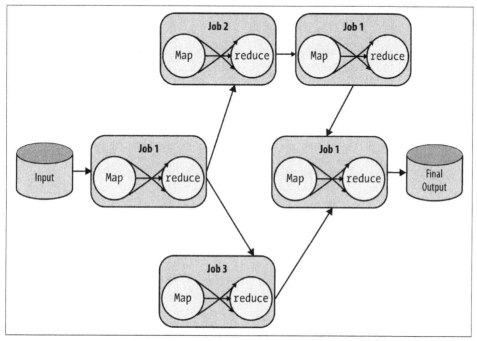

Figure 3-3. Data flow job chaining is an extension of linear chaining

Map-Only Jobs

When considering job chains and job dependencies, it's helpful to note that the possibility of map-only jobs exists. Map-only jobs fall into two categories: those where you would require no aggregation and those where you are actively trying to avoid the shuffle and sort phase—either to maintain data order or to optimize the execution of the job.

To execute a map-only job, simply set the number of reducers to 0. With Hadoop Streaming, you can specify the number of reducers via the `-numReduceTasks` flag. Reduce-only jobs are also possible, by using an identity mapper, as discussed in Chapter 5. "Map-only" jobs that require sorting can be executed with the identity reducer.

To compute the Pearson correlation coefficient, and to illustrate job chaining, we will use the formula for a sample Pearson correlation as given by Wikipedia in the equation that follows. Our input data will be key/value pairs of data where the key is a dependent variable, y, and the value is a vector of dependent variables, and x_i is the variable with which we want to determine the correlation with y.

Equation 3-1. A formula for computing the sample Pearson correlation coefficient

$$r = r_{xy} = \frac{\sum_{i=1}^{n}\left(x_i - \bar{x}\right)\left(y_i - \bar{y}\right)}{\sqrt{\sum_{i=1}^{n}\left(x_i - \bar{x}\right)^2}\sqrt{\sum_{i=1}^{n}\left(y_i - \bar{y}\right)^2}}$$

Our first map reduce job will compute n and the mean of x and y as follows:

```
class VariablePairsMapper(Mapper):

    def map(self):
        # Compute the pairwise count and sum for each x, y pair.
        # The output key is the index of the x in the vector
        for y, vector in self:
            for x, i in enumerate(vector):
                self.emit(i, (1, x, y) )


class PairsMeanReducer(Reducer):

    def reduce(self):
        for key, values in self:
            # Load all of the values into memory so that we can iterate twice.
            values = list(values)

            # Compute the sum of x, y and the number of items
            sx, sy, sn = 0
            for (n, x, y) in values:
                sn += n
                sx += x
                sy += y

            # Compute the mean of x and y
            xbar = sx / n
            ybar = sy / n

            # Emit the mean of x and y along with each x, y pair.
            for (n, x, y) in values:
                self.emit(key, (x, y, xbar, ybar))
```

Now that we have the mean values in hand, we can compute the covariance and standard deviations in order to compute the final Pearson correlation coefficient in a second job. To do this, we need to pass through the *same* input data a second time, and include the output of the first job as input to this job. To simplify this and for illustration purposes only, we have emitted each *x,y* pair along with its associated mean as the output to the first job:

```python
import math


class PearsonMapper(Mapper):

    def map(self):
        # Compute the differences between x and xbar and y and ybar
        # Emit the product of the differences as well as their squares
        for i, (x, y, xbar, ybar) in self:
            xdiff = x-xbar
            ydiff = y-ybar
            self.emit(i, xdiff*ydiff, xdiff**2, ydiff**2)


class PearsonReducer(Reducer):

    def reduce(self):
        for key, values in self:
            # Compute the sum of the difference product and squares.
            sxyd = 0
            sxd2 = 0
            syd2 = 0

            for (xyd, x2d, y2d) in values:
                sxyd  += xyd
                sxd2 += x2d
                syd2 += y2d

            # Emit the correlation coefficient
            r = sxyd / (math.sqrt(sxd2) * math.sqrt(xyd2))
            self.emit(key, r)
```

While this isn't the most efficient method of implementing a parallel Pearson coefficient, it hopefully demonstrates a clear example of job chaining. The primary consideration is how to output the data from job 1 such that job 2 can conduct its work. Moving from this simple introduction to more complex topics, in Chapter 5 we will explore *pairs* and *stripes*, which make complex computations like this more feasible. While manual job chaining is possible (executing the first job, then the second on the command line), this isn't ideal. In Chapter 8, we explore *data flows* and how to put chained jobs together with higher-order tools.

Conclusion

Hadoop Streaming is an important tool that enables data scientists who want to program in R or Python (rather than Java) to immediately start using Hadoop and MapReduce, in particular. For a long time, Hadoop Streaming was the only game in town if you wanted to do big data in Python. However, for more complex jobs or algorithms, particularly ones that required optimization like combiners or partitioners, the Java API was required.

Things have dramatically changed since then, however, particularly for Python developers. In the following chapter, we discuss Spark, a dramatically different computing framework on Hadoop, which ships with a native Python API (and soon one in R). Spark is quickly becoming the data science platform of choice, particularly because tools like DataFrames and a large array of analytical packages are being built on it.

However, MapReduce and Hadoop Streaming have not been completely subsumed by Spark. Batch jobs, particularly those that are run often (e.g., extract, transform, and load [ETL] operations or other data wrangling and cleaning processes) are actually more suited to MapReduce if only for the built-in shuffle and sort. Moreover, MapReduce and Hadoop Streaming are well built and well tested, and can be trusted for mission-critical applications. In the end, and because the programming model is so similar, most practical big data is now conducted with *both* MapReduce and Spark, each well suited to its specific type of application.

CHAPTER 4

In-Memory Computing with Spark

Together, HDFS and MapReduce have been the foundation of and the driver for the advent of large-scale machine learning, scaling analytics, and big data appliances for the last decade. Like most platform technologies, the maturation of Hadoop has led to a stable computing environment that is general enough to build specialist tools for tasks such as graph processing, micro-batch processing, SQL querying, data warehousing, and machine learning. However, as Hadoop became more widely adopted, more specializations were required for a wider variety of new use cases, and it became clear that the batch processing model of MapReduce was not well suited to common workflows including iterative, interactive, or on-demand computations upon a single dataset.

The primary MapReduce abstraction (specification of computation as a mapping then a reduction) is parallelizable, easy to understand, and hides the details of distributed computing, thus allowing Hadoop to guarantee correctness. However, in order to achieve coordination and fault tolerance, the MapReduce model uses a pull execution model that requires intermediate writes of data back to HDFS. Unfortunately, the input/output (I/O) of moving data from where it's stored to where it needs to be computed upon is the largest time cost in any computing system; as a result, while MapReduce is incredibly safe and resilient, it is also necessarily slow on a per-task basis. Worse, almost all applications must chain multiple MapReduce jobs together in multiple steps, creating a data flow toward the final required result. This results in huge amounts of intermediate data written to HDFS that is not required by the user, creating additional costs in terms of disk usage.

To address these problems, Hadoop has moved to a more general resource management framework for computation: YARN. Whereas previously the MapReduce application allocated resources (processors, memory) to jobs specifically for mappers and reducers, YARN provides more general resource access to Hadoop applications. The result is that specialized tools no longer have to be decomposed into a series of Map-Reduce jobs and can become more complex. By generalizing the management of the cluster, the programming model first imagined in MapReduce can be expanded to include new abstractions and operations.

Spark is the first fast, general-purpose distributed computing paradigm resulting from this shift, and is rapidly gaining popularity particularly because of its speed and adaptability. Spark primarily achieves this speed via a new data model called resilient distributed datasets (RDDs) that are stored in memory while being computed upon, thus eliminating expensive intermediate disk writes. It also takes advantage of a directed acyclic graph (DAG) execution engine that can optimize computation, particularly iterative computation, which is essential for data theoretic tasks such as optimization and machine learning. These speed gains allow Spark to be accessed in an interactive fashion (as though you were sitting at the Python interpreter), making the user an integral part of computation and allowing for data exploration of big datasets that was not previously possible, bringing the cluster to the data scientist.

 Because directed acyclic graphs are commonly used to describe the steps in a data flow, the term DAG is used often when discussing big data processing. In this sense, DAGs are directed because one step or steps follow after another, and *acylic* because a single step does not repeat itself. When a data flow is described as a DAG, it eliminates costly synchronization and makes parallel applications easier to build.

In this chapter, we introduce Spark and resilient distributed datasets. This is the last chapter describing the nuts and bolts of doing analytics with Hadoop. Because Spark implements many applications already familiar to data scientists (e.g., DataFrames, interactive notebooks, and SQL), we propose that at least initially, Spark will be the primary method of cluster interaction for the novice Hadoop user. To that end, we describe RDDs, explore the use of Spark on the command line with `pyspark`, then demonstrate how to write Spark applications in Python and submit them to the cluster as Spark jobs.

Spark Basics

Apache Spark is a cluster-computing platform that provides an API for distributed programming similar to the MapReduce model, but is designed to be fast for interactive queries and iterative algorithms.[1] It primarily achieves this by caching data required for computation in the memory of the nodes in the cluster. In-memory clus-

---

1 Holden Karau, Andy Konwinski, Patrick Wendell, and Matei Zaharia, *Learning Spark*, (O'Reilly, 2015).

ter computation enables Spark to run iterative algorithms, as programs can check-point data and refer back to it without reloading it from disk; in addition, it supports interactive querying and streaming data analysis at extremely fast speeds. Because Spark is compatible with YARN, it can run on an existing Hadoop cluster and access any Hadoop data source, including HDFS, S3, HBase, and Cassandra.

Importantly, Spark was designed from the ground up to support big data applications and data science in particular. Instead of a programming model that only supports map and reduce, the Spark API has many other powerful distributed abstractions similarly related to functional programming, including sample, filter, join, and collect, to name a few. Moreover, while Spark is implemented in Scala, programming APIs in Scala, Java, R, and Python makes Spark much more accessible to a range of data scientists who can take fast and full advantage of the Spark engine.

In order to understand the shift, consider the limitations of MapReduce with regards to iterative algorithms. These types of algorithms apply the same operation many times to blocks of data until they reach a desired result. For example, optimization algorithms like gradient descent are iterative; given some target function (like a linear model), the goal is to optimize the parameters of that function such that the error (the difference between the predicted value of the model and the actual value of the data) is minimized. Here, the algorithm applies the target function with one set of parameters to the entire dataset and computes the error, afterward slightly modifying the parameters of the function according to the computed error (descending down the error curve). This process is repeated (the iterative part) until the error is mini-mized below some threshold or until a maximum number of iterations is reached.

This basic technique is the foundation of many machine learning algorithms, particu-larly supervised learning, in which the correct answers are known ahead of time and can be used to optimize some decision space. In order to program this type of algo-rithm in MapReduce, the parameters of the target function would have to be mapped to every instance in the dataset, and the error computed and reduced. After the reduce phase, the parameters would be updated and fed into the next MapReduce job. This is possible by chaining the error computation and update jobs together; how-ever, on each job the data would have to be read from disk and the errors written back to it, causing significant I/O-related delay.

Instead, Spark keeps the dataset in memory as much as possible throughout the course of the application, preventing the reloading of data between iterations. Spark programmers therefore do not simply specify map and reduce steps, but rather an entire series of data flow transformations to be applied to the input data before per-forming some action that requires coordination like a reduction or a write to disk. Because data flows can be described using directed acyclic graphs (DAGs), Spark's execution engine knows ahead of time how to distribute the computation across the cluster and manages the details of the computation, similar to how MapReduce abstracts distributed computation.

By combining acyclic data flow and in-memory computing, Spark is extremely fast particularly when the cluster is large enough to hold all of the data in memory. In fact, by increasing the size of the cluster and therefore the amount of available memory to hold an entire, very large dataset, the speed of Spark means that it can be used *interactively*—making the user a key participant of analytical processes that are running on the cluster. As Spark evolved, the notion of user interaction became essential to its model of distributed computation; in fact, it is probably for this reason that so many languages are supported.

Spark's generality also meant that it could be used to build higher-level tools for implementing SQL-like computations, graph and machine learning algorithms, and even interactive notebooks and data frames—all familiar tools to data scientists, but in a cluster-computing context. Before we get into the details of *how* Spark implements general distributed computing, it's useful to get a sense of what tools are available in Spark.

The Spark Stack

Spark is a general-purpose distributed computing abstraction and can run in a stand-alone mode. However, Spark focuses purely on *computation* rather than *data storage* and as such is typically run in a cluster that implements data warehousing and cluster management tools. In this book, we are primarily interested in Hadoop (though Spark distributions on Apache Mesos and Amazon EC2 also exist). When Spark is built with Hadoop, it utilizes YARN to allocate and manage cluster resources like processors and memory via the `ResourceManager`. Importantly, Spark can then access any Hadoop data source—for example HDFS, HBase, or Hive, to name a few.

Spark exposes its primary programming abstraction to developers through the Spark Core module. This module contains basic and general functionality, including the API that defines resilient distributed datasets (RDDs). RDDs, which we will describe in more detail in the next section, are the essential functionality upon which all Spark computation resides. Spark then builds upon this core, implementing special-purpose libraries for a variety of data science tasks that interact with Hadoop, as shown in Figure 4-1.

The component libraries are not integrated into the general-purpose computing framework, making the Spark Core module extremely flexible and allowing developers to easily solve similar use cases with different approaches. For example, Hive will be moving to Spark, allowing an easy migration path for existing users; GraphX is based on the Pregel model of vertex-centric graph computation, but other graph libraries that leverage gather, apply, scatter (GAS) style computations could easily be implemented with RDDs. This flexibility means that specialist tools can still use

Spark for development, but that new users can quickly get started with the Spark components that already exist.

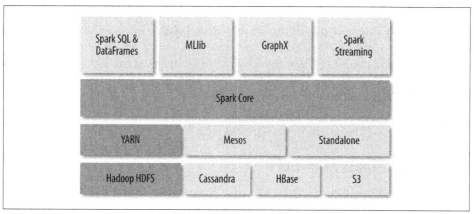

Figure 4-1. Spark is a computational framework designed to take advantage of cluster management platforms like YARN and distributed data storage like HDFS

The primary components included with Spark are as follows:

Spark SQL

Originally provided APIs for interacting with Spark via the Apache Hive variant of SQL called HiveQL; in fact, you can still directly access Hive via this library. However, this library is moving toward providing a more general, structured data-processing abstraction, DataFrames. DataFrames are essentially distributed collections of data organized into columns, conceptually similar to tables in relational databases.

Spark Streaming

Enables the processing and manipulation of unbounded streams of data in real time. Many streaming data libraries (such as Apache Storm) exist for handling real-time data. Spark Streaming enables programs to leverage this data similar to how you would interact with a normal RDD as data is flowing in.

MLlib

A library of common machine learning algorithms implemented as Spark operations on RDDs. This library contains scalable learning algorithms (e.g., classifications, regressions, etc.). that require iterative operations across large datasets. The Mahout library, formerly the big data machine learning library of choice, will move to Spark for its implementations in the future.

GraphX

A collection of algorithms and tools for manipulating graphs and performing parallel graph operations and computations. GraphX extends the RDD API to include operations for manipulating graphs, creating subgraphs, or accessing all vertices in a path.

These components combined with the Spark programming model provide a rich methodology of interacting with cluster resources. It is probably because of this completeness that Spark has become so immensely popular for distributed analytics. Instead of learning multiple tools, the basic API remains the same across components and the components themselves are easily accessed without extra installation. This richness and consistency comes from the primary programming abstraction in Spark that we've mentioned a few times up to this point, resilient distributed datasets, which we will explore in more detail in the next section.

Resilient Distributed Datasets

In Chapter 2, we described Hadoop as a distributed computing framework that dealt with two primary problems: how to distribute data across a cluster, and how to distribute computation. The distributed data storage problem deals with high availability of data (getting data to the place it needs to be processed) as well as recoverability and durability. Distributed computation intends to improve the performance (speed) of a computation by breaking a large computation or task into smaller, independent computations that can be run simultaneously (in parallel) and then aggregated to a final result. Because each parallel computation is run on an individual node or computer in the cluster, a distributed computing framework needs to provide consistency, correctness, and fault-tolerant guarantees for the whole computation. Spark does not deal with distributed data storage, relying on Hadoop to provide this functionality, and instead focuses on reliable distributed computation through a framework called resilient distributed datasets.

RDDs are essentially a programming abstraction that represents a read-only collection of objects that are partitioned across a set of machines. RDDs can be rebuilt from a lineage (and are therefore fault tolerant), are accessed via parallel operations, can be read from and written to distributed storages (e.g., HDFS or S3), and most importantly, can be cached in the memory of worker nodes for immediate reuse. As mentioned earlier, it is this in-memory caching feature that allows for massive speedups and provides for *iterative computing* required for machine learning and user-centric *interactive analyses*.

RDDs are operated upon with functional programming constructs that include and expand upon map and reduce. Programmers create new RDDs by loading data from an input source, or by transforming an existing collection to generate a new one. The history of applied transformations is primarily what defines the RDD's *lineage*, and because the collection is *immutable* (not directly modifiable), transformations can be reapplied to part or all of the collection in order to recover from failure. The Spark

API is therefore essentially a collection of operations that create, transform, and export RDDs.

 Recovering from failure in Spark is very different than in Map-Reduce. In MapReduce, data is written as sequence files (binary flat files containing typed key/value pairs) to disk between each interim step of processing. Processes therefore pull data between map, shuffle and sort, and reduce. If a process fails, then another process can start pulling data. In Spark, the collection is stored in memory and by keeping checkpoints or cached versions of earlier parts of an RDD, its lineage can be used to rebuild some or all of the collection.

The fundamental programming model therefore is describing how RDDs are created and modified via programmatic operations. There are two types of operations that can be applied to RDDs: *transformations* and *actions*. Transformations are operations that are applied to an existing RDD to create a new RDD—for example, applying a filter operation on an RDD to generate a smaller RDD of filtered values. Actions, however, are operations that actually return a result back to the Spark driver program —resulting in a coordination or aggregation of all partitions in an RDD. In this model, map is a transformation, because a function is passed to every object stored in the RDD and the output of that function maps to a new RDD. On the other hand, an aggregation like reduce is an action, because reduce requires the RDD to be repartitioned (according to a key) and some aggregate value like sum or mean computed and returned. Most actions in Spark are designed solely for the purpose of output—to return a single value or a small list of values, or to write data back to distributed storage.

An additional benefit of Spark is that it applies transformations "lazily"—inspecting a complete sequence of transformations and an action before executing them by submitting a job to the cluster. This lazy-execution provides significant storage and computation optimizations, as it allows Spark to build up a lineage of the data and evaluate the complete transformation chain in order to compute upon only the data needed for a result; for example, if you run the first() action on an RDD, Spark will avoid reading the entire dataset and return just the first matching line.

Programming with RDDs

Programming Spark applications is similar to other data flow frameworks previously implemented on Hadoop. Code is written in a driver program that is evaluated lazily on the driver-local machine when submitted, and upon an action, the driver code is distributed across the cluster to be executed by workers on their partitions of the RDD. Results are then sent back to the driver for aggregation or compilation. As illustrated in Figure 4-2, the driver program creates one or more RDDs by parallelizing a dataset from a Hadoop data source, applies operations to transform the RDD, then invokes some action on the transformed RDD to retrieve output.

 We've used the term *parallelization* a few times, and it's worth a bit of explanation. RDDs are partitioned collections of data that allow the programmer to apply operations to the entire collection in *parallel*. It is the partitions that allow the parallelization, and the partitions themselves are computed boundaries in the list where data is stored on different nodes. Therefore "parallelization" is the act of partitioning a dataset and sending each part of the data to the node that will perform computations upon it.

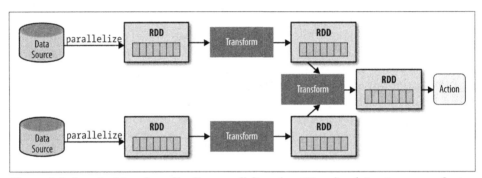

Figure 4-2. A typical Spark application parallelizes (partitions) a dataset across a cluster into RDDs

A typical data flow sequence for programming Spark is as follows:

1. Define one or more RDDs, either through accessing data stored on disk (e.g., HDFS, Cassandra, HBase, or S3), parallelizing some collection, transforming an existing RDD, or by caching. Caching is one of the fundamental procedures in Spark—storing an RDD in the memory of a node for rapid access as the computation progresses.

2. Invoke operations on the RDD by passing closures (here, a function that does not rely on external variables or data) to each element of the RDD. Spark offers many high-level operators beyond map and reduce.

3. Use the resulting RDDs with aggregating actions (e.g., count, collect, save, etc.). Actions kick off the computation on the cluster because no progress can be made until the aggregation has been computed.

A quick note on variables and closures, which can be confusing in Spark. When Spark runs a closure on a worker, any variables used in the closure are copied to that node, but are maintained within the local scope of that closure. If external data is required, Spark provides two types of shared variables that can be interacted with by all workers in a restricted fashion: *broadcast variables* and *accumulators*. Broadcast variables are distributed to all workers, but are read-only and are often used as lookup tables or stopword lists. Accumulators are variables that workers can "add" to using associative operations and are typically used as counters. These data structures are similar to the MapReduce distributed cache and counters, and serve a similar role. However, because Spark allows for general interprocess communication, these data structures are perhaps used in a wider variety of applications.

Closures are a cool-kid functional programming technique, and make distributed computing possible. They serve as a means for providing lexically scoped name binding, which basically means that a closure is a function that includes its own independent data environment. As a result of this independence, a closure operates with no outside information and is thus parallelizable. Closures are becoming more common in daily programming, often used as callbacks. In other languages, you may have heard them referred to as *blocks* or *anonymous functions*.

Although the following sections provide demonstrations showing how to use Spark for performing distributed computation, a full guide to the many transformations and actions available to Spark developers is beyond the scope of this book. A full list of supported transformations and actions, as well as documentation on usage, can be found in the Spark Programming Guide (*http://spark.apache.org/docs/latest/programming-guide.html*). In the next section, we'll take a look at how to use Spark interactively to employ transformations and actions on the command line without having to write complete programs.

Spark Execution

A brief note on the execution of Spark: essentially, Spark applications are run as independent sets of processes, coordinated by a SparkContext in a driver program. The context will connect to some cluster manager (e.g., YARN), which allocates system resources. Each worker in the cluster is managed by an executor, which is in turn managed by the SparkContext. The executor manages computation as well as storage and caching on each machine. The interaction of the driver, YARN, and the workers is shown in Figure 4-3.

It is important to note that application code is sent from the driver to the executors, and the executors specify the context and the various tasks to be run. The executors communicate back and forth with the driver for data sharing or for interaction. Drivers are key participants in Spark jobs, and therefore, they should be on the same network as the cluster. This is different from Hadoop code, where you might submit a job from anywhere to the ResourceManager, which then handles the execution on the cluster.

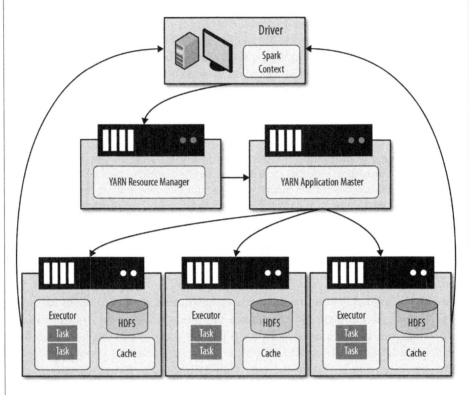

Figure 4-3. In the Spark execution model, the driver program is an essential part of processing

With this in mind, Spark applications can actually be submitted to the Hadoop cluster in two modes: yarn-client and yarn-cluster. In yarn-client mode, the driver is run inside of the client process as described, and the ApplicationMaster simply manages the progression of the job and requests resources. However, in yarn-cluster mode, the driver program is run inside of the ApplicationMaster process, thus releasing the client process and proceeding more like traditional MapReduce jobs. Programmers would use yarn-client mode to get immediate results or in an interactive mode and yarn-cluster for long-running jobs or ones that do not require user intervention.

Interactive Spark Using PySpark

For datasets that fit into the memory of a cluster, Spark is fast enough to allow data scientists to interact and explore big data from an interactive shell that implements a Python REPL (read-evaluate-print loop) called pyspark. This interaction is similar to how you might interact with native Python code in the Python interpreter, writing commands on the command line and receiving output to stdout (there are also Scala and R interactive shells). This type of interactivity also allows the use of interactive notebooks, and setting up an iPython or Jupyter notebook with a Spark environment is very easy.

In this section, we'll begin exploring how to use RDDs with pyspark, as this is the easiest way to start working with Spark. In order to run the interactive shell, you will need to locate the pyspark command, which is in the *bin* directory of the Spark library. Similar to how you may have a $HADOOP_HOME (an environment variable pointing to the location of the Hadoop libraries on your system), you should also have a $SPARK_HOME. Spark requires no configuration to run right off the bat, so simply downloading the Spark build for your system is enough. Replacing $SPARK_HOME with the download path (or setting your environment), you can run the interactive shell as follows:

```
hostname $ $SPARK_HOME/bin/pyspark
[… snip …]
>>>
```

PySpark automatically creates a SparkContext for you to work with, using the local Spark configuration. It is exposed to the terminal via the sc variable. Let's create our first RDD:

```
>>> text = sc.textFile("shakespeare.txt")
>>> print text
shakespeare.txt MappedRDD[1] at textFile at  NativeMethodAccessorImpl.java:-2
```

The textFile method loads the complete works of William Shakespeare (*http://bit.ly/ 16c7kPV*) from the local disk into an RDD named text. If you inspect the RDD, you can see that it is a MappedRDD and that the path to the file is a relative path from the current working directory (pass in a correct path to the *shakespeare.txt* file on your system). Similar to our MapReduce example in Chapter 2, let's start to transform this RDD in order to compute the "Hello, World" of distributed computing and implement the word count application using Spark:

```
>>> from operator import add
>>> def tokenize(text):
...     return text.split()
...
>>> words = text.flatMap(tokenize)
```

We imported the operator add, which is a named function that can be used as a closure for addition. We'll use this function later. The first thing we have to do is split our text into words. We created a function called tokenize whose argument is some piece of text and returns a list of the tokens (words) in that text by simply splitting on whitespace. We then created a new RDD called words by transforming the text RDD through the application of the flatMap operator, and passed it the closure tokenize.

At this point, we have an RDD of type PythonRDD called words; however, you may have noticed that entering these commands has been instantaneous, although you might have expected a slight processing delay as the entirety of Shakespeare was split into words. Because Spark performs lazy evaluation, the execution of the processing (read the dataset, partition across processes, and map the tokenize function to the collection) has not occurred yet. Instead, the PythonRDD describes what needs to take place to create this RDD and in so doing, maintains a lineage of how the data got to the words form.

We can therefore continue to apply transformations to this RDD without waiting for a long, possibly erroneous or non-optimal distributed execution to take place. As described in Chapter 2, the next steps are to map each word to a key/value pair, where the key is the word and the value is a 1, and then use a reducer to sum the 1s for each key. First, let's apply our map:

```
>>> wc = words.map(lambda x: (x,1))
>>> print wc.toDebugString()
(2) PythonRDD[3] at RDD at PythonRDD.scala:43
 |  shakespeare.txt MappedRDD[1] at textFile at NativeMethodAccessorImpl.java:-2
 |  shakespeare.txt HadoopRDD[0] at textFile at
NativeMethodAccessorImpl.java:-2
```

Instead of using a named function, we will use an anonymous function (with the lambda keyword in Python). This line of code will map the lambda to each element of words. Therefore, each x is a word, and the word will be transformed into a tuple (word, 1) by the anonymous closure. In order to inspect the lineage so far, we can use the toDebugString method to see how our PipelinedRDD is being transformed. We can then apply the reduceByKey action to get our word counts and then write those word counts to disk:

```
>>> counts = wc.reduceByKey(add)
>>> counts.saveAsTextFile("wc")
```

Once we finally invoke the action saveAsTextFile, the distributed job kicks off and you should see a lot of INFO statements as the job runs "across the cluster" (or simply as multiple processes on your local machine). If you exit the interpreter, you should see a directory called wc in your current working directory:

```
hostname $ ls wc/
_SUCCESS    part-00000 part-00001
```

Each part file represents a partition of the final RDD that was computed by various processes on your computer and saved to disk. If you use the head command on one of the part files, you should see tuples of word count pairs:

```
hostname $ head wc/part-00000
(u'fawn', 14)
(u'Fame.', 1)
(u'Fame,', 2)
(u'kinghenryviii@7731', 1)
(u'othello@36737', 1)
(u'loveslabourslost@51678', 1)
(u'1kinghenryiv@54228', 1)
(u'troilusandcressida@83747', 1)
(u'fleeces', 1)
(u'midsummersnightsdream@71681', 1)
```

Note that in a MapReduce job, the keys would be sorted due to the mandatory intermediate shuffle and sort phase between map and reduce. Spark's repartitioning for reduction does not necessarily utilize a sort because all executors can communicate with each other and as a result, the preceding output is not sorted lexicographically. Even without the sort, however, you are guaranteed that each key appears only once across all part files because the reduceByKey operator was used to aggregate the counts RDD. If sorting is necessary, you could use the sort operator to ensure that all the keys are sorted before writing them to disk.

Writing Spark Applications

Writing Spark applications in Python is similar to working with Spark in the interactive console because the API is the same. However, instead of typing commands into an interactive shell, you need to create a complete, executable driver program to submit to the cluster. This involves a few housekeeping tasks that were automatically taken care of in pyspark—including getting access to the SparkContext, which was automatically loaded by the shell.

Many Spark programs are therefore simple Python scripts that contain some data (shared variables), define closures for transforming RDDs, and describe a step-by-step execution plan of RDD transformation and aggregation. A basic template for writing a Spark application in Python is as follows:

```
## Spark Application - execute with spark-submit

## Imports
from pyspark import SparkConf, SparkContext

## Shared variables and data
APP_NAME = "My Spark Application"

## Closure functions
```

```
## Main functionality
def main(sc):
    """
    Describe RDD transformations and actions here.
    """
    pass

if __name__ == "__main__":
    # Configure Spark
    conf = SparkConf().setAppName(APP_NAME)
    conf = conf.setMaster("local[*]")
    sc   = SparkContext(conf=conf)

    # Execute main functionality
    main(sc)
```

This template exposes the top-down structure of a Python Spark application: imports allow various Python libraries to be used for analysis as well as Spark components such as GraphX or SparkSQL. Shared data and variables are specified as module constants, including an identifying application name that is used in web UIs, for debugging, and in logging. Job-specific closures or custom operators are included with the driver program for easy debugging or to be imported in other Spark jobs, and finally some main method defines the analytical methodology that transforms and aggregates RDDs, which is run as the driver program.

Veteran Python programmers should note the use of the if __name__ == '__main__' (usually called ifmain) statement, in which the Spark configuration and SparkContext are defined and passed to the main function. The use of the ifmain allows us to easily import driver code into other Spark contexts, without creating a new context or configuration and executing a job (on import, the name won't be __main__). In particular, Spark programmers will routinely import code from applications into an iPython/Jupyter notebook or the pyspark interactive shell to explore the analysis before running a job on a larger dataset.

The driver program defines the entirety of the Spark execution; for example, to stop or exit the program in code, programmers can use sc.stop() or sys.exit(0). This control extends to the execution environment as well—in this template, a Spark cluster configuration, local[*] is hardcoded into the SparkConf via the setMaster method. This tells Spark to run on the local machine using as many processes as available (multiprocess, but not distributed computation). While you can specify where Spark executes on the command line using spark-submit, driver programs often select this based on an environment variable using os.environ. Therefore, while developing Spark jobs (e.g., using a DEBUG variable), the job can be run locally, but in production run across the cluster on a larger data set.

Writing Spark applications is certainly different than writing MapReduce applications because of the flexibility provided by the many transformations and actions, as well as the more flexible programming environment. In the following section, we take a look at a complete analysis that leverages the centrality of the driver program to compute data across a cluster to create a visualization as output.

Visualizing Airline Delays with Spark

In Chapter 3, we explored using Hadoop Streaming and MapReduce to compute the average flight delay per airport using the US Department of Transportation's on-time flight dataset (*http://bit.ly/1Dz76xB*). This kind of computation—parsing a CSV file and performing an aggregate computation—is an extremely common use case of Hadoop, particularly as CSV data is easily exported from relational databases. This dataset, which records all US domestic flight departure and arrival times along with their delays, is also interesting because while a single month is easily computed upon, the entire dataset would benefit from distributed computation due to its size.

In this example, we'll use Spark to perform an aggregation of this dataset, in particular determining which airlines were the most delayed in April 2014. We will specifically look at the slightly more advanced (and Pythonic) techniques we can use due to the increased flexibility of the Spark Python API. Moreover, we will show how central the driver program is to the computation by pulling the results back and displaying a visualization on the driver machine using matplotlib (a task that would take two steps using traditional MapReduce).

In order to get a feel for how Spark applications are structured, and to see the template described in the previous section in action, we will first inspect a 10,000-foot view of the complete structure of the program with the details snipped out:

```
## Imports
import csv
import matplotlib.pyplot as plt

from StringIO import StringIO
from datetime import datetime
from collections import namedtuple
from operator import add, itemgetter
from pyspark import SparkConf, SparkContext

## Module constants
APP_NAME = "Flight Delay Analysis"
DATE_FMT = "%Y-%m-%d"
TIME_FMT = "%H%M"

fields   = ('date', 'airline', 'flightnum', 'origin', 'dest', 'dep',
            'dep_delay', 'arv', 'arv_delay', 'airtime', 'distance')
Flight   = namedtuple('Flight', fields)
```

```
## Closure functions
def parse(row):
    """
    Parses a row and returns a named tuple.
    """
    pass


def split(line):
    """
    Operator function for splitting a line with csv module
    """
    pass


def plot(delays):
    """
    Show a bar chart of the total delay per airline
    """
    pass


## Main functionality
def main(sc):
    """
    Describe the transformations and actions used on the dataset, then plot
    the visualization on the output using matplotlib.
    """
    pass


if __name__ == "__main__":
    # Configure Spark
    conf = SparkConf().setMaster("local[*]")
    conf = conf.setAppName(APP_NAME)
    sc   = SparkContext(conf=conf)

    # Execute main functionality
    main(sc)
```

This snippet of code, while long, provides a good overview of the structure of an actual Spark program. The imports show the usual use of a mixture of standard library tools as well as a third-party library, matplotlib. As with Hadoop Streaming, any third-party code that is not part of the standard library must be either pre-installed on the cluster or shipped with the job. For code that need only be executed on the driver and not in the executors (e.g., matplotlib), you can use a try/except block and capture ImportErrors.

As with Hadoop Streaming, any third-party Python dependencies that are not part of the Python standard library must be pre-installed on *each* node in the cluster. However, unlike Hadoop Streaming, the fact that there are two contexts, the driver context and the executor context, means that some heavyweight libraries (particularly visualization libraries) can be installed only on the driver machine, so long as they are not used in a closure passed to a Spark operation that will execute on the cluster. To prevent errors, wrap imports in a `try/except` block and capture `ImportErrors`.

The application then defines some data that is configurable, including the date and time format for parsing datetime strings and the application name. A specialized `name dtuple` data structure is also created in order to create lightweight and accessible parsed rows from the input data. This information should be available to all executors, but is lightweight enough to not require a broadcast variable. Next, the processing functions, `parse`, `split`, and `plot` are defined, as well as a `main` function that uses the `SparkContext` to define the actions and transformations on the airline dataset. Finally, the `ifmain` configures Spark and executes the `main` function.

With this high-level overview complete, let's dive deeper into the specifics of the code, starting with the `main` method that defines the primary Spark operations and the analytical methodology:

```
## Main functionality
def main(sc):
    """
    Describe the transformations and actions used on the dataset, then plot
    the visualization on the output using matplotlib.
    """

    # Load the airlines lookup dictionary
    airlines = dict(sc.textFile("ontime/airlines.csv").map(split).collect())

    # Broadcast the lookup dictionary to the cluster
    airline_lookup = sc.broadcast(airlines)

    # Read the CSV data into an RDD
    flights = sc.textFile("ontime/flights.csv").map(split).map(parse)

    # Map the total delay to the airline (joined using the broadcast value)
    delays  = flights.map(lambda f: (airline_lookup.value[f.airline],
                                     add(f.dep_delay, f.arv_delay)))

    # Reduce the total delay for the month to the airline
    delays  = delays.reduceByKey(add).collect()
    delays  = sorted(delays, key=itemgetter(1))

    # Provide output from the driver
    for d in delays:
```

```
    print "%0.0f minutes delayed\t%s" % (d[1], d[0])

# Show a bar chart of the delays
plot(delays)
```

Our first job is to load our two data sources from disk: first, a lookup table of airline codes to airline names, and second, the flight instances dataset. The dataset *airlines.csv* is a small jump table that allows us to join airline codes with the full airline name; however, because this dataset is small enough, we don't have to perform a distributed join of two RDDs. Instead we store this information as a Python dictionary and broadcast it to every node in the cluster using `sc.broadcast`, which transforms the local Python dictionary into a broadcast variable.

The creation of this broadcast variable and execution is as follows. First, an RDD is created from the text file on the local disk called *airlines.csv* (note the relative path). Creation of the RDD is required because this data could be coming from a Hadoop data source, which would be specified with a URI to the location (e.g., *hdfs://* for HDFS data or *s3://* for S3, etc.). Note if this file was simply on the local machine, then loading it into an RDD is not necessary. The `split` function is then mapped to every element in the dataset, as discussed momentarily. Finally, the `collect` action is applied to the RDD, which brings the data back from the cluster to the driver as a Python list. Because the `collect` action was applied, when this line of code executes, a job is sent to the cluster to load the RDD, split it, then return the context to the driver program:

```
def split(line):
    """
    Operator function for splitting a line with csv module
    """
    reader = csv.reader(StringIO(line))
    return reader.next()
```

The `split` function parses each line of text using the `csv` module by creating a file-like object with the line of text using `StringIO`, which is then passed into the `csv.reader`. Because there is only a single line of text, we can simply return `reader.next()`. While this method of CSV parsing may seem pretty heavyweight, it allows us to more easily deal with delimiters, escaping, and other nuances of CSV processing. For larger datasets, a similar methodology is applied to entire files using `sc.wholeTextFiles` to process many CSV files that are split into blocks of 128 MB each (e.g., the block size and replication on HDFS):

```
def parse(row):
    """
    Parses a row and returns a named tuple.
    """

    row[0] = datetime.strptime(row[0], DATE_FMT).date()
    row[5] = datetime.strptime(row[5], TIME_FMT).time()
```

```
row[6]  = float(row[6])
row[7]  = datetime.strptime(row[7], TIME_FMT).time()
row[8]  = float(row[8])
row[9]  = float(row[9])
row[10] = float(row[10])
return Flight(*row[:11])
```

Next, the `main` function loads the much larger *flights.csv*, which needs to be computed upon in a parallel fashion using an RDD. After splitting the CSV rows, we map the `parse` function to the CSV row, which converts dates and times to Python dates and times, and casts floating-point numbers appropriately. The output of this function is a `namedtuple` called `Flight` that was defined in the module constants section of the application. Named tuples are lightweight data structures that contain record information such that data can be accessed by name—for example, `flight.date` rather than position (e.g., `flight[0]`). Like normal Python tuples, they are immutable, so they are safe to use in processing applications because the data can't be modified. Additionally, they are much more memory and processing efficient than dictionaries, and as a result, provide a noticeable benefit in big data applications like Spark where memory is at a premium.

With an RDD of `Flight` objects in hand, the final transformation is to map an anonymous function that transforms the RDD to a series of key/value pairs where the key is the name of the airline and the value is the sum of the arrival and departure delays. At this point, besides the creation of the airlines dictionary, no execution has been performed on the collection. However, once we begin to sum the per airline delays using the `reduceByKey` action and the `add` operator, the job is executed across the cluster, then collected back to the driver program.

At this point, the cluster computation is complete, and we proceed in a sequential fashion on the driver program. The delays are sorted by delay magnitude in the memory of the client program. Note that this is possible for the same reason that we created the airlines lookup table as a broadcast variable: the number of airlines is small and it is more efficient to sort in memory. However, if this RDD was extremely large, a distributed sort using `rdd.sort` could be used. Finally, instead of writing the results to disk, the output is printed to the console. If this dataset were big, the `rdd.first` action might be used to take the first n items rather than printing the entire dataset, or by using `rdd.saveAsTextFile` to write the data back to our local disk or to HDFS.

Finally, because we have the data available in the driver, we can visualize the results using `matplotlib` as follows:

```
def plot(delays):
    """
    Show a bar chart of the total delay per airline
    """
    airlines = [d[0] for d in delays]
    minutes  = [d[1] for d in delays]
```

```
index    = list(xrange(len(airlines)))

fig, axe = plt.subplots()
bars = axe.barh(index, minutes)

# Add the total minutes to the right
for idx, air, min in zip(index, airlines, minutes):
    if min > 0:
        bars[idx].set_color('#d9230f')
        axe.annotate(" %0.0f min" % min, xy=(min+1, idx+0.5), va='center')
    else:
        bars[idx].set_color('#469408')
        axe.annotate(" %0.0f min" % min, xy=(10, idx+0.5), va='center')

# Set the ticks
ticks = plt.yticks([idx+ 0.5 for idx in index], airlines)
xt = plt.xticks()[0]
plt.xticks(xt, [' '] * len(xt))

# Minimize chart junk
plt.grid(axis = 'x', color ='white', linestyle='-')

plt.title('Total Minutes Delayed per Airline')
plt.show()
```

Hopefully this example illustrates the interplay of the cluster and the driver program (sending out for analytics, then bringing results back to the driver), as well as the role of Python code in a Spark application. To run this code (presuming that you have a directory called *ontime* with the two CSV files in the same directory), use the spark-submit command as follows:

```
hostname $ spark-submit app.py
```

Because we hardcoded the master as localhost[*] in the configuration under the ifmain, this command creates a Spark job with as many processes as are available on the localhost. It will then begin executing the transformations and actions specified in the main function with the local SparkContext. First it loads the jump table as an RDD, collect, and broadcast it to all processes, then it loads the flight data RDD and processes it to compute the average delays in a parallel fashion.

Once the context and the output from the collect is returned to the driver, we can visualize the result using matplotlib, as shown in Figure 4-4. The final result shows that the total delays (in minutes) in April 2014 span from arriving early for those you're flying Hawaiian or Alaskan Airlines, to an aggregate total delay for most big airlines. The novelty here is not in the visualization of the analysis, but in the one-step process of submitting a parallel executing job, and in a reasonable amount of user time, displaying a result. Consequently, applications like these that deliver on-demand analyses directly to users for immediate insights are becoming increasingly common.

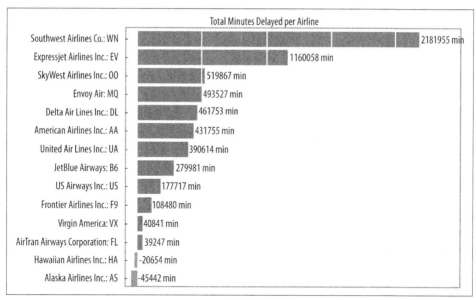

Figure 4-4. Visualization of the most delayed airlines in our dataset

Conclusion

While Spark was originally intended to address MapReduce's limitations in performing iterative algorithms, it has now developed into a full-fledged, general-purpose distributed computation engine. Spark has evolved to cover a wide range of big data
processing workloads that utilize the general-purpose engine, rather than by implementing specialized systems. Because Spark is 10–20 times faster than traditional
MapReduce, you might then ask where Spark fits in the Hadoop ecosystem. While it's
premature to say that Spark is the certain successor to MapReduce, Spark is gaining
an amazing amount of traction in organizations and companies that have already
adopted Hadoop but are in need of a platform that can perform near real-time computations using existing cluster resources. However, we should keep in mind that at
least as of now, Spark should be considered an extension of, not a replacement for,
Hadoop and MapReduce, and can coexist quite well with the rest of the Hadoop ecosystem.

Spark doesn't solve the distributed storage problem (usually Spark gets its data from
HDFS), but it does provide a rich functional programming API for distributed computation. This framework is built upon the idea of *resilient distributed datasets*. RDDs
are a programming abstraction that represents a partitioned collection of objects,
allowing for distributed operations to be performed upon them. RDDs are fault tolerant (the resilient part), and most importantly, can be stored in memory on worker

nodes for immediate reuse. In-memory storage provides for faster and more easily expressed iterative algorithms as well as enabling real-time interactive analyses.

Because the Spark library has an API available in Python, R, Scala, and Java, as well as built-in modules for machine learning, streaming data, graph algorithms, and SQL-like queries, it has rapidly become one of the most important distributed computation frameworks that exist today. When coupled with YARN, Spark serves to augment (not replace) existing Hadoop clusters, and will be an important part of big data in the future, opening up new avenues of data science exploration.

This chapter is far from a complete introduction to Spark; instead, it serves to introduce the Spark computing framework and resilient distributed datasets, and provide insight about how to interact with and program for Spark. Because this book is targeted toward a data science audience that knows Python or R, Spark probably feels a bit more native than Hadoop Streaming for analytics. Throughout the rest of the book, we use both Hadoop Streaming and Spark to conduct computations, but for the most part—especially where machine learning is concerned—we will primarily be using Spark.

CHAPTER 5

Distributed Analysis and Patterns

MapReduce and Spark allow developers and data scientists the ability to easily conduct *data parallel* operations, where data is distributed to multiple processing nodes and computed upon simultaneously, then reduced to a final output. YARN provides simple *task parallelism* by allowing a cluster to perform multiple different operations simultaneously by allocating free computational resources to perform individual tasks. Parallelism reduces the amount of time required to perform a single computation, thereby unlocking datasets that are measured in petabytes, analyzed at thousands of records per second, or composed of multiple heterogeneous data sources. However, most parallel operations like the ones described to this point are simple, leading to the question, how can data scientists conduct advanced data analysis at scale?

The primary principle of conducting large-scale analytics can be summarized by the quip from Creighton Abrams: "When eating an elephant, take one bite at a time." Whereas single operations take many small bites of the data, these operations must be composed into a step-by-step sequence called a *data flow* to be organized into more meaningful results. Data flows may fork and merge, allowing for both task and data parallelism if two operations can be computed simultaneously, but the sequence must maintain the property that data is fed sequentially from an input data source to a final output. For that reason, data flows are described as *directed acyclic graphs* (DAGs). It is important, therefore, to realize that if an algorithm, analysis, or other non-trivial computation can be expressed as a DAG, then it can be parallelized on Hadoop.

Unfortunately, it also quickly becomes apparent that many algorithms aren't easily converted into DAGs, and are therefore unsuitable for this type of parallelism. Algorithms that cannot be described as a directed data flow include those that maintain or update a single data structure throughout the course of computation (requiring some shared memory) or computations that are dependent on the results of another at intermediate steps (requiring intermediate interprocess communication). Algorithms that introduce cycles, particularly iterative algorithms that are not bounded by a finite number of cycles, are also not easily described as DAGs.

There are tools and techniques that address requirements for cyclicity, shared memory, or interprocess communication in both MapReduce and Spark, but to make use of these tools, algorithms must be rewritten to a distributed form. Rather than rewrite algorithms, a less technical but equally effective approach is usually employed: design a data flow that decomposes the input domain into a smaller output that fits into the memory of a single machine, run the sequential algorithm on that output, then validate that analysis across the cluster with another data flow (e.g., to compute error).

It is because of the widespread use of this approach that Hadoop is often said to be a preprocessor that unlocks the potential of large datasets by reducing them into increasingly manageable chunks through every operation. A common rule of thumb is use either MapReduce or Spark to articulate data down to a computational space that can fit into 128 GB of memory (a cost-effective hardware requirement for a single machine). This rule is often called "last-mile" computing because it moves data from an extremely large space to a place close enough, the last mile, that allows for accurate analyses or application-specific computations.

In this chapter, we explore patterns for parallel computations in the context of data flows that reduce or decompose the computational space into a more manageable one. We begin by discussing key-based computations, a requirement for MapReduce and also essential to Spark. This leads us to a discussion of patterns for summarization, indexing, and filtering, which are key components to most decomposition algorithms. In this context, we will discuss applications for statistical summarization, sampling, search, and binning. We conclude by surveying three preprocessing techniques for computing regression, classification, and clustering style analyses.

 This chapter serves as an introduction to the methods used in the Hadoop ecosystem, which are bundled into other projects and discussed in the final four chapters of the book. This chapter discusses algorithms expressed as data flows, while Chapter 8 goes on to talk about tools for composing data flows, including higher-level APIs like Pig and Spark Data Frames. Many of the filtering and summarization algorithms discussed in this chapter are more easily expressed as structured queries, whose execution on Hadoop with Hive is discussed in Chapter 7. Finally, the components in these chapters, including the use of Sckit-Learn models, serve as a first step toward understanding machine learning with Spark's MLlib, discussed in Chapter 9.

This chapter also presents standard algorithms that are used routinely for data analytics, including statistical summarization (the parallel "describe" command), parallel grep, TF-IDF, and canopy clustering. Through these examples, we will clarify the basic mechanics of both MapReduce and Spark.

Computing with Keys

The first step toward understanding how data flows work in practice is to understand the relationship between key/value pairs and parallel computation. In MapReduce, *all data* is structured as key/value pairs in both the map and reduce stages. The key requirement relates primarily to reduction, as aggregation is grouped by the key, and parallel reduction requires partitioning of the *keyspace*—in other words, the domain of key values such that a reducer task sees all values for that key. If you don't necessarily have a key to group by (which is actually very common), you could reduce to a single key that would force a single reduction on all mapped values. However, in this case, the reduce phase would not benefit from parallelism.

Although often ignored (especially in the mapper, where the key is simply a document identifier), keys allow the computation to work on sets of data simultaneously. Therefore, a data flow expresses the relation of one set of values to another, which should sound familiar, especially presented in the context of more traditional data management—structured queries on a relational database. Similar to how you would not run multiple individual queries for an analysis of different dimensions on a database like PostgreSQL, MapReduce and Spark computations look to perform grouping operations in parallel, as shown by the mean computation grouped by key in Figure 5-1.

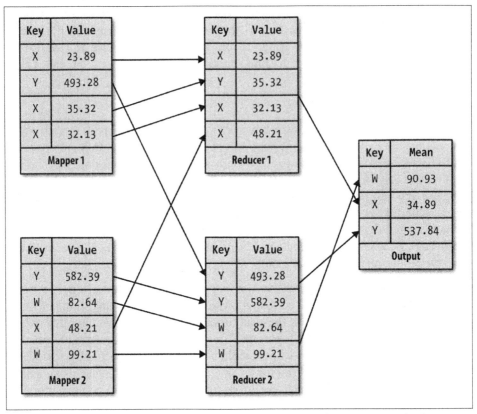

Figure 5-1. Keys allow parallel reduction by partitioning the keyspace to multiple reducers

Moreover, keys can maintain information that has already been reduced at one stage in the data flow, automatically parallelizing a result that is required for the next step in computation. This is done using compound keys—a technique discussed in the next section that shows that keys do not need to be simple, primitive values. Keys are so useful for these types of computations, in fact, that although they are not strictly required in computations with Spark (an RDD can be a collection of simple values), most Spark applications require them for their analyses, primarily using groupByKey, aggregateByKey, sortByKey and reduceByKey actions to collect and reduce.

Compound Keys

Keys need not be simple primitives such as integers or strings; instead, they can be compound or complex types so long as they are both *hashable* and *comparable*. Comparable types must at the very least expose some mechanism to determine equality (for shuffling) and some method of ordering (for sorting). Comparison is usually accomplished by mapping some type to a numeric value (e.g., months of the year to the integers 1–12) or through a lexical ordering. Hashable types in Python are any immutable type, the most notable of which is the tuple. Tuples can contain mutable types (e.g., a tuple of lists), however, so a hashable tuple is one that is composed of immutable types. Mutable types such as lists and dictionaries can be transformed into immutable tuples:

```
# Transform a list into a tuple
key = tuple(['a', 'b', 'c'])

# Transform a dictionary into a tuple of tuples
key = {'a': 1, 'b': 2}
key = tuple(key.items())
```

Compound keys are used in two primary ways: to facet the keyspace across multiple dimensions and to carry key-specific information forward through computational stages that involve the values alone. Consider web log records of the following form:

```
local - - [30/Apr/1995:21:18:07 -0600] "GET 7448.html HTTP/1.0" 404 -
local - - [30/Apr/1995:21:18:42 -0600] "GET 7448.html HTTP/1.0" 200 980
remote - - [30/Apr/1995:21:22:56 -0600] "GET 4115.html HTTP/1.0" 200 1363
remote - - [30/Apr/1995:21:26:29 -0600] "GET index.html HTTP/1.0" 200 2881
```

Web log records are a typical data source of big data computations on Hadoop, as they represent per-user clickstream data that can be easily mined for insight in a variety of domains; they also tend to be very large, dynamic semistructured datasets, well suited to operations in Spark and MapReduce. Initial computation on this dataset requires a frequency analysis; for example, we can decompose the text into two daily time series, one for local traffic and the other for remote traffic using a compound key:

```
import re
from datetime import datetime

# Parse datetimes in the log record
dtfmt = "%d/%b/%Y:%H:%M:%S %z"

# Parse log records using a regular expression
linre = re.compile(r'^(\w+) \- \- \[(.+)\] "(.+)" (\d+) ([\d\-]+)$')

def parse(line):
    # Match the log record against our regular expression
    match = linre.match(line)
    if match is not None:
        # The regular expression has groups to extract the source, timestamp,
        # the request, the status code, and the byte size of the response.
        parts = match.groups()

        # Parse the datetime and return the source, along with the year and day.
        date = datetime.strptime(parts[1], dtfmt).timetuple()
        return (parts[0], date.tm_year, date.tm_yday)
```

This function can be used in a mapper to parse each line of the log file, or passed as a closure to the `map` method of an RDD loaded from text files. The `parse` function uses a date format and a regular expression to parse the line, then emits a compound key composed of the traffic type, the year, and the day of the year. This key is associated with a counter (e.g., a 1) that can be passed into a sum reducer to get a frequency-based time series. Mapping yields the following data from the preceding dataset:

```
('local', 1995, 120)    1
('local', 1995, 120)    1
('remote', 1995, 120)   1
('remote', 1995, 120)   1
```

Compound keys that are used as *complex* keys allow computations to occur across a faceted keyspace (e.g., the source of the network traffic, the year, and the day, and are the most common use case for compound keys). Another common use case is to propagate key-specific information to downstream computations (e.g., computations that are dependent on the reduction, or per-key aggregated values). By having the reducer associate its computation with the key (particularly values like counts or floats), this information is maintained with the key for more complex computation.

 Both MapReduce and Spark's Java and Scala APIs require strong typing for both keys and values. In Hadoop terms, this means that compound keys and structured values need to be defined as classes that implement the `Writable` interface, and keys must also implement the `WritableComparable` interface. These tools allow Java and Scala developers lightweight and extensible serialization of data structures, which minimize network traffic and aid in shuffle and sort operations. Python developers, however, have the overhead of string serialization and deserialization of tuples and Python primitives. In order to serialize nested data structures, use the `json` module. For more complex jobs, binary serialization formats such as Protocol Buffers, Avro, or Parquet may speed up the processing time by minimizing network traffic.

Compound data serialization

The final consideration when using compound keys (and complex values) is to understand *serialization* and *deserialization* of the compound data. *Serialization* is the process of turning an object in memory into a stream of bytes such that it can be written to disk or transmitted across the network (*deserialization* is the reverse process). This process is essential, particularly in MapReduce, as keys and values are written (usually as strings) to disk between map and reduce phases. However, it is also essential to understand in Spark, where intermediate jobs may preprocess data for further computation.

By default in Spark, the Python API uses the `pickle` module for serialization, which means that any data structures you use must be pickle-able. While the `pickle` module is extremely efficient, this constraint can be a gotcha in Spark programming, particularly when passing closures (functions that don't depend on global values, usually anonymous lambda ones). With MapReduce Streaming, you must serialize both the key and the value as a string, separated by a specified character, by default a tab (\t). The question becomes, is there a way to serialize compound keys (and values) as strings more efficiently?

One common first attempt is to simply serialize an immutable type (e.g., a tuple) using the built-in `str` function, converting the tuple into a string that can be easily pickled or streamed. The problem then shifts to deserialization; using the `ast` (abstract syntax tree) in the Python standard library, we can use the `literal_eval` function to evaluate stringified tuples back into Python tuple types as follows:

```
import ast

def map(key, val):
    # Parse the compound key, which is a tuple.
    key = ast.literal_eval(key)

    # Write out the new key as a string
    return (str(key), val)
```

As both keys and values get more complex, it is also generally useful to consider other data structures for serialization, particularly more compact ones to reduce network traffic or to translate to a string value to ensure safety. For example, a common representation for structured data is Base64-encoded JSON because it is compact, uses only ASCII characters, and is easily serialized and deserialized with the standard library as follows:

```
import json
import base64

def serialize(data):
    """
    Returns the Base64-encoded JSON representation of the data (keys or values)
    """
    return base64.b64encode(json.dumps(data))

def deserialize(data):
    """
    Decodes Base64 JSON-encoded data
    """
    return json.loads(base64.b64decode(data))
```

However, take care when using more complex serial representations; often there is a trade-off in the computational complexity of serialization versus the amount of space used. Many types of parallel algorithms can be implemented faster and more simply with tuple strings or a tab-delimited format, particularly when care is taken in managing how keys are passed throughout the computation. In the next section, we'll take a look at common key-based computing patterns used in both MapReduce and Spark.

Keyspace Patterns

The notion of computing with keys allows you to manage sets of data and their relations. However, keys are also a primary piece of the computation, and as such, they must be managed in addition to the data. In this section, we explore several patterns that impact the *keyspace*, specifically the explode, filter, transform, and identity patterns. These common patterns are used to construct larger patterns and complete algorithms by operating on the association between keys and values.

For the following examples, we will consider a dataset of orders whose key is the order ID, customer ID, and timestamp, and whose value is a list of universal product codes (UPCs) for the products purchased in the order as follows:

```
1001, 1063457, 2014-09-16 12:23:33, 098668259830, 098668318865
1002, 0171488, 2014-12-11 03:05:03, 098668318865
1003, 1022739, 2015-01-03 13:01:54, 098668275427, 098668331789, 098668274321
```

Transforming the keyspace

The most common key-based operation is a transformation of the input key domain, which can be conducted either in a `map` or a `reduce`. Transforming the keyspace during mapping causes a repartitioning (division) of the data during aggregation, while transforming the keyspace during reduction serves to reorganize the output (or the input to following computations). The most common transformation functions are direct assignment, compounding, splitting, and inversion.

Direct assignment drops the input key, which is usually entirely ignored, and constructs a new key from the input value or another source (e.g., a random key). Consider the case of loading raw or semi-structured data from text, CSV, or JSON. The input key in this case is a line or document ID, which is typically dropped in favor of some data-specific value.

Compounding and its opposite operation, *splitting*, manage compound keys as discussed in the previous section. Compounding constructs or adds to a compound key, increasing the faceting of the key relation. Splitting breaks apart a compound key and uses only a smaller piece of it. Generally compounding and splitting also split and compound the value in a way such that a compound key receives its new data from the split value or vice versa, ensuring that no data is lost. It is, however, appropriate to also drop unneeded data and eliminate extraneous information via compounding or splitting.

Inversion swaps keys and values, a common pattern particularly in chained Map-Reduce jobs or in Spark operations that are dependent on an intermediate aggregation (particularly a groupby). For example, in order to sort a dataset by value rather than by key, it is necessary to first map the inversion of the key and value, perform a sortByKey or utilize the shuffle and sort in MapReduce, then re-invert in the reduce or with another map.

Consider a job to sort our orders by the number of products in each order, along with the date, which will use all of the keyspace transformations identified earlier:

```
# Load orders into an RDD and parse the CSV
orders = sc.textFile("orders.csv").map(split)

# Key assignment: (orderid, customerid, date), products
orders = orders.map(lambda r: ((r[0], r[1], r[2]), r[3:]))

# Compute the order size and split the key to orderid, date
orders = orders.map(lambda (k, v): ((k[0], parse_date(k[2])), len(v)))

# Invert the key and value to sort
orders = orders.map(lambda (k, v): ((v, k[1]), k[0]))

# Sort the orders by key
orders = orders.sortByKey(ascending=False)

# Reinvert the key/value space so that we key on order ID again
orders = orders.map(lambda (k,v ): (v, k))

# Get the top ten order IDs by size and date
print orders.take(10)
```

This example is perhaps a bit verbose for the required task, but it does demonstrate each type of transformation as follows:

1. First, the dataset is loaded from a CSV using the split method discussed in Chapter 4.

2. At this point, orders is only a collection of lists, so we assign keys by breaking the value into the IDs and date as the key, and associate it with the list of products as the value.

3. The next step is to get the length of the products list (number of products ordered) and to parse the date, using a closure that wraps a date format for date time.strptime; note that this method splits the compound key and eliminates the customer ID, which is unnecessary.

4. In order to sort by order size, we need to invert the size value with the key, also splitting the date from the key so we can also sort by date.

5. After performing the sort, this function reinverts so that each order can be identified by size and date.

The following snippet demonstrates what happens to the first record throughout each map in the Spark job:

```
0. "1001, 1063457, 2014-09-16 12:23:33, 098668259830, 098668318865"
1. [1001, 1063457, 2014-09-16 12:23:33, 098668259830, 098668318865]
2. ((1001, 1063457, 2014-09-16 12:23:33), [098668259830, 098668318865])
3. ((1001, datetime(2014, 9, 16, 12, 23, 33), 2)
4. ((2, datetime(2014, 9, 16, 12, 23, 33)), 1001)
5. (1001, (2, datetime(2014, 9, 16, 12, 23, 33)))
```

Through this series of transformations, the client program can then take the top 10 orders by size and date, and print them out after the distributed computation.

The explode mapper

The explode mapper generates multiple intermediate key/value pairs for a single input key. Generally this is done by a combination of a key shift and splitting of the value into multiple parts, as we've already seen in the word count example in Chapter 2, where the single lineno/line pair into the mapper was output as several new key/value pairs, word/1, by splitting the line on space. An explode mapper can also generate many intermediate pairs by dividing a value into its constituent parts and reassigning them with the key.

In our example, we can explode the list of products per order value to order/product pairs, as in the following code:

```
def order_pairs(key, products):
    # Returns a list of order id, product pairs
    pairs = []

    for product in products:
        pairs.append((key[0], product))

    return pairs

orders = orders.flatMap(order_pairs)
```

Applying this mapper to our input dataset produces the following output:

```
1001, 098668259830
1001, 098668318865
1002, 098668318865
1003, 098668275427
1003, 098668331789
1003, 098668274321
```

Note the use of the flatMap operation on the RDD, which is specifically designed for explode mapping. It operates similarly to the regular map; however, the function can yield a sequence instead of a single item, which is then chained into a single collection (rather than an RDD of lists). No such restriction exists in MapReduce and Hadoop Streaming, any number of pairs can be emitted from a map function (or none at all).

The filter mapper

Although we will discuss filtering (particularly statistical sampling) in more detail later in the chapter, here we will mention filtering as it relates to key operations. Filtering is often essential to limit the amount of computation performed in a reduce stage, particularly in a big data context. It is also used to partition a computation into two paths of the same data flow, a sort of data-oriented branching in larger algorithms that is specifically designed for extremely large datasets. Consider extending our orders example (in Spark) where we only select orders from 2014:

```
from functools import partial

def year_filter(item, year=None):
    key, val = item
    if parse_date(key[2]).year == year:
        return True
    return False

orders = orders.filter(partial(year_filter, year=2014))
```

Spark provides a filter operation that takes a function and transforms the RDD such that only elements on which the function returns True are retained. This example shows a more advanced use of a closure and a general filter function that can take any year. The partial function creates a closure whose year argument to year_filter is always 2014, allowing for a bit more versatility. MapReduce code is similar but requires a bit more logic:

```
def YearFilterMapper(Mapper):

    def __init__(self, year, **kwargs):
        super(YearFilterMapper, self).__init__(**kwargs)
        self.year = year

    def map(self):
        for key, value in self:
            if parse_date(key[2]).year == self.year:
                self.emit(key, value)

if __name__ == "__main__":
    mapper = YearFilterMapper(2014)
    mapper.map()
```

It is completely acceptable for a mapper to not emit anything, therefore the logic for a filter mapper is to only emit when the condition is met. The same flexibility as in the partial method is provided by using our class-based Mapper, and simply instantiating the class with the year we would like to filter upon. More advanced Spark and MapReduce apps will likely accept the year as input on the command to run the job.

Filtering produces the same data as our input, with the last order record (order 1003) removed as it was in 2015:

```
1001, 1063457, 2014-09-16 12:23:33, 098668259830, 098668318865
1002, 0171488, 2014-12-11 03:05:03, 098668318865
```

The identity pattern

The final keyspace pattern that is commonly used in MapReduce (although generally not in Spark) is the Identity function. This is simply a pass-through, such that identity mappers or reducers return the same value as their input (e.g., as in the *identity function*, $f(x) = x$). Identity mappers are typically used to perform multiple reductions in a data flow. When an identity reducer is employed in MapReduce, it makes the job the equivalent of a sort on the keyspace. Identity mappers and reducers are implemented simply as follows:

```
class IdentityMapper(Mapper):

    def map(self):
        for key, value in self:
            self.emit(key, value)


class IdentityReducer(Reducer):

    def reduce(self):
        for key, values in self:
            for value in values:
                self.emit(key, value)
```

Identity reducers are generally more common because of the optimized shuffle and sort in MapReduce. However, identity mappers are also very important, particularly in chained MapReduce jobs where the output of one reducer must immediately be reduced again by a secondary reducer. In fact, it is because of the phased operation of MapReduce that identity reducers are required; in Spark, because RDDs are lazily evaluated, identity closures are not necessary.

Pairs versus Stripes

Data scientists are accustomed to working with data represented as vectors, matrices, or data frames. Linear algebra computations tend to be optimized on single core machines, and algorithms in machine learning are implemented using low-level data structures like the multi-dimensional arrays provided in the numpy library. These structures, while compact, are not available in a big data context, however, simply because of the magnitude of data. Instead, there are two ways that matrices are commonly represented: by *pairs* and by *stripes*. Both pairs and stripes are examples of key-based computation.

To explain the motivation behind this example, consider the problem of building a word co-occurrence matrix for a text-based corpus (like word count, this is the problem that typically demonstrates pairs versus stripes.[1]) Word co-occurrences can be used to create a statistical model of language that can be used in many applications, including machine translation, sentence generation, etc.

The word co-occurrence matrix as shown in Figure 5-2 is a square matrix of size NxN, where N is the vocabulary (the number of unique words) in the corpus. Each cell $W_{i,j}$ contains the number of times both word w_i and word w_j appear together in a sentence, paragraph, document, or other fixed-length window. This matrix is sparse, particularly with aggressive stopword filtering because most words only co-occur with very few other words on a regular basis.

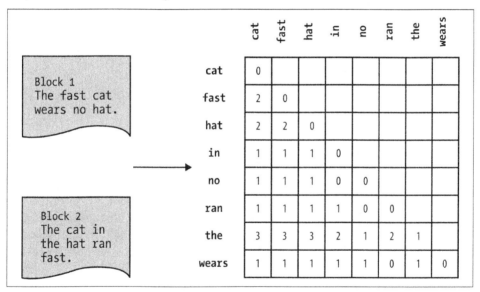

	cat	fast	hat	in	no	ran	the	wears
cat	0							
fast	2	0						
hat	2	2	0					
in	1	1	1	0				
no	1	1	1	0	0			
ran	1	1	1	1	0	0		
the	3	3	3	2	1	2	1	
wears	1	1	1	1	1	0	1	0

Block 1
The fast cat wears no hat.

Block 2
The cat in the hat ran fast.

Figure 5-2. A word co-occurrence matrix demonstrates the frequency of terms appearing together in the same block of text, such as a sentence

The *pairs* approach maps every cell in the matrix to a particular value, where the pair is the compound key i,j. Reducers therefore work on per-cell values to produce a final, cell-by-cell matrix. This is a reasonable approach, which yields output where

---

[1] Introduced by Jimmy Lin and Chris Dyer in *Data-Intensive Text Processing with MapReduce* (*http://bit.ly/1PcgEmB*).

each $W_{i,j}$ is computed upon and stored separately. Using a sum reducer, the mapper is as follows (see Chapter 3 for more on text processing and tokenization using NLTK):

```
from itertools import combinations

class WordPairsMapper(Mapper):

    def map(self):
        for docid, document in self:
            tokens = list(self.tokenize(document))
            for pair in combinations(sorted(tokens), 2):
                self.emit(pair, 1)
```

The most essential part of this approach is to ensure lexicographic *ordering* of the tokens by sorting them with the `sorted` built-in. Pairs must be ordered in a symmetric matrix, where $W_{i,j}$ is equal to $W_{j,i}$, otherwise the keys (b,a) and (a,b) would not be reduced together. Note that the `combinations` function from the `itertools` library respects the ordering of its input list. Here is the input:

```
"See Spot run, run Spot, run!"
```

The pairs of the word co-occurrence matrix would be aggregated as follows:

```
(run, run), 6
(run, see), 3
(run, spot), 6
(see, run), 3
(see, spot), 2
(spot, run), 6
(spot, see), 2
(spot, spot), 1
```

While the pairs approach is easy to implement and understand, it causes a lot of intermediate pairs that must be transmitted across the network both during the Map-Reduce shuffle and sort phase, and during `groupByKey` operations to shuffle values between partitions in an RDD. Moreover, the pairs approach is not well suited to computations that require an entire row (or column) of data.

The stripes approach was initially conceived as an optimization to reduce the number of intermediate pairs and reduce network communication in order to make jobs faster. However, it also quickly became an essential tool in many algorithms that need to perform fast per-element computations—for example, relative frequencies or other statistical operations. Instead of pairs, a per-term associative array (a Python dictionary) is constructed in the mapper and emitted as a value:

```
from collections import Counter

class WordStripeMapper(Mapper):

    def map(self):
        for docid, document in self:
```

```
        tokens = list(self.tokenize(document))

        for i, term in enumerate(tokens):
            # Create a new stripe for each term
            stripe = Counter()

            for j, token in enumerate(tokens):
                # Don't count the term's co-occurrence with itself
                if i != j:
                    stripe[token] += 1

            # Emit the term and the stripe
            self.emit(term, stripe)


class StripeSumReducer(Reducer):

    def reduce(self):
        for key, values in self:
            stripe = Counter()

            # Add all the mapped counters together
            for value in values:
                for token, count in value.iteritems():
                    # For each token, count add the collector stripe
                    stripe[token] += count

        self.emit(key, stripe)
```

The mapper and reducer for stripes are a bit more complex. Two nested loops over all the tokens are required in the mapper, and care must be taken to ensure that the term is not counted with itself. The `enumerate` built-in allows us to track the index of the term in both loops, allowing us to skip identical indices rather than terms (which may actually co-occur if the term is repeated in the text). The `Counter` in the `collections` library is a useful data structure that is essentially a dictionary whose default value is an `int`. The reducer then needs to sum the dictionaries per element, constructing a total count of all counters from the mappers. For the same input, the output is now the more compact:

```
run,  ((run, 6), (see, 3), (spot, 6))
see,  ((run, 3), (spot, 2))
spot, ((run, 6), (see, 2), (spot, 1))
```

The stripes approach is not only more compact in its representation, but also generates fewer and simpler intermediary keys, thus optimizing sorting and shuffling of data or other optimizations. However, the stripes object is heavier, both in terms of processing time as well as the serialization requirements, particularly if the stripes get very large. There is a limit to the size of a stripe, particularly in very dense matrices, which may take a lot of memory to track single occurrences.

Pairs and stripes concludes our discussion of computing with keys. As you can see, most big data computations rely on key-based computing to provide and maintain relations between sets of data in order to ensure proper distribution across different mappers and reducers. Large-scale computing performed on both Spark and Map-Reduce require a shift in the way we think about traditional approaches to standard computations, if only because of the size. In the next section, we'll build upon this shift in thinking by proposing specific design patterns that are commonly implemented for decomposition toward last-mile computing.

Design Patterns

Design patterns are a special term in software design: generic, reusable solutions for a particular programming challenge. Design patterns should typically be language-agnostic, and refer not only to the implementation details of the pattern, but generally to a design or construction strategy. Probably the most common software design pattern is the model-view-controller (MVC) pattern that is very popular in web development, and implemented in many languages from Ruby to Java.

Similarly, we can explore functional design patterns for solving parallel computations in both MapReduce and Spark. These patterns show a generic strategy and principle that can be used in more complex or domain-specific roles. In fact, we have already seen an example in the pairs and stripes patterns used to compute word co-occurrence. Both pairs and stripes can be applied to more general computation.

In their book *MapReduce Design Patterns*, Donald Miner and Adam Shook explore 23 design patterns for common MapReduce jobs. They loosely categorize them as follows:

Summarization
Provide a summary view of a large dataset in terms of aggregations, grouping, statistical measures, indexing, or other high-level views of the data.

Filtering
Create subsets or samples of the data based on a fixed set of criteria, without modifying the original data in any way.

Data Organization
Reorganize records into a meaningful pattern in a way that doesn't necessarily imply grouping. This task is useful as a first step to further computations.

Joins
Collect related data from disparate sources into a unified whole.

Metapatterns
Implement job chaining and job merging for complex or optimized computations. These are patterns associated with other patterns.

Input and output

Transform data from one input source to a different output source using data manipulation patterns, either internal to HDFS or from external sources.

This section explores techniques for summarization and filtering in detail for both MapReduce and Spark, as well as discussing more generally the construction of data flows and job chaining for MapReduce. We will do so by presenting several specific applications that reveal the patterns, but one pattern should become quickly apparent: these techniques generally decompose or transform the input data to a smaller source of data for last-mile computation.

Summarization

Summarization attempts to describe the largest amount of information about a dataset as simply as possible. We are accustomed to executive summaries that highlight the primary take-aways of a longer document without getting into the details. Similarly, descriptive statistics attempt to summarize the relationships between observations by measuring their central tendency (mean, median), their dispersion (standard deviation), the shape of their distribution (skewness), or the dependence of variables on each other (correlation).

Key-based computation takes summarization to the next step by naturally grouping data together (another form of summarization) and aggregating some value that generally describes the key, which hopefully lead to insights. These can be simple analyses like computing the poorest performing airport or airline in terms of delay to more complex analyses that infer how weather, distance, or other factors affect performance. Many times summarization is the first step to larger generalizations and predictions, such as the computation of word co-occurrence as a language model, or a frequency analysis that describes a probability distribution.

MapReduce and Spark in principle apply a sequence of summarizations distilling the most specific form of the data (each individual record) to a more general form. Broadly speaking, we are most familiar with summarization as characterized by the following operations:

- Aggregation (collection to a single value such as the mean, sum, or maximum)
- Indexing (the functional mapping of a value to a set of values)
- Grouping (selection or division of a set into multiple sets)

In this section, we explore patterns for both aggregation and indexing (grouping is easily accomplished via key-based techniques discussed earlier). In particular, we'll explore a parallel statistical description of a dataset—such as the describe command in Pandas and how aggregation is implemented. Then we'll explore two indexing techniques: inverted indexing and document summarization by term frequency-inverse document frequency (TF-IDF).

Aggregation

An aggregation function in the context of MapReduce and Spark is one that takes two input values and produces a single output value and is also *commutative* and *associative* so that it can be computed in parallel. As a review, commutativity states that the order does not matter to a binary operation (e.g., given some operation, ✤, a ✤ b = b ✤ a). Associativity states that a computation is the same regardless of how the inputs are grouped, (a ✤ b) ✤ c = a ✤ (b ✤ c). Addition and multiplication are commutative and associative, whereas subtraction and division are not.

Aggregation is the general application of an operation on a collection to create a smaller collection (gathering together), and reduction is generally considered an operation that reduces a collection into a single value. Aggregation can also be thought of as the application of a series of smaller reductions. With this context, it's easy to see why associativity and commutativity are necessary for parallelism; given a reduction a ✤ b ✤ c ✤ d, the potential for shuffling due to networking or other physical constraints means that order must not matter. Associativity allows one process to compute a ✤ b, another to compute c ✤ d, and one or the other to send their result to perform the final ✤ operation.

Consider the standard dataset descriptors: mean, median, mode, minimum, maximum, and sum. Of these, *summation*, *minimum*, and *maximum* are easily implemented because they are both associative and commutative. *Mean*, *median*, and *mode*, however, are not. For both median and mode, some ordering is typically required, and mean experiences a loss in precision when computed in a grouped fashion because of division. Although there are parallel approximations for these computations, it is important to be aware that some care should be taken when performing these types of analyses. Rather than go over each of these computations individually, we will look at a single MapReduce job to describe an entire dataset.

Statistical summarization

At this point, we have two key concepts that allow us to begin to treat our datasets in an analytical fashion: first, we can use keys as relations to define meaningful subsets of our data, and second, we can implement multiple computations simultaneously using a variety of approaches, including job chaining, keyspace management, or mechanisms such as pairs and stripes. We can simplify and summarize large datasets by grouping instances into keys and describing the per-key properties similar to the `describe` command in Pandas.

Although we have already seen examples for computing per-key means and counts, these types of analyses are usually run initially to get a sense of a larger dataset. Particularly with high velocity big data (data that changes at a dramatic rate), running regular descriptive jobs can give you a sense of what is changing and how. Rather than implementing a MapReduce job for each descriptive metric individually (costly), we're going to run all six jobs together in a single batch, computing the count, sum, mean, standard deviation, and range (minimum and maximum).

The basic strategy will be to map a collection of counter values for each computation we want to make on a per-key basis. The reducer will then apply each operation independently to each item in the value collection, using each as necessary to compute the final output (e.g., mean depends on both a count and a sum). Here is the basic outline for such a mapper:

```
class StatsMapper(Mapper):

    def map(self):
        for key, value in self:
            try:
                value = float(value)
                self.emit(key, (1, value, value ** 2))
            except ValueError:
                # Could not parse the value, ignore.
                pass
```

In this case, the three operations that will be directly reduced are count, sum, and sum of squares. Therefore, this mapper emits on a per-key basis, a 1 for count, the value for summation, and the square of the value for the sum of the squares. The reducer uses the count and sum to compute the mean, the value to compute the range, and the count, sum, and sum of squares to compute the standard deviation as follows:

```
from ast import literal_eval as make_tuple

class StatsReducer(Reducer):

    def reduce(self):
        for key, values in self:
            # Parse the values from the mapper
            values = make_tuple(values)

            count   = 0
            delay   = 0.0
            square  = 0.0
            minimum = None
            maximum = None

            for value in values:
                count  += value[0]
                delay  += value[1]
                square += value[2]
```

```
            if minimum is None or value[1] < minimum:
                minimum = value[1]

            if maximum is None or value[1] > maximum:
                maximum = value[1]

        mean   = delay / float(count)
        stddev = math.sqrt((square-(delay**2)/count)/count-1)

        self.emit(key, (count, mean, stddev, minimum, maximum))
```

This job exemplifies the use of complex data types as output and intermediate values in MapReduce, and is really the first example of moving toward more advanced analytical approaches. The reducer utilizes the `ast.literal_eval` mechanism of deserialization to parse the value tuple, then performs a *single* loop over the data values (you would have to load all of the values into memory, for example, as a list to make multiple passes) to compute the various sums, minimums, and maximums.

However, whereas a reducer in MapReduce has access to an iterable of all values associated with a single key, in Spark this computation has to be modified slightly. Instead of being able to apply an operation that accepts a collection as input, you must be able to apply your operation to pairs of input at a time, and because the result of one application is the first input to the second application, the operation must be associative and commutative. For example, given the input `[5, 2, 7]`, you cannot simply apply `sum` to the collection, but rather `add` as follows: `add(add(5, 2), 7)`. Therefore, our mapper must extend the value with minimum and maximum counters, such that the minimum and maximum values are tracked with each value through the reduction as follows:

```
def counters(item):
    """
    Parses a key/value pair into the key and summary counters.
    A counter is as follows: (count, total, square, minimum, maximum).
    """
    key, value = item # Break apart the item tuple

    try:
        value = float(value)
        self.emit(key, (1, value, value ** 2, value, value))
    except ValueError:
        # Could not parse the value, ignore.
        pass

def aggregation(first, second):
    """
    For two (key, counter) items, perform summary aggregations.
    """
    count1, total1, squares1, min1, max1 = first
    count2, total2, squares2, min2, max2 = second
```

```
        minimum = min((min1, min2))
        maximum = max((max1, max2))
        count   = count1 + count2
        total   = total1 + total2
        squares = squares1 + squares2

        return (count, total, squares, minimum, maximum)

    def summary(aggregate):
        """
        Compute summary statistics from aggregation.
        """
        (key, (count, total, square, minimum, maximum)) = aggregate

        mean   = total / float(count)
        stddev = math.sqrt((square-(total**2)/count)/count-1)

        return (key, (count, mean, stddev, minimum, maximum))


    def main(sc):
        """
        Primary analysis mechanism for Spark application
        """

        # Given a dataset of key/value pairs, map to counters
        dataset = dataset.map(counters)

        # Perform summary aggregation by key
        dataset = dataset.reduceByKey(aggregation)
        dataset = dataset.map(summary)

        # Write the results out to disk
        dataset.saveAsTextFile("dataset-summary")
```

The data flow in the Spark job is interesting because of the rule for reduceByKey functions. Instead of being able to track the minimum and maximum values as we iterate, we have to annotate the result of our computation with the *last seen* minimum and maximum and propagate it as the computation continues to reduce. For this reason, we can't simply perform our final computation during the aggregation, and another map is needed to finalize the summarization across the (much smaller) aggregated RDD.

The describe example provides a useful pattern for computing multiple features simultaneously and returning them as a vector. This pattern is reused often, particularly in the machine learning context, where multiple procedures might be required in order to produce an instance to train on (e.g., quadratic computations, normalization, imputation, joins, or more specific machine learning tasks). Understanding the difference between aggregation implementations in MapReduce versus Spark can make a lot of difference in tracking down bugs and porting code from MapReduce to Spark and vice versa.

Indexing

In contrast to aggregation-based summarization techniques, *indexing* takes a many-to-many approach. While aggregation collects several records into a single record, indexing associates several records to one or more indices. In databases, an index is a specialized data structure that is used for fast lookups, usually a binary-tree (B-Tree). In Hadoop/Spark, indices perform a similar function, though rather than being maintained and updated, they are typically generated as a first step to downstream computation that will require fast lookups.

Text indexing has a special place in the Hadoop algorithm pantheon due to Hadoop's original intended use for creating search applications. When dealing with only a small corpus of documents, it may be possible to scan the documents looking for the search term like grep does. However, as the number of documents and queries increases, this quickly becomes unreasonable. In this section, we take a look at two types of text-based indices, the more common inverted index, as well as term frequency-inverse document frequency (TF-IDF), a numerical statistic that is associated with an index and is commonly used for machine learning.

Inverted index

An *inverted index* is a mapping from an index term to locations in a set of documents (in contrast to forward indexing, which maps from documents to index terms). In full text search, the index terms are search terms: usually words or numbers with stopwords removed (e.g., very common words that are meaningless in search). Most search engines also employ some sort of stemming or lemmatization: multiple words with the same meaning are categorized into a single word class (e.g., "running", "ran", "runs" is indexed by the single term "run").

The search example shows the most common use case for an inverted index: it quickly allows the search algorithm to retrieve the subset of documents that it must rank and return without scanning every single document. For example, for the query "running bear", the index can be used to look up the intersection of documents that contain the term "running" and the term "bear". A simple ranking system might then be employed to return documents where the search terms are close together rather than far apart in the document (though obviously modern search ranking systems are far more complex than this).

The search example can be generalized, however, to a machine learning context. The index term does not necessarily have to be text; it can be any piece of a larger record. Moreover, the task of using an index to simplify or speed up downstream computation (like the ranking) is common. Depending on how the index is created, there can be a trade-off between performance and accuracy, or, given a stochastic index, between precision and recall.

Let's consider some preprocessed text that has a document ID and a line number as a key and the line text as a value. This style of preprocessing can be used for any user-driven text like a message board or reviews, but in this case, we'll take a look at the complete works of Shakespeare's plays. In particular, we want to create an index that gives us character associations; therefore, instead of the mapping of character to line that we already have, we want to summarize to character and starting line, so that we can see which characters follow each other. Each line in the corpus is represented as follows:

```
hamlet@15261        HAMLET    O, that this too too solid flesh would melt
hamlet@15261                  Thaw and resolve itself into a dew!
```

The first part of the line is the `title@lineno` identifier, then a TAB char (\t), the name of the character, a second TAB char, and the line of the play. If the same character is speaking across multiple lines, a double TAB character separates the identifier from the text. In order to create an inverted index of speaking characters, we would use an identity reducer and the following mapper (note that the same algorithm is easily implemented with Spark):

```
class CharacterIndexMapper(Mapper):

    def map(self):
        for row in self:
            row = row.split("\t")          # split the tab parts
            if not len(row) >= 3: continue  # ensure we have data

            if row[1] != "":
                # If we have a character, emit the name and the docid/lineno.
                self.emit(row[1], row[0])
```

 This Shakespeare character index example illustrates a couple of key points concerning indexing. First, the index term can be anything (here a character name). Second, the algorithm, while very straightforward, is highly dependent on the structure of the input data (e.g., we knew to search for tab splits to find the character name). Finally, this example also highlights the use of some of the map/reduce patterns we've seen earlier—in this case, the identity reducer. Moving forward, this data structure can be used to create a graph of dialog between characters, which can then be used to analyze community or character similarity. The key point is that inverted indices are typically the first step in downstream computations.

The output of the character index job is a list of character names, each of which corresponds to a list of lines where that character starts speaking. This can be used as a lookup table or as input to other types of analysis.

TF-IDF

Term frequency-inverse document frequency (TF-IDF) is now probably the most commonly used form of text-based summarization and is currently the most commonly used feature of documents in text-based machine learning. TF-IDF is a metric that defines the relationship between a term (a word) and a document that is part of a larger corpus. In particular, it attempts to define how important that word is to that particular document given the word's relative frequency in other documents.

The term frequency, $tf_{i,k}$, is the number of times a given term, i appears in a document, j, and is typically used to measure the relevance of that word to the document. Consider a document about American politics—we might say that terms like "democracy" or "election" appear more frequently than terms like "luminal" and are therefore more relevant to the overall discourse of the document. On the other hand, term frequency by itself will over-emphasize commonly occurring words like "speaking", which might appear in both scientific and political topics given a combined corpus. Therefore, the document frequency of a term i, df_i, that is the number of documents the term appears in, is used to offset the term frequency. Namely, the log-scaled inverse of the ratio of documents the term appears in to the total number of documents, N, is multiplied against the term frequency. A higher TF-IDF score means that the given word appears frequently in the target document, but infrequently in the rest of corpus. TF-IDF for a term i in a document j:

$$w_{i,j} = tf_{i,j} \times \log\left(\frac{N}{df_i}\right)$$

This measure was originally used for topic modeling of documents, a form of clustering that attempts to associate documents with a common theme. It's easy to see that documents that share terms with a high TF-IDF are probably related to each other, as those terms appear infrequently given the rest of the corpus. For similar reasons, TF-IDF is now widely incorporated into other machine learning tasks, including classification, automatic question answering, and even social network or web analysis where there is unstructured data.

We include this algorithm with indexing for a similar reason that we included the simpler inverted indexing example: it creates a data structure that is typically used for downstream computations and machine learning. Moreover, this more complex example highlights something we've only touched upon in other sections: the use of job chaining to compute a single algorithm. With that in mind, let's take a look at the MapReduce implementation of TF-IDF.

Our strategy is to use keyspace patterns to propagate required data throughout all three of our jobs. The first job computes the term frequency per document with a simple word count that also maintains the document ID for the term. The second job computes the total number of documents the word appears in. Finally, the last job computes the TF-IDF using the information propagated through to the end by the first two jobs. The first job is as follows:

```
class TermFrequencyMapper(Mapper):

    def __init__(self, *args, **kwargs):
        """
        Initialize the tokenizer and stopwords.
        """
        super(TermFrequencyMapper, self).__init__(*args, **kwargs)

        self.stopwords = set()
        self.tokenizer = re.compile(r'\W+')

        # Read the stopwords from the text file.
        with open('stopwords.txt') as stopwords:
            for line in stopwords:
                self.stopwords.add(line.strip())

    def tokenize(self, text):
        """
        Tokenizes and normalizes a line of text (yields only non-stopwords
        that aren't digits, punctuation, or empty strings).
        """
        for word in re.split(self.tokenizer, text):
            if word and word not in self.stopwords and word.isalpha():
                yield word

    def map(self):
        for docid, line in self:
            # Otherwise, tokenize the line and emit every (word, docid).
            for word in self.tokenize(line):
                self.emit((word, docid), 1)


class SumReducer(Reducer):

    def reduce(self):
        for key, values in self:
            total = sum(int(count[1]) for count in values)
            self.emit(key, total)
```

In order to compute terms in our document, we'll go a bit further than simply splitting on space. Here we'll use a regular expression to tokenize our text, which can get

Design Patterns | 113

more complex as your indexing requires. We also read in a list of stopwords from a *stopwords.txt* file, which will need to be included with the job. Our `tokenization` method therefore simply uses a regular expression to split, and filters out stopwords, numbers, and punctuation. More advanced tokenizers can also stem the word, or normalize it (e.g., make it all lowercase). The first job emits (`term`, `docid`) keys with the frequency as the value.

The second job is composed of a mapper and reducer, as follows:

```python
class DocumentTermsMapper(Mapper):

    def map(self):
        for line in self:
            key, tf = line.split(self.sep)   # Split line into key, val parts
            word, docid = make_tuple(key)    # Parse the tuple string
            self.emit(word, (docid, tf, 1))  # Emit word and data with counter

class DocumentTermsReducer(Reducer):

    def reduce(self):
        for word, values in self:
            # Load the values into memory to make multiple passes and parse
            values = [make_tuple(value) for value in values]

            # Pass 1: compute the document frequency of the terms
            terms = sum(int(item[2]) for item in values)

            # Pass 2: emit a value for every docid associated with the word
            for docid, tf, num in values:
                self.emit((word, docid), (int(tf), terms))
```

The mapper for this job is another count mapper to sum the document frequency of the term; it also changes the keyspace, maintaining the document term frequency and adding the document ID to the values. This has the effect that we can reduce by word, where every value is a document. The reducer therefore requires two passes over the data—one to sum, and the other to perform a per-document keyspace change. In order to do this it must buffer the tuples (`docid`, `tf`, `count`) in memory, using a list comprehension to load the data from its generator. If there are many documents containing the word (think high-frequency words like "the"), this computation might not fit into memory. It is for this reason that stopword lists are so important to computing TF-IDF. Other solutions include using temporary disk storage for the intermediary data, or implementing another in-between MapReduce job, one for the sum, the second for the keyspace change:

```python
class TFIDFMapper(Mapper):

    def __init__(self, *args, **kwargs):
        self.N = kwargs.pop("documents")
        super(TFIDFMapper, self).__init__(*args, **kwargs)
```

```
def map(self):
    for line in self:
        key, val = map(make_tuple, line.split(self.sep))
        tf, n = (int(x) for x in val)
    if n > 0:
        idf = math.log(self.N/n)
        self.emit(key, idf*tf)
```

The final job is a map-only one, as we already have the keys we want to compute on—the pairs (`word, docid`) emitted from the last reducer. This can be easily implemented using an identity reducer. Here, we simply parse the line into tuples of ints, and so long as the frequency is greater than zero, we compute the TF-IDF. Note that we need one extra piece of information, the number of documents in the corpus, which was not computed along the way.

Although this job seems complex, envision the execution as a data flow: as pieces of the computation are produced, they are added to the flow of data. The key/value choices are motivated by the next step in the computation. And, crucially, the original input is only traversed a single time by this computation, allowing for linear dependency in the job. This data flow mindset is also required for the Spark implementation of the TF-IDF computation, as follows:

```
def tokenize(document, stopwords=None):
    """
    Tokenize and return (docid, word) pairs with a counter.
    """

    def line_tokenizer(lines):
        """
        Inner generator for word tokenization line by line.
        """
        for line in lines:
            for word in re.split(tokenizer, line):
                if word and word not in stopwords.value and word.isalpha():
                    yield word

    docid, lines = document
    return [
        ((docid, word), 1) for word in line_tokenizer(lines)
    ]


def term_frequency(v1, v2):
    """
    Compute the term frequency by splitting the complex value.
    """
    docid, tf, count1  = v1
    _docid, _tf, count2 = v2
    return (docid, tf, count1 + count2)
```

```
def tfidf(args):
    """
    Compute the TF-IDF given a ((word, docid), (tf, n)) argument.
    Note that N_DOCS must be defined in advance, and is the number of docs
    in the corpus (n is the document frequency of the word).
    """
    (key, (tf, n)) = args
    if n > 0:
        idf = math.log(N_DOCS/n)
        return (key, idf*tf)


def main(sc):
    """
    Primary analysis mechanism for Spark application
    """

    # Load stopwords from the dataset
    with open('stopwords.txt', 'r') as words:
        stopwords = frozenset([
            word.strip() for word in words.read().split("\n")
        ])

    # Broadcast the stopwords across the cluster
    stopwords = sc.broadcast(stopwords)

    # Phase 1: tokenize and compute document frequency.
    # Note: assumed we have a corpus of (docid, text) pairs.
    docfreq = corpus.flatMap(partial(tokenize, stopwords=stopwords))
    docfreq = docfreq.reduceByKey(add)

    # Phase 2: compute term frequency, then perform keyspace change.
    trmfreq = docfreq.map(lambda (key, tf): (key[1], (key[0], tf, 1)))
    trmfreq = trmfreq.reduceByKey(term_frequency)
    trmfreq = trmfreq.map(
        lambda (word, (docid, tf, n)): ((word, docid), (tf, n))
    )

    # Phase 3: compute the tf-idf of each word, document pair.
    tfidfs = trmfreq.map(tfidf)
```

The Spark job similarly loads stopwords from disk, then broadcasts them to the rest of the cluster. We can then flatMap a partial of the tokenize function that embeds the stopwords broadcast value as the default argument. Here we use flatMap because the tokenize function will generate a list of token counts for each line in the document (which requires the use of the inner line_tokenizer function). Finally, we map our Spark-implemented term_frequency and tfidif functions to each document. Note that because reduceByKey is called twice, and some final action will need to be applied to the `tfidfs` RDD, this Spark job similarly has three data flows, like the MapReduce job.

Filtering

Filtering is one of the primary methods of coarse-grained data reduction for downstream computation. Unlike aggregation methods, which reduce the input space through a high-level overview over a set of groups, filtering is intended to reduce the computational space through omission. In the keyspace section, we explored filtering as it applied to mappers. In fact, many filtering tasks are a perfect fit for map-only jobs, which do not require reducers because mappers are so well suited to this task. This can be considered filtering by predicate or by selection, similar to a `where` clause in a SQL statement.

Other filtering tasks may leverage reducers in order to accumulate a representative dataset or to perform some per-values filtering constraint. Examples of this style of filtering include finding the n-largest or n-smallest values, performing deduplication, or subselection. A very common filtering task in analytics is sampling: creating a smaller, representative dataset that is well distributed relative to the larger dataset (depending on the type of distribution you are expecting to achieve). Data-oriented subsamples are used in development, to validate machine-learning algorithms (e.g., cross-validation) or to produce other statistical computations (e.g., power).

Generically we might implement filtering as a function that takes a single record as input. If the evaluation returns true, the record is emitted; otherwise, it is dropped. In this section, we explore sortless *n*-largest/smallest, sampling techniques, as well as more advanced filtering using Bloom filters to improve performance.

Top n records

The top n records (and conversely the bottom n records) methodology is a cardinality comparison filter that requires both a mapper and reducer to work. The basic principle is to have each mapper yield its top n items, and then the reducer will similarly choose the top n items from the mappers. If n is relatively small (at least in comparison to the rest of the dataset) a single reducer should be able to handle this computation with ease because at most n records will come from each mapper:

```
import bisect

class TopNMapper(Mapper):

    def __init__(self, n, *args, **kwargs):
        self.n = n
        super(TopNMapper, self).__init__(*args, **kwargs)

    def map(self):
```

```
            items = []
            for value in self:
                # maintain sorted list of items
                bisect.insort(items, value)

            for item in items[-self.n:]:
                # emit the top n values from the mapper
                self.emit(None, item)


    class TopNReducer(object):

        def __init__(self, n, *args, **kwargs):
            self.n = n
            super(TopNReducer, self).__init__(*args, **kwargs)

        def reduce(self):
            items = []
            for _, values in self:
                for value in values:
                    bisect.insort(items, value)

            for item in items[-self.n:]:
                # emit the top n values from the mapper
                self.emit(None, item)
```

Here both the mapper and the reducer use the `bisect` module to insert values into a
list in ascending sorted order. In order to get the biggest *n* values, a slice with a negative index is used, thereby selecting the last *n* values in the sorted list. To get the
smallest *n*, you would simply slice off the first *n* values in the list. Using `None` as the
key ensures that only a single reducer is used. Note that in Spark, the rich RDD API
gives you the ability to use the `top` and `takeOrdered` actions, such that you don't have
to implement this yourself. Note that for both Spark and MapReduce, the records
need to be comparable for sorting, which may require strict parsing; for example, in
Python, `'14' > 22` can be `True`.

The primary benefit of this methodology is that a complete sort does not have to
occur over the entire dataset. Instead, the mappers each sort their own subset of the
data, and the reducer sees only n times the number of mappers worth of data. This
code can be optimized a few ways, but the primary optimization relates to the data
structure being used. In the next section, we will examine the use of a `heap` over the
`bisect` module for implementing similar functionality.

Simple random sample

Simple random samples are subsets of a dataset where each record is equally likely to
belong to the subset. In this case, the `evaluation` function does not care about the
content or structure of the record, but instead utilizes some random number genera-

tor to evaluate whether to emit the record. The question is how to ensure that every element has an equal likelihood of being selected.

A first approach if we don't exactly need a specific sample of size n but rather some percentage of records is to simply use a random number generator to produce a number and compare it to the desired threshold size. The range of values available to the random number generator along with the threshold determines what approximate percentage of records will be emitted. Generally speaking, random number generators return a value between 0 and 1—so direct comparison to a percentage will yield the intended result! For example, if we want to sample 20% of our dataset, we might write a mapper as follows:

```python
import random

class PercentSampleMapper(Mapper):

    def __init__(self, *args, **kwargs):
        self.percentage = kwargs.pop("percentage")
        super(PercentSampleMapper, self).__init__(*args, **kwargs)

    def map(self):
        for _, val in self:
            if random.random() < self.percentage:
                self.emit(None, val)

if __name__ == '__main__':
    mapper = PercentSampleMapper(sys.stdin, percentage=0.20)
    mapper.map()
```

The PercentSampleMapper is initialized with a percentage keyword argument, which is popped off the generic keyword arguments in __init__. This job will return approximately 20% of the original dataset because while each record is equally likely to have a random number that is less than 0.2, that is likely to occur only approximately 20% of the times it is called. If this is run as a map-only job with no reducer, a myriad of tiny files will be written to disk that matches the number of mappers. Utilizing a single identity reducer will ensure that these values are all collected into a single file.

However, what if you want a specific sample size, n? In order to ensure that each method is equally likely, you would have to randomly select an element n times without replacement in order to ensure each record has an equal chance of being selected. One way to do this is to shuffle the records, select a random number between 0 and N-1 where N is the number of records, and emitting the record at that index. Shuffle again, and select a random number between 0 and N-2, and so forth.

Statisticians might be tempted to employ sampling techniques like *reservoir sampling*, which in a single-process context are able to efficiently sample on data streams or a large dataset. Generally speaking, when you employ any probability distribution in a mapper, you must be careful because there is no guarantee that a mapper will see the same data across runs, that each mapper will get the same amount of data, or that there is a specific ordering to the mapping process. These vagaries could lead to some mappers having higher or lower expected likelihoods. A (correct) reaction is to then move the work to a reducer or aggregation; however, this action may negate the benefits of multi-process execution on a cluster! While there are distributed reservoir sampling algorithms, let this caution serve as a reminder that sequential and parallel implementations of the same algorithm can often be very different!

In order to parallelize the shuffle method, we can think about a deck of cards that is equally dealt to four players. If we want to sample 4 cards with an equal likelihood of selection, we can simply have each player shuffle their part of the deck and deal you 4 cards each; you can then select the top 4 cards from your 16 cards. If you toss the cards in the air to each player instead of dealing them evenly, such that each player may not get an even number of cards, this method still ensures that each card is equally likely to be selected. The question then becomes; how can we shuffle our records using Hadoop such that we achieve better performance?

The answer is to assign every record a random floating-point number between 0 and 1 in the mapper. The mapper will then emit the top n records. Similarly, the reducer will emit only the top n records it sees from its mappers. Although this mechanism still only allows a single reducer, the reducer gets a limited subset of the data (e.g., n times the number of mappers), which should be able to fit in the reducer's memory. Because every row has an equal probability of having one of the n top random numbers, we have achieved a random sample:

```
import random, heapq

class SampleMapper(Mapper):

    def __init__(self, n, *args, **kwargs):
        self.n = n
        super(SampleMapper, self).__init__(*args, **kwargs)

    def map(self):
        # initialize our heap as a list with n zeros
        heap = [0 for x in xrange(self.n)]

        for value in self:
            # maintain a heap of only n largest values
            heapq.heappushpop(heap, (random.random(), value))
```

```
        for item in heap:
            # emit the sampled values
            self.emit(None, item)


class SampleReducer(Mapper):

    def __init__(self, n, *args, **kwargs):
        self.n = n
        super(SampleReducer, self).__init__(*args, **kwargs)

    def reduce(self):
        # initialize our heap as a list with n zeros
        heap = [0 for x in xrange(self.n)]

        for _, values in self:
            for value in values:
                heapq.heappushpop(heap, make_tuple(value))

        for item in heap:
            # emit the sampled values
            self.emit(None, item[1])
```

We could have used the `bisect` module as in the top *n* records approach, but for the sake of variety, we have used a heap data structure to maintain a list in memory of only the n largest random values. This further reduces the memory requirements of both the mappers, and in particular, the reducer, such that only n values are held in memory at a time. Our mapper (and similarly our reducer), initializes a list of length n whose values are zero. The `heapq.heappushpop` function pushes the new value into the heap, then pops the smallest value off (and does so much faster than sequential calls to `heapq.push` and `heapq.pop`).

Bloom filtering

A *bloom filter* is an efficient probabilistic data structure used to perform set membership testing. A bloom filter is really no different from any other evaluation function, except that a preliminary computation must be made to gather "hot values" (members of the exclusion set), which we would like to filter against. The benefit is that a bloom filter is compact (making even large sets very easy to transmit to every mapper on the cluster) and fast to test membership.

Bloom filters suffer, however, from false positives—in other words, saying something belongs to the set when it does not; however, they guarantee that any exclusion does not belong in the membership set—there are no false negatives). Therefore, the expression x `in bloom` evaluates to either "x is probably in the set" or "x is definitely not in the set". These semantics will certainly define how you construct your bloom filter, considering the trade-off between the size of the filter set, the number of possible elements in your data, and what can be held in memory for both mappers and reducers. If you're willing to have some fuzziness, most bloom filters can be constructed with a threshold for the probability of a false negative, by increasing or decreasing the size of the bloom filter.

In order to construct a bloom filter, you will first have to build it. Bloom filters work by applying several hashes to input data, then by setting bits in a bit array according to the hash. Once the bit array is constructed, it can be used to test membership by applying hashes to the test data and seeing if the relevant bits are 1 or not. The bit array construction can either be parallelized by using rules to map distinct values to a reducer that constructs the bloom filter, or it can be a living, versioned data structure that is maintained by other processes.

In this example, we will use a third-party library, `pybloomfiltermmap`, which can be installed using `pip`. There are a few third-party bloom filter libraries for Python, but this one exposes the best API for creating a configurable filter. Let's consider an example in which we are including tweets based on whether they contain a hashtag or @ reply that is in a whitelist of terms and usernames. In order to create the bloom filter, we load our data from disk, and save the bloom filter to an `mmap` file as follows:

```
from pybloomfilter import BloomFilter

bloom = BloomFilter(1000000, 0.1, 'twitter.bloom')

for prefix, path in (('#', 'hashtags.txt'), ('@', 'handles.txt')):
    with open(path, 'r') as f:
        for word in f:
            bloom.add(prefix + word.strip())
```

This example creates a bloom filter with a capacity of one million elements, and an error rate of 0.1. Under the hood, it uses these parameters to select an optimal number, k, where k is the number of required hash functions to guarantee that error threshold for the given capacity. There is a trade-off in performance and space — the lower the capacity and lower the error rate, the more hash functions are required, thus a slower computation; the higher the capacity, the bigger the bloom filter will have to be. After reading our hashtags and Twitter handles from files on disk (and prefixing them appropriately), our bloom filter will be written to disk in a file called *twitter.bloom*.

To employ this in a Spark context:

```
ELEMS = re.compile(r'[#@][\w\d]+')

def tweet_filter(tweet, bloom=None):
    for elem in ELEMS.findall(tweet['text']):
        if elem in bloom.value:
            return True
```

```
# Load the bloom filter from disk and parallelize it
bloom = sc.broadcast(BloomFilter.open('twitter.bloom'))

# Load JSON tweets from disk and parse them
tweets = sc.textFile('tweets').map(json.loads)
tweets = tweets.filter(partial(tweet_filter, bloom=bloom))
```

Our tweet filter is created using the `functools.partial` function to create a closure with the bloom filter broadcast variable, which was loaded from disk on the driver. The `tweet_filter` function uses a regular expression to extract all hashtags and @ replies, then checks if they are in the bloom filter; if so, it returns `True`, thus retaining all elements in the RDD that match our whitelist.

Bloom filters are potentially the most complex data structure that you will use on a regular basis performing analytics in Hadoop. They are included here not because of their complexity, but rather to show how the combination of performance and correctness can affect distributed computation. As a data scientist practicing big data, you will probably find that stochastic methods will add value to timely computations that are necessary for further analyses.

Toward Last-Mile Analytics

In this chapter, we've looked at many data analysis patterns, from working with keys to routine patterns for aggregation and filtering. There has been one overriding theme: the decomposition of data from a much larger input to a more manageable one of a smaller size. Using the tools that we have discussed in this chapter, this section looks at a strategy for computing an end-to-end predictive model.

Many machine learning techniques use generalized linear models (GLM) under the hood to estimate a response variable given some input data and an error distribution. The most commonly used GLM is a linear regression (others include logistic and Poisson regressions), which models the continuous relationship between a dependent variable Y and one or more independent variables, X. That relationship is encoded by a set of *coefficients* and an *error term* as follows:

$$Y = \beta_0 + \beta_1 X_1 + \cdots + \beta_n X_n + \epsilon$$

At the risk of glossing over this very important topic too quickly, we can state that the computation of the β coefficients is the primary goal of fitting the model to existing data. This is generally done via an optimization algorithm that finds the set of coefficients that minimizes the amount of error given some dataset with observations for X and Y. Note that linear regression can be considered a *supervised* machine learning method, as the "correct" answers (the X and Y variables that we fit the model to) are known in advance.

Optimization algorithms like ordinary least squares or stochastic gradient descent are iterative; that is, they make multiple passes over the data. In a big data context, reading a complete dataset multiple times for each optimization iteration can be prohibitively time consuming, particularly for on-demand analytics or development. Spark makes things a bit better with distributed machine learning algorithms and in-memory computing exposed in its MLlib, which we discuss in Chapter 9. However, for extremely large datasets, or smaller time windows, even Spark can take too long; and if Spark doesn't have the model or distributed algorithm you'd like to implement, then the many gotchas of distributed programming could limit your analytical choices.

The general solution is the one we've proposed throughout this chapter: decompose your problem by transforming the input dataset into a smaller one, until it fits in memory. Once the dataset is reduced to an in-memory computation, it can be analyzed using standard techniques, then validated across the entire dataset. For a linear regression, we could take a simple random sample of the dataset, perform feature extraction on the sample, build our linear model, then validate the model by computing the mean square error of the entire dataset.

Fitting a Model

Consider a specific example where we have a dataset that originates from news articles or blog posts and a prediction task where we want to determine the number of comments in the next 24 hours. Given the raw HTML pages from a web crawl, the data flow may be as follows:

1. Parse HTML page for metadata and separate the main text and the comments.
2. Create an index of comments/commenters to blog post associated with a timestamp.
3. Use the index to create instances for our model, where an instance is a blog post and the comments in a 24-hour sliding window.
4. Join the instances with the primary text data (for both comments and blog test).
5. Extract the features of each instance (e.g., number of comments in the first 24 hours, the length of the blog post, the amount of time from the window to the publication time, bag of words features, day of week, etc.).
6. Sample the instance features.
7. Build a linear model in memory using Scikit-Learn or Statsmodels.
8. Compute the mean squared error or coefficient of determination across the entire dataset of instance features.

This data flow shows that there are many pre-preprocessing jobs that need only be run once or a few times (e.g., the feature extraction needs to be rerun throughout the feature analysis lifecycle). However, the model sampling and validation process could run fairly routinely. Once this is up and running, we might even have a live model, where new information is fed into the data pipeline and the model is refit and validated again.

At this point, let's assume that through techniques we've already learned we've managed to arrive at a dataset that has all features extracted. Using the sampling technique we saw earlier in the chapter, we can take a smaller dataset and save it to disk, and build a linear model with Scikit-Learn:

```
import pickle
import numpy as np
from sklearn import linear_model

# Load data from tab-delimited file on disk
data = np.loadtxt('sample.txt')

# The target is the first column (the key) and X is the value
y = data[:,0]
X = data[:,1:]

# Instantiate and fit our linear model
clf = linear_model.Ridge(alpha=1.0, fit_intercept=True)
clf.fit(X, y)

# Write the model as a pickle to disk
with open('clf.pickle', 'wb') as f:
    pickle.dump(clf, f)
```

This snippet of code uses the np.loadtxt function to load our sample data from disk, which in this case must be a tab-delimited file of instances where the first column is the target value and the remaining columns are the features. This type of output matches what might happen when key/value pairs are written to disk from Spark or MapReduce, although you will have to collect the data from the cluster into a single file, and ensure it is correctly formatted. The data is then fit to a *ridge regression*, a linear regression that has regularization applied to prevent overfitting the model.

Validating Models

In order to use this model in the cluster to evaluate our performance, we have two choices. First, we could write the Scikit-Learn linear model properties, clf.coef_ (coefficients) and clf.intercept_ (error term) to disk and then load those parameters into our MapReduce or Spark job and compute the error ourselves. However, this requires us to implement a prediction function for every single model we may want to use. Instead, we will use the pickle module to dump the model to disk, then load it to every node in the cluster to make our prediction. We can now write boilerplate Scikit-Learn model error estimation, and use any model we would like in Scikit-Learn as we're engaging in hypothesis-driven development (e.g., tuning parameters, performing feature analysis, or model selection).

In order to validate our model, we must compute the mean square error (MSE) across the entire dataset. Error is defined as the difference between the actual and predicted values, $y - \hat{y}$. We compute the mean of the square error to ensure that there are no negative values (which would reduce error). To do this, we simply need a mean reducer and a mapper that can load the model and compute the square error:

```python
import pickle

class MSEMapper(Mapper):

    def __init__(self, model, *args, **kwargs):
        super(MSEMapper, self).__init__(*args, **kwargs)

        # Load our model from disk
        with open(model, 'rb') as f:
            self.clf = pickle.load(f)


    def map(self):
        for row in self:
            # Parse the floating-point values in the row
            row = map(float, row)
            y = row[0]
            X = row[1:]

            yhat = self.clf.predict(x)

            self.emit(_, (y-yhat) ** 2)
```

In Spark, we can use an accumulator to sum the square error, and broadcast the model across the cluster as follows:

```python
def cost(row, clf=None):
    """
    Computes the square error given the row.
    """
    return (row[0] - clf.predict(row[1:])) ** 2


def main(sc):
    """
    Primary analysis mechanism for Spark application
    """

    # Load the model from the pickle file
    with open('clf.pickle', 'rb') as f:
```

```
        clf = sc.broadcast(model.load(f))


        # Create an accumulator to sum the squared error
        sum_square_error = sc.accumulator(0)

        # Load and parse the blog data
        blogs = sc.textFile("blogData").map(float)

        # Map the cost function and accumulate the sum
        error = blogs.map(partial(cost, clf=clf))
        error.foreach(lambda cost: sum_square_error.add(cost))

        # Print and compute the mean
        print sum_square_error.value / error.count()
```

Using the `pickle` module to serialize Scikit-Learn models is a great way to get started on machine learning with much larger datasets. Workflows will often include the storage of the pickled models in a database blob field, then loaded and validated across the cluster on demand. More advanced big data and scaling require machine learning libraries like Mahout and Spark's MLlib, which we discuss in a bit more detail in Chapter 9. Of course, there is also a second inflection point for models that are either so recently developed they don't have a distributed counterpart, or cannot be parallelized. Either way, using the sample, train, validate strategy can be a very effective tool in your analytical toolkit.

Conclusion

At the start of this book, we began by describing the data science process in the context of big data, particularly thinking about building data products and the data science pipeline. We then necessarily had to move from those more general topics into a more specific discussion of distributed computing, MapReduce, and Spark. At the beginning of this chapter, you should have felt comfortable understanding *how* distributed computation works, and how you might implement a job on a Hadoop cluster, but not necessarily *what* to implement. This chapter was designed to give you a feel for the variety of distributed computing patterns, as well as introduce a number of analytics in order to convey how large-scale analyses might be adapted from other data processing workflows.

The first thing we nailed down was the idea of computing with keys, a natural parallelization technique that gives us the ability to operate on multiple sets or domains simultaneously. Rather than making several, independent queries, key-based computation allows us to apply operations to multiple sets simultaneously. Understanding how to compute with keys is essential to understanding MapReduce, and is extremely relevant to Spark computing as well. To that end, we introduced several key-based patterns for both mappers and reducers, implemented in both MapReduce and Spark.

We then moved on to discussing design patterns for higher-level algorithms and operations. We looked at summarization, indexing, and filtering patterns, but presented alongside very common analyses like TF-IDF, describe, and random sampling. These patterns and algorithms were selected to present Hadoop in a more analytical context, rather than a computational one. Finally, we looked at a case study for an end-to-end analysis using "last-mile computing" to compute a linear regression. We described a basic initial strategy of decomposing the input domain, performing in-memory computation, and then validating that computation across the cluster. This strategy serves many parts of the data pipeline, including powering on a variety of analyses in an agile, hypothesis-driven development workflow.

This chapter serves as the glue between the first and second parts of the book. Whereas the first half looked at the bare metal and details of computing on Hadoop, the second half will view Hadoop more as a data management tool. The upcoming chapters focus on the Hadoop ecosystem and the tools used to enable the data pipeline in a cluster. We look at data mining and warehousing using Hive, ingestion with Sqoop, data flows with higher-order tools such as Pig and Spark, and finally, machine learning with the Spark MLlib. This chapter started us down that road, as a bridge between what is possible with the bare metal, and what might come next using the various libraries.

PART II

Workflows and Tools for Big Data Science

The second part of *Data Analytics with Hadoop* explores higher-level tools and workflows for practicing data scientists. Although a foundational knowledge of Hadoop, MapReduce, and Spark is required to understand what kind of analyses can be conducted at scale, the day-to-day efforts of a data scientist engaging in big data will generally revolve around the ecosystem of tools built on top of Hadoop. Generally speaking, we have organized these final chapters around the data product pipeline presented in Chapter 1.

Chapter 6 discusses data warehousing and data mining and introduces Hive and HBase for both relational and columnar data storage and queries. Chapter 7 identifies the need for ingestion utilities to get data into HDFS and looks at structured methods using Sqoop, as well as less structured ingestion using Flume. Chapter 8 explores higher-level APIs for analytics: Apache Pig and Spark DataFrames. Chapter 9 discusses machine learning and computational methods using Spark MLlib. Finally, Chapter 10 wraps things up and takes a complete view of doing data science by summarizing the integration of the workflows discussed in the previous chapters of this part.

## CHAPTER 6

Data Mining and Warehousing

As data analysts, we often prefer to focus on the task of mining data for meaningful insights or applying predictive modeling methods on data that has already been curated, cleaned, and staged for our analysis. However, in most traditional enterprise data environments, there is a tremendous amount of engineering and technical resources that go into funneling and organizing this data into a unified data warehouse before any meaningful data analysis can happen.

The *enterprise data warehouse* (EDW) has thus become the linchpin in most organizations that process and analyze data at scale. However, because the overwhelming majority of EDWs utilize some form of relational database management system (RDBMS) as the primary storage and querying engine, much of the effort in setting up new data analysis projects is spent on up-front schema design and extract, transform, and load (ETL) operations. It's estimated that ETL consumes 70–80% of data warehousing costs, risks, and implementation time.[1] This overhead makes it costly to perform even modest levels of data analysis prototyping or exploratory analysis.

RDBMSs present another limitation in the face of the rapidly expanding diversity of data types that we need to store and analyze, which can be unstructured (emails, multimedia files) or semi-structured (clickstream data) in nature. The velocity and variety of this data often demands the ability to evolve the schema in a "just-in-time" manner, which is very tough to support in a traditional DW.

It's for these reasons that Hadoop has become the most disruptive technology in the data warehousing and data mining space. Hadoop's separation of storage from processing enables organizations to store their raw data in HDFS without necessitating

---

1 Kimball Group, "New Directions for ETL" (*https://channels.theinnovationenterprise.com/articles/new-directions-for-etl*).

ETLs to conform the data into a single unified data model. Moreover, with YARN's generalized processing layer, we're able to directly access and query the raw data from multiple perspectives and using different methods (SQL, non-SQL) as appropriate for the particular use case. Hadoop thus not only enables exploratory analysis and data mining prototyping, it opens the floodgates to new types of data and analysis.

This chapter is an introduction to some of the primary frameworks and tools that enable data warehousing and data mining functions in Hadoop. We'll explore Hadoop's most popular SQL-based querying engine, Hive, as well as a NoSQL database for Hadoop, HBase. Finally, we'll run through some other notable Hadoop projects in the data warehousing space.

Structured Data Queries with Hive

Apache Hive is a "data warehousing" framework built on top of Hadoop. Hive provides data analysts with a familiar SQL-based interface to Hadoop, which allows them to attach structured schemas to data in HDFS and access and analyze that data using SQL queries. Hive has made it possible for developers who are fluent in SQL to leverage the scalability and resilience of Hadoop without requiring them to learn Java or the native MapReduce API.

Hive provides its own dialect of SQL called the Hive Query Language, or HQL. HQL supports many commonly used SQL statements, including data definition statements (DDLs) (e.g., CREATE DATABASE/SCHEMA/TABLE), data manipulation statements (DMSs) (e.g., INSERT, UPDATE, LOAD), and data retrieval queries (e.g., SELECT). Hive also supports integration of custom user-defined functions, which can be written in Java or any language supported by Hadoop Streaming, that extend the built-in functionality of HQL.

Hive commands and HQL queries are compiled into an *execution plan* or a series of HDFS operations and/or MapReduce jobs, which are then executed on a Hadoop cluster. Thus, Hive has inherited certain limitations from HDFS and MapReduce that constrain it from providing key online transaction processing (OLTP) features that one might expect from a traditional database management system. In particular, because HDFS is a write-once, read-many (WORM) file system and does not provide in-place file updates, Hive is not very efficient for performing row-level inserts, updates, or deletes. In fact, these row-level updates are only recently supported as of Hive release 0.14.0 (*https://issues.apache.org/jira/browse/HIVE-5317*).

Additionally, Hive queries entail higher-latency due to the overhead required to generate and launch the compiled MapReduce jobs on the cluster; even small queries that would complete within a few seconds on a traditional RDBMS may take several minutes to finish in Hive.

On the plus side, Hive provides the high-scalability and high-throughput that you would expect from any Hadoop-based application, and as a result, is very well suited to batch-level workloads for online analytical processing (OLAP) of very large datasets at the terabyte and petabyte scale.

In this section, we explore some of Hive's primary features and write HQL queries to perform data analysis. We assume that you have installed Hive to run on Hadoop in pseudo-distributed mode. The steps for installing Hive can be found in Appendix B.

The Hive Command-Line Interface (CLI)

Hive's installation comes packaged with a handy command-line interface (CLI), which we will use to interact with Hive and run our HQL statements. To start the Hive CLI from the $HIVE_HOME:

```
~$ cd $HIVE_HOME
/srv/hive$ bin/hive
```

This will initiate the CLI and bootstrap the logger (if configured) and Hive history file, and finally display a Hive CLI prompt:

```
hive>
```

At any time, you can exit the Hive CLI using the following command:

```
hive> exit;
```

Hive can also run in non-interactive mode directly from the command line by passing the filename option, -f, followed by the path to the script to execute:

```
~$ hive -f ~/hadoop-fundamentals/hive/init.hql
~$ hive -f ~/hadoop-fundamentals/hive/top_50_players_by_homeruns.hql >>
~/homeruns.tsv
```

Additionally, the quoted-query-string option, -e, allows you to run inline commands from the command line:

```
~$ hive -e 'SHOW DATABASES;'
```

You can view the full list of Hive options for the CLI by using the -H flag:

```
~$ hive -H

usage: hive
 -d,--define <key=value>          Variable substitution to apply to hive
                                   commands. e.g. -d A=B or --define A=B
    --database <databasename>     Specify the database to use
 -e <quoted-query-string>         SQL from command line
 -f <filename>                    SQL from files
 -H,--help                        Print help information
 -h <hostname>                    connecting to Hive Server on remote host
    --hiveconf <property=value>   Use value for given property
    --hivevar <key=value>         Variable substitution to apply to hive
```

```
                               commands. e.g. --hivevar A=B
  -i <filename>                Initialization SQL file
  -p <port>                    connecting to Hive Server on port number
  -S,--silent                  Silent mode in interactive shell
  -v,--verbose                 Verbose mode (echo executed SQL to the
                               console)
```

Non-interactive mode is very handy for running saved scripts, but the CLI gives us the ability to easily debug and iterate on queries in Hive.

Hive Query Language (HQL)

In this section, we'll learn how to write HiveQL (HQL) statements to create a Hive database, load the database with data that resides in HDFS, and perform query-based analysis on the data. The data referenced in this section can be found in the GitHub repository within the */data* directory.

Creating a database

Creating a database in Hive is very similar to creating a database in a SQL-based RDBMS, by using the CREATE DATABASE or CREATE SCHEMA statement:

```
hive> CREATE DATABASE log_data;
```

When Hive creates a new database, the schema definition data is stored in the *Hive metastore*. Hive will raise an error if the database already exists in the metastore; we can check for the existence of the database by using IF NOT EXISTS:

```
hive> CREATE DATABASE IF NOT EXISTS log_data;
```

We can then run SHOW DATABASES to verify that our database has been created. Hive will return all databases found in the metastore, along with the default Hive database:

```
hive> SHOW DATABASES;
OK
default
log_data
Time taken: 0.085 seconds, Fetched: 2 row(s)
```

Additionally, we can set our working database with the USE command:

```
hive> USE log_data;
```

Now that we've created a database in Hive, we can describe the layout of our data by creating table definitions within that database.

Creating tables

Hive provides a SQL-like CREATE TABLE statement, which in its simplest form takes a table name and column definitions:

```
CREATE TABLE apache_log (
    host STRING,
    identity STRING,
    user STRING,
    time STRING,
    request STRING,
    status STRING,
    size STRING,
    referer STRING,
    agent STRING
);
```

However, because Hive data is stored in the file system, usually in HDFS or the local file system, the CREATE TABLE command also takes optional clauses to specify the row format with the ROW FORMAT clause that tells Hive how to read each row in the file and map to our columns. For example, we could indicate that the data is in a delimited file with fields delimited by the tab character:

```
hive> CREATE TABLE shakespeare (
    lineno STRING,
    linetext STRING
)
ROW FORMAT DELIMITED
    FIELDS TERMINATED BY '\t';
```

In the case of the Apache access log, each row is structured according to the Common Log Format (*https://httpd.apache.org/docs/1.3/logs.html#common*). Fortunately, Hive provides a way for us to apply a regex to known record formats to *deserialize* or parse each row into its constituent fields. We'll use the Hive serializer-deserializer row format option, SERDE, and the contributed RegexSerDe library to specify a regex with which to deserialize and map the fields into columns for our table. We'll need to manually add the *hive-serde* JAR from the *lib* folder to the current hive session in order to use the RegexSerDe package:

```
hive> ADD JAR /srv/hive/lib/hive-serde-0.13.1.jar;
```

And now let's drop the apache_log table that we created previously, and re-create it to use our custom serializer:

```
hive> DROP TABLE apache_log;

hive> CREATE TABLE apache_log (
    host STRING,
    identity STRING,
    user STRING,
    time STRING,
    request STRING,
    status STRING,
    size STRING,
    referer STRING,
    agent STRING
```

```
)
ROW FORMAT SERDE 'org.apache.hadoop.hive.serde2.RegexSerDe'
WITH SERDEPROPERTIES ("input.regex" = "([^ ]*) ([^ ]*) ([^ ]*) (-|\\[[^\\]]
*\\])([^ \"]*|\"[^\"]*\") (-|[0-9]*) (-|[0-9]*)(?: ([^ \"]*|\".*\") ([^ \"]
*|\".*\"))?", "output.format.string" = "%1$s %2$s %3$s %4$s %5$s %6$s %7$s
%8$s %9$s")
STORED AS TEXTFILE;
```

Once we've created the table, we can use DESCRIBE to verify our table definition:

```
hive> DESCRIBE apache_log;
OK
host                    string                  from deserializer
identity                string                  from deserializer
user                    string                  from deserializer
time                    string                  from deserializer
request                 string                  from deserializer
status                  string                  from deserializer
size                    string                  from deserializer
referrer                string                  from deserializer
agent                   string                  from deserializer
Time taken: 0.553 seconds, Fetched: 9 row(s)
```

Note that in this particular table, all columns are defined with the Hive primitive data type, string. Hive supports many other primitive data types that will be familiar to SQL users and generally correspond to the primitive types supported by Java (*https://cwiki.apache.org/confluence/display/Hive/LanguageManual+DDL*). A list of these primitive data types is provided in Table 6-1.

Table 6-1. Hive primitive data types

Type	Description	Example
TINYINT	8-bit signed integer, from -128 to 127	127
SMALLINT	16-bit signed integer, from -32,768 to 32,767	32,767
INT	32-bit signed integer	2,147,483,647
BIGINT	64-bit signed integer	9,223,372,036,854,775,807
FLOAT	32-bit single-precision float	1.99
DOUBLE	64-bit double-precision float	3.14159265359
BOOLEAN	True/false	true
STRING	2 GB max character string	hello world
TIMESTAMP	Nanosecond precision	1400561325

In addition to the primitive data types, Hive also supports complex data types, listed in Table 6-2, that can store a collection of values.

Table 6-2. Hive complex data types

Type	Description	Example
ARRAY	Ordered collection of elements. The elements in the array must be of the same type.	`recipients ARRAY<email:STRING>`
MAP	Unordered collection of key/value pairs. Keys must be of primitive types and values can be of any type.	`files MAP<filename:STRING, size:INT>`
STRUCT	Collection of elements of any type.	`address STRUCT<street:STRING, city:STRING, state:STRING, zip:INT>`

This may seem awkward at first, because relational databases generally don't support collection types, but instead store associated collections in separate tables to maintain *first normal form* and minimize data duplication and the risk of data inconsistencies. However, in a big data system like Hive where we are processing large volumes of unstructured data by sequentially scanning off disk, the ability to read embedded collections provides a huge benefit in retrieval performance.[2]

For a complete reference of Hive's supported table and data type options, refer to the documentation in the Apache Hive Language Manual (*https://cwiki.apache.org/conflu ence/display/Hive/LanguageManual*).

Loading data

With our table created and schema defined, we are ready to load the data into Hive. It's important to note one important distinction between Hive and traditional RDBMSs with regards to schema enforcement: Hive does not perform any verification of the data for compliance with the table schema, nor does it perform any transformations when loading the data into a table.

Traditional relational databases enforce the schema on *writes* by rejecting any data that does not conform to the schema as defined; Hive can only enforce queries on schema *reads*. If in reading the data file, the file structure does not match the defined schema, Hive will generally return null values for missing fields or type mismatches and attempt to recover from errors. Schema on read enables a very fast initial load, as the data is not read, parsed, and serialized to disk in the database's internal format. Load operations are purely copy/move operations that move data files into locations corresponding to Hive tables (*https://cwiki.apache.org/confluence/display/Hive/LanguageManual+DML*).

Data loading in Hive is done in batch-oriented fashion using a bulk `LOAD DATA` command or by inserting results from another query with the `INSERT` command. To start,

---

2 Capriolo et al., *Programming Hive* (O'Reilly).

let's copy our Apache log data file (*http://ita.ee.lbl.gov/html/contrib/Calgary-HTTP.html*) to HDFS and then load it into the table we created earlier:

```
~$ hadoop fs -mkdir statistics
~$ hadoop fs -mkdir statistics/log_data
~$ hadoop fs -copyFromLocal ~/hadoop-fundamentals/data/log_data/apache.log \
    statistics/log_data/
```

You can verify that the *apache.log* file was successfully uploaded to HDFS with the `tail` command:

```
~$ hadoop fs -tail statistics/log_data/apache.log
```

Once the file has been uploaded to HDFS, return to the Hive CLI and use the `log_data` database:

```
~$ $HIVE_HOME/bin/hive

hive> use log_data;
OK
Time taken: 0.221 seconds
```

We'll use the `LOAD DATA` command and specify the HDFS path to the logfile, writing the contents into the `apache_log` table:

```
hive> LOAD DATA INPATH 'statistics/log-data/apache.log'
OVERWRITE INTO TABLE apache_log;

Loading data to table log_data.apache_log
rmr: DEPRECATED: Please use 'rm -r' instead.
Deleted hdfs://localhost:9000/user/hive/warehouse/log_data.db/apache_log
Table log_data.apache_log stats: [numFiles=1, numRows=0, totalSize=52276758,
rawDataSize=0]
OK
Time taken: 0.902 seconds
```

`LOAD DATA` is Hive's bulk loading command. `INPATH` takes an argument to a path on the default file system (in this case, HDFS). We can also specify a path on the local file system by using `LOCAL INPATH` instead. Hive proceeds to move the file into the warehouse location. If the `OVERWRITE` keyword is used, then any existing data in the target table will be deleted and replaced by the data file input; otherwise, the new data is added to the table.

Once the data has been copied and loaded, Hive outputs some statistics on the loaded data; although the `num_rows` reported is 0, you can verify the actual count of rows by running a `SELECT COUNT` (output truncated):

```
hive> SELECT COUNT(1) FROM apache_log;
Total MapReduce jobs = 1
Launching Job 1 out of 1
...
OK
```

```
726739
Time taken: 34.666 seconds, Fetched: 1 row(s)
```

As you can see, when we run this Hive query it actually executes a MapReduce job to perform the aggregation. After the MapReduce job has executed, you should see that the apache_log table now contains 726,739 rows.

Data Analysis with Hive

Now that we've defined a schema and loaded data into Hive, we can perform actual data analysis on our data by running HQL queries against the Hive database. In this section, we will write and run HQL queries to determine the peak months in remote traffic hits based on the Apache access log data we imported earlier.

Grouping

In the previous section, we loaded an Apache access logfile into a Hive table called apache_log, with rows consisting of web log data in the Apache Common Log Format (*http://httpd.apache.org/docs/2.2/logs.html#accesslog*):

```
127.0.0.1 - frank [10/Oct/2000:13:55:36 -0700] "GET /apache_pb.gif HTTP/1.0" 200
2326
```

Consider a MapReduce program that computes the number of hits per calendar month; although this is a fairly simple group-count problem, implementing the MapReduce program still requires a decent level of effort to write the mapper, reducer, and main function to configure the job, in addition to the effort of compiling and creating the JAR file. However with Hive, this problem is as simple and intuitive as running a SQL GROUP BY query:

```
hive> SELECT
        month,
        count(1) AS count
      FROM (SELECT split(time, '/')[1] AS month FROM apache_log) l
      GROUP BY month
      ORDER BY count DESC;
OK
Mar 99717
Sep 89083
Feb 72088
Aug 66058
Apr 64984
May 63753
Jul 54920
Jun 53682
Oct 45892
Jan 43635
Nov 41235
Dec 29789
```

```
NULL    1903
Time taken: 84.77 seconds, Fetched: 13 row(s)
```

Both the Hive query and the MapReduce program perform the work of tokenizing the input and extracting the month token as the aggregate field. In addition, Hive provides a succinct and natural query interface to perform the grouping, and because our data is structured as a Hive table, we can easily perform other ad hoc queries on any of the other fields:

```
hive> SELECT host, count(1) AS count FROM apache_log GROUP BY host
ORDER BY count;
```

In addition to count, Hive also supports other aggregate functions to compute the sum, average, min, max as well as statistical aggregations for variance, standard deviation, and covariance of numeric columns. When using these built-in aggregate functions, you can improve the performance of the aggregation query by setting the following property to true:

```
hive> SET hive.map.aggr = true;
```

This setting tells Hive to perform "top-level" aggregation in the map phase, as opposed to aggregation after performing a GROUP BY. However, be aware that this setting will require more memory.[3] A full list of built-in aggregate functions can be found in "Hive Operators and User-Defined Functions (UDFs)" (*http://bit.ly/1r1RnGC*) in the Hive documentation.

Using Hive also provides us with the convenience of easily storing our computations. We can create new tables to store the results returned by these queries for later record-keeping and analysis:

```
hive> CREATE TABLE
        remote_hits_by_month
        AS
        SELECT
            month,
            count(1) AS count
        FROM (
            SELECT split(time, '/')[1] AS month
            FROM apache_log
            WHERE host == 'remote'
            ) l
        GROUP BY month
        ORDER BY count DESC;
```

The CREATE TABLE AS SELECT (CTAS) operation can be very useful in deriving and building new tables based on filtered and aggregated data from existing Hive tables.

---

3 Edward Capriolo, Dean Wampler, and Jason Rutherglen *Programming Hive* (O'Reilly).

Aggregations and joins

We've covered some of the conveniences that Hive offers in querying and aggregating data from a single, structured dataset, but Hive really shines when performing more complex aggregations across multiple datasets.

In Chapter 3, we developed a MapReduce program to analyze the on-time performance of US airlines based on flight data collected by the Research and Innovative Technology Administration (RITA) Bureau of Transportation Studies (TransStats) (*http://1.usa.gov/1r1RJ09*). The on-time dataset was normalized in that chapter to include all required data within a single data file; however, in reality, the data as downloaded from RITA's website actually includes codes that must be cross-referenced against separate lookup datasets for the airline and carrier codes. The April 2014 data has been included in the GitHub repo, under *data/flight_data*.

Each row of the on-time flight data in *ontime_flights.tsv* includes an integer value that represents the code for AIRLINE_ID (such as 19805) and a string value that represents the code for CARRIER (such as "AA"). AIRLINE_ID codes can be joined with the corresponding code in the *airlines.tsv* file in which each row contains the code and corresponding description:

```
19805   American Airlines Inc.: AA
```

Accordingly, CARRIER codes can be joined with the corresponding code in *carriers.tsv*, which contains the code and corresponding airline name and effective dates:

```
AA  American Airlines Inc. (1960 - )
```

Implementing these joins in a MapReduce program would require either a map-side join to load the lookups in memory, or reduce-side join in which we'd perform the join in the reducer. Both methods require a decent level of effort to write the MapReduce code to configure the job, but with Hive, we can simply load these additional lookup datasets into separate tables and perform the join in a SQL query.

Assuming that we've uploaded our data files to HDFS or local file system, let's start by creating a new database for our flight data:

```
hive> CREATE DATABASE flight_data;
OK
Time taken: 0.741 seconds
```

And then define schemas and load data for the on-time data and lookup tables (output omitted and newlines added for readability):

```
hive> CREATE TABLE flights (
        flight_date DATE,
        airline_code INT,
        carrier_code STRING,
        origin STRING,
        dest STRING,
```

```
            depart_time INT,
            depart_delta INT,
            depart_delay INT,
            arrive_time INT,
            arrive_delta INT,
            arrive_delay INT,
            is_cancelled BOOLEAN,
            cancellation_code STRING,
            distance INT,
            carrier_delay INT,
            weather_delay INT,
            nas_delay INT,
            security_delay INT,
            late_aircraft_delay INT
        )
        ROW FORMAT DELIMITED
        FIELDS TERMINATED BY '\t'
        STORED AS TEXTFILE;

hive> CREATE TABLE airlines (
            code INT,
            description STRING
        )
        ROW FORMAT DELIMITED
        FIELDS TERMINATED BY '\t'
        STORED AS TEXTFILE;

hive> CREATE TABLE carriers (
            code STRING,
            description STRING
        )
        ROW FORMAT DELIMITED
        FIELDS TERMINATED BY '\t'
        STORED AS TEXTFILE;

hive> CREATE TABLE cancellation_reasons (
            code STRING,
            description STRING
        )
        ROW FORMAT DELIMITED
        FIELDS TERMINATED BY '\t'
        STORED AS TEXTFILE;

hive> LOAD DATA LOCAL INPATH
        '${env:HOME}/hadoop-fundamentals/data/flight_data/ontime_flights.tsv'
        OVERWRITE INTO TABLE flights;

hive> LOAD DATA LOCAL INPATH
        '${env:HOME}/hadoop-fundamentals/data/flight_data/airlines.tsv'
        OVERWRITE INTO TABLE airlines;

hive> LOAD DATA LOCAL INPATH
```

```
          '${env:HOME}/hadoop-fundamentals/data/flight_data/carriers.tsv'
      OVERWRITE INTO TABLE carriers;

hive> LOAD DATA LOCAL INPATH
      '${env:HOME}/hadoop-fundamentals/data/flight_data/
      cancellation_reasons.tsv'
      OVERWRITE INTO TABLE cancellation_reasons;
```

To get a list of airlines and their respective average departure delays, we can simply perform a SQL JOIN on flights and airlines on the airline code and then use the aggregate function AVG() to compute the average depart_delay grouped by the airline description:

```
hive> SELECT
          a.description,
          AVG(f.depart_delay)
      FROM airlines a
      JOIN flights f ON a.code = f.airline_code
      GROUP BY a.description;

AirTran Airways Corporation: FL 8.035840978593273
Alaska Airlines Inc.: AS    4.746143501305276
American Airlines Inc.: AA  10.085038790027395
American Eagle Airlines Inc.: MQ    11.048787878787879
Delta Air Lines Inc.: DL    8.149843785719728
ExpressJet Airlines Inc.: EV    15.762459814292642
Frontier Airlines Inc.: F9  12.319591084296967
Hawaiian Airlines Inc.: HA  2.872051586628203
JetBlue Airways: B6 12.090553084509766
SkyWest Airlines Inc.: OO   10.086447897294379
Southwest Airlines Co.: WN  14.722817981677437
US Airways Inc.: US 7.363223345079652
United Air Lines Inc.: UA   11.124291343587137
Virgin America: VX  9.98681228106326
Time taken: 22.786 seconds, Fetched: 14 row(s)
```

As you can see, performing joins in Hive versus MapReduce provides pretty significant savings in coding effort. More importantly, the structured Hive data schema that we've defined gives us the ability to add or change queries with ease; let's update our query to instead return the average departure delay grouped by carrier:

```
hive> SELECT
          c.description,
          AVG(f.depart_delay)
      FROM carriers c
      JOIN flights f ON c.code = f.carrier_code
      GROUP BY c.description;

Aces Airlines (1992 - 2003) 9.98681228106326
AirTran Airways Corporation (1994 - )   8.035840978593273
Alaska Airlines Inc. (1960 - ) 4.746143501305276
American Airlines Inc. (1960 - )    10.085038790027395
```

```
American Eagle Airlines Inc. (1998 - )   11.048787878787879
Atlantic Southeast Airlines (1993 - 2011)   15.762459814292642
Delta Air Lines Inc. (1960 - )  8.149843785719728
ExpressJet Airlines Inc. (2012 - )  15.762459814292642
Frontier Airlines Inc. (1960 - 1986)   8.035840978593273
Frontier Airlines Inc. (1994 - )    12.319591084296967
Hawaiian Airlines Inc. (1960 - )    2.872051586628203
JetBlue Airways (2000 - )   12.090553084509766
Simmons Airlines (1991 - 1998)  11.048787878787879
SkyWest Airlines Inc. (2003 - ) 10.086447897294379
Southwest Airlines Co. (1979 - )    14.722817981677437
US Airways Inc. (1997 - )   7.363223345079652
USAir (1988 - 1997) 7.363223345079652
United Air Lines Inc. (1960 - ) 11.124291343587137
Virgin America (2007 - )    9.98681228106326
Time taken: 22.76 seconds, Fetched: 19 row(s)
```

Hive can be a good fit for use cases such as these, where we are working with datasets that lend themselves to a structured table-based format, and the computations that we are interested in are batch-oriented, OLAP queries, rather than real-time, row-oriented, OLTP transactions. For more information and further reading on using and optimizing Hive, we recommend the excellent, example-driven book *Programming Hive* (O'Reilly).

HBase

In the previous section, we learned how we could use Hive to perform SQL-based analysis on large, structured datasets stored in HDFS. However, we observed that while Hive provides a familiar data manipulation paradigm within Hadoop, it doesn't change the storage and processing paradigm, which still utilizes HDFS and Map-Reduce in a batch-oriented fashion.

Recall that because HDFS is designed as a write-once, read-many (WORM) file system, it is optimized for sequential reads and not efficient for use cases that require frequent or fast row-level updates to the data. This data access pattern is often called "random access" and the number of applications that require such real-time, low-latency read/write access are growing rapidly. Take, for example, the explosion of real-time sensor and telemetry applications, such as those used by NOAA (*https://www.ncdc.noaa.gov/data-access/land-based-station-data*) to gather weather data from remote stations or by NASA's Deep Space Network (*https://solarsystem.nasa.gov/basics/bsf18-1.php*) to record data transmissions from unmanned spacecraft. These applications must store and process an enormous volume of event data from potentially numerous transmission devices at an extremely fast rate, while ensuring data correctness or *consistency* when querying that data. Thus, for use cases that require random, real-time read/write access to data, we need to look outside of standard MapReduce and Hive for our data persistence and processing layer.

The conventional relational approach also presents a modeling challenge for many data analytics applications. Applications like Facebook's real-time analytics application "Insights for Websites" platform, which tracks over 200,000 events per second,[4] or StumbleUpon (*http://www.stumbleupon.com*)'s real-time recommendation system[5] record heavy volumes of data events from many sources concurrently. These types of real-time applications need to record high volumes of time-based events that tend to have many possible structural variations. The data may be keyed on a certain value, like User, but the value is often represented as a collection of arbitrary metadata. Take, for example, two events, "Like" and "Share", which require different column values, as shown in Table 6-3.

Table 6-3. Unstructured events

Event ID	Event Timestamp	Event Type	User ID	Post ID	Comment	Receiver User ID
1	1370139285	Like	jjones	521		
2	1370139285	Share	smith	237	This is hilarious!	342
3	1370139285	Share	emiller	963	Great article	

These types of data applications entail *sparse* data storage requirements. In a relational model, rows are sparse but columns are not. That is, upon inserting a new row to a table, the database allocates storage for every column regardless of whether a value exists for that field or not. However, in applications where data is represented as a collection of arbitrary fields or sparse columns, each row may use only a subset of available columns, which can make a standard relational schema both a wasteful and awkward fit.

NoSQL and Column-Oriented Databases

NoSQL databases were developed in response to the scale and agility challenges that face many modern applications today. NoSQL is a broad term that generally refers to non-relational databases and encompasses a wide collection of data storage models, including graph databases, document databases, key/value data stores and column-family databases.

HBase is classified as a column-family or column-oriented database, modeled on Google's BigTable architecture (*http://research.google.com/archive/bigtable.html*). This architecture allows HBase to provide:

---

4 Alex Himel, "Building Realtime Insights" (*https://www.facebook.com/note.php?note_id=10150103900258920*), Facebook Engineering note, March 15, 2011.

5 Katie Gray, "Why We Love HBase" (*http://www.stumbleupon.com/blog/why-we-love-hbase/*), StumbleUpon Official Blog, November 18, 2010.

- Random (row-level) read/write access

- Strong consistency

- "Schema-less" or flexible data modeling

The schema-less trait is a result of how HBase approaches data modeling, which is very different from how relational databases approach data modeling. HBase organizes data into *tables* that contain *rows*. Within a table, rows are identified by their unique *row key*, which do not have a data type and are instead stored and treated as a *byte array*. Row keys are similar to the concept of primary keys in relational databases, in that they are automatically indexed; in HBase, table rows are sorted by their row key and because row keys are byte arrays, almost anything can serve as a row key from strings to binary representations of longs or even serialized data structures. HBase stores its data as key/value pairs, where all table lookups are performed via the table's row key, or unique identifier to the stored record data.

Data within a row is grouped into *column families*, which consist of related columns. Visually, you can picture an HBase table that holds census data for a given population where each row represents a person and is accessed via a unique ID rowkey, with column families for personal data which contains columns for name and address, and demographic info which contains columns for birthdate and gender. This example is shown in Figure 6-1.

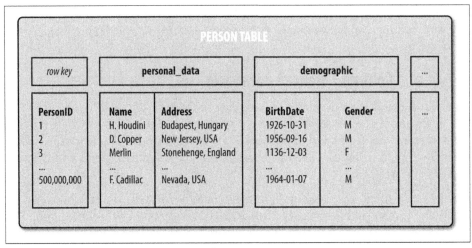

Figure 6-1. Census data as an HBase schema

Storing data in columns rather than rows has particular benefits for data warehouses and analytical databases where aggregates are computed over large sets of data with potentially sparse values, where not all columns values are present. Although column families are very flexible, in practice a column family is not entirely schema-less. Column families are actually defined up front before we can begin inserting data into a particular row and column, because they impact the physical arrangement of data stored in HBase.[6] However, the actual columns that make up a row can be determined and created on an as-needed basis. In fact, each row can have a different set of columns. Figure 6-2 shows an example HBase table with two rows where first row key utilizes three column families and the second row key utilizes just one column.

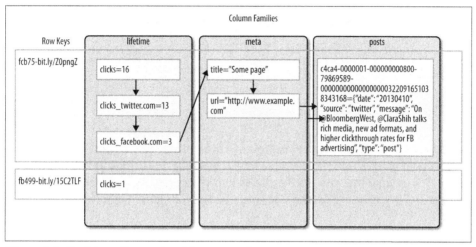

Figure 6-2. Social media events with sparse columns

Another interesting feature of HBase and BigTable-based column-oriented databases is that the table cells, or the intersection of row and column coordinates, are versioned by timestamp, stored as a long integer representing milliseconds since January 1, 1970 UTC. HBase is thus also described as being a multidimensional map where time provides the third dimension, as shown in Figure 6-3. The time dimension is indexed in decreasing order, so that when reading from an HBase store, the most recent values are found first. The contents of a cell can be referenced by a {`rowkey`, `column`, `timestamp`} tuple, or we can scan for a range of cell values by time range.

---

6 Amandeep Khurana, "Introduction to HBase Schema Design," *;login:*, October 2012, Volume 37, Number 5.

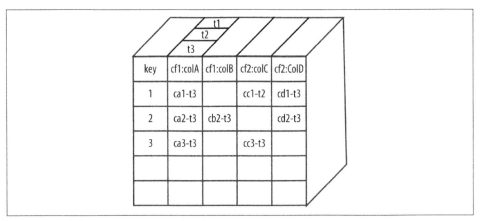

Figure 6-3. HBase timestamp versioning

Now that we've covered the key features of HBase schema design, we'll learn how to design and query a simple HBase table for a hypothetical real-time link-sharing application. We assume that you have installed and configured HBase within your development environment. The steps to install and configure HBase are covered in Appendix B.

Real-Time Analytics with HBase

HBase schemas can be created or updated with the HBase Shell or with the Java API, using the HBaseAdmin (*https://hbase.apache.org/apidocs/org/apache/hadoop/hbase/client/HBaseAdmin.html*) interface class. Additionally, HBase supports a number of other clients that can be used to support non-Java programming languages, including a REST API interface, Thrift, and Avro.[7] These clients act as proxies that wrap the native Java API.

For the purposes of this HBase overview, we define and work with the HBase shell to design a schema for a linkshare tracker that tracks the number of times a link has been shared. However, in a real-world setting, you would write your application using the native Java API or supported client libraries. If creating an external gateway client, consider your use case carefully. Applications requiring high-throughput may find it advantageous to use a purely binary format like Thrift or Avro, while a REST API may be a better approach for a lower frequency of requests that are large in size.

---

[7] See "Apache HBase Book External APIs" (*http://hbase.apache.org/book.html#external_apis*) in the Apache HBase Reference Guide.

Generating a schema

When designing schemas in HBase, it's important to think in terms of the column-family structure of the data model and how it affects data access patterns. While schema definition for traditional relational databases is primarily driven by the accurate representation of the entities and relationships and performance considerations like joins and indexes, successful HBase schema definition tends to be driven by the intended use cases of the application. Furthermore, because HBase doesn't support joins and provides only a single indexed rowkey, we must be careful to ensure that the schema can fully support all use cases. Often this involves de-normalization and data duplication with nested entities.

The good news is that because HBase allows dynamic column definition at runtime, we have quite a bit of flexibility even after table creation to modify and scale our schema.

Namespaces, tables, and column families

So what aspects of the schema must we carefully consider up front? First, we need to declare the table name, and at least one column-family name at the time of table definition. We can also declare our own optional namespace (supported as of Apache HBase v0.96.0) to serve as a logical grouping of tables, analogous to a database in relational database systems.[8] If no namespace is declared, HBase will use the `default` namespace:

```
hbase> create 'linkshare', 'link'
0 row(s) in 1.5740 seconds
```

We just created a single table called `linkshare` in the default namespace with one column-family, named `link`. To alter the table after creation, such as changing or adding column families, we need to first disable the table so that clients will not be able to access the table during the `alter` operation:

```
hbase> disable 'linkshare'
0 row(s) in 1.1340 seconds

hbase> alter 'linkshare', 'statistics'
Updating all regions with the new schema...
1/1 regions updated.
Done.
0 row(s) in 1.1630 seconds
```

We can then re-enable the table using the `enable` command:

```
hbase> enable 'linkshare'
0 row(s) in 1.1930 seconds
```

---

8 See "Namespace" (*http://hbase.apache.org/book.html#namespace*) in the Apache HBase Reference Guide.

And then use the `describe` command to verify that the table contains the two expected column families with the default configurations:

```
hbase> describe 'linkshare'

Table linkshare is ENABLED
COLUMN FAMILIES DESCRIPTION
{NAME => 'link', DATA_BLOCK_ENCODING => 'NONE', BLOOMFILTER => 'ROW',
REPLICATION_SCOPE => '0', COMPRESSION => 'NONE', VERSIONS => '1',
TTL => 'FOREVER', MIN_VERSIONS => '0', KEEP_DELETED_CELLS => 'FALSE',
BLOCKSIZE => '65536', IN_MEMORY => 'false', BLOCKCACHE => 'true'}
{NAME => 'statistics', DATA_BLOCK_ENCODING => 'NONE',
BLOOMFILTER => 'ROW', REPLICATION_SCOPE => '0', VERSIONS => '1',
COMPRESSION => 'NONE', MIN_VERSIONS => '0', TTL => 'FOREVER',
KEEP_DELETED_CELLS => 'FALSE', BLOCKSIZE => '65536',
IN_MEMORY => 'false', BLOCKCACHE => 'true'}
2 row(s) in 0.1290 seconds
```

We've created a single HBase table (`linkshare`) with two column families (`link` and `statistics`), but our table does not yet contain any rows. Before we insert row data, we need to determine how to design our row key.

Row keys

Good row key design affects not only how we query the table, but the performance and complexity of data access. By default, HBase stores rows in sorted order by row key, so that similar keys are stored to the same RegionServer. While this enables faster range scans, it could also lead to uneven load on particular servers (called Region-Server hotspotting) during read/write operations. Thus, in addition to enabling our data access use cases, we also need to be mindful to account for row key distribution across regions.

For the current example, let's assume that we will use the unique reversed link URL for the row key. But we highly recommended that you read "HBase and Schema Design" (*http://hbase.apache.org/0.94/book/schema.html*) in the Apache HBase Reference Guide for case studies on good row key design.

Inserting data with put

Now our table is ready to start storing data. In our `linkshare` application, we want to store descriptive data about the link, such as its title, while maintaining a frequency counter that tracks the number of times the link has been shared.

We can insert, or put, a value in a cell at the specified table/row/column and optionally timestamp coordinates. To put a cell value into table `linkshare` at row with row key `org.hbase.www` under column-family link and column title marked with the current timestamp, do:

```
hbase> put 'linkshare', 'org.hbase.www', 'link:title', 'Apache HBase'
hbase> put 'linkshare', 'org.hadoop.www', 'link:title', 'Apache Hadoop'
hbase> put 'linkshare', 'com.oreilly.www', 'link:title', 'O\'Reilly.com'
```

The put operation works great for inserting a value for a single cell, but for incrementing frequency counters, HBase provides a special mechanism to treat columns as counters. Otherwise, under heavy load, we could face significant contention for these rows as we would need to lock the row, read the value, increment it, write it back, and finally unlock the row for other writers to be able to access the cell.[9]

To increment a counter, we use the command incr instead of put:

```
hbase> incr 'linkshare', 'org.hbase.www', 'statistics:share', 1
(COUNTER VALUE is now 1)

hbase> incr 'linkshare', 'org.hbase.www', 'statistics:like', 1
(COUNTER VALUE is now 1)
```

The last option passed is the increment value, which in this case is 1. Incrementing a counter will return the updated counter value, but you can also access a counter's current value any time using the get_counter command, specifying the table name, row key, and column:

```
hbase> incr 'linkshare', 'org.hbase.www', 'statistics:share', 1
(COUNTER VALUE is now 2)

hbase> get_counter 'linkshare', 'org.hbase.www', 'statistics:share', 'dummy'
COUNTER VALUE = 2
```

The get_counter method is used to decode the byte-array value of the counter and return the integer value. Unfortunately, the latest HBase build includes a bug in the shell command for getting the counter value, which expects a fourth argument that is never used. As a result, we'll need to pass in a fourth dummy value:

```
hbase> get_counter 'linkshare', 'org.hbase.www', 'statistics:share', 'dummy'
COUNTER VALUE = 2
```

HBase provides two general methods to retrieve data from a table: the get command performs lookups by row key to retrieve attributes for a specific row, and the scan command, which takes a set of filter specifications and iterates over multiple rows based on the indicated specifications.

Get row or cell values

In its simplest form, the get command accepts the table name followed by the row key, and returns the most recent version timestamp and cell value for all columns in the row:

---

9 Lars George, *HBase: The Definitive Guide* (O'Reilly).

```
hbase> get 'linkshare', 'org.hbase.www'

COLUMN                          CELL
 link:title                     timestamp=1422145743298, value=Apache HBase
 statistics:like                timestamp=1422153344211,
     value=\x00\x00\x00\x00\x00\x00\x00\x1F
 statistics:share               timestamp=1422153337498,
     value=\x00\x00\x00\x00\x00\x00\x00\x02
3 row(s) in 0.0310 seconds
```

Note that the `statistics:share` column returns the value in its byte array representation, printing the separate bytes as hexadecimal values. To display the integer representation of the counter value, use the `get_counter` command mentioned in the previous section.

The `get` command also accepts an optional dictionary of parameters to specify the column(s), timestamp, timerange, and version of the cell values we want to retrieve. For example, we can specify the column(s) of interest:

```
hbase> get 'linkshare', 'org.hbase.www', {COLUMN => 'link:title'}
hbase> get 'linkshare', 'org.hbase.www', {COLUMN => ['link:title',
    'statistics:share']}
```

There is also a shortcut to specify column parameters in a `get` by just appending the comma-delimited column names after the row key:

```
hbase> get 'linkshare', 'org.hbase.www', 'link:title'
hbase> get 'linkshare', 'org.hbase.www', 'link:title', 'statistics:share'
hbase> get 'linkshare', 'org.hbase.www', ['link:title', 'statistics:share']
```

To specify a time range of values we are interested in, we pass in a TIMERANGE parameter with start and end timestamps in milliseconds:

```
hbase> get 'linkshare', 'org.hbase.www', {TIMERANGE => [1399887705673,
    1400133976734]}
```

If instead of explicit timestamp ranges we want to pull back cell values based on a certain number of previous versions, we can specify the column of interest and use the VERSIONS parameter to specify the number of versions to retrieve:

```
hbase> get 'linkshare', 'org.hbase.www', {COLUMN => 'statistics:share',
    VERSIONS => 2}
```

While this type of range query may not seem as interesting for a counter value that increments by 1, it does provide us the means to determine the rate at which the share counter is incremented, which we could use to determine the virality of the link. Additionally, these types of range filters can be especially useful for performing "as-of-time" queries—for example, inspecting metrics identified between a certain time range of interest.

Scan rows

A `scan` operation is akin to database cursors or iterators, and takes advantage of the underlying sequentially sorted storage mechanism, iterating through row data to match against the scanner specifications. With `scan`, we can scan an entire HBase table or specify a range of rows to scan.

Using `scan` is similar to using the `get` command; it also accepts COLUMN, TIMESTAMP, TIMERANGE, and FILTER parameters. However, instead of specifying a single row key, you can specify an optional STARTROW and/or STOPROW parameter, which can be used to limit the scan to a specific range of rows. If neither STARTROW nor STOPROW are provided, the `scan` operation will scan through the entire table.

You can, in fact, call `scan` with the table name to display all the contents of a table:

```
hbase> scan 'linkshare'

ROW                     COLUMN+CELL
com.oreilly.www         column=link:title, timestamp=1422153270279,
value=O'Reilly.com
org.hadoop.www          column=link:title, timestamp=1422153262507,
value=Apache Hadoop
org.hbase.www           column=link:title, timestamp=1422145743298,
value=Apache HBase
org.hbase.www           column=statistics:like, timestamp=1422153344211,
    value=\x00\x00\x00\x00\x00\x00\x00\x1F
org.hbase.www           column=statistics:share, timestamp=1422153337498,
    value=\x00\x00\x00\x00\x00\x00\x00\x02
3 row(s) in 0.0290 seconds
```

Keep in mind that the rows in HBase are stored in lexicographical order.[10] For example, numbers going from 1 to 100 will be ordered like this:

```
1,10,100,11,12,13,14,15,16,17,18,19,2,20,21,...,9,91,92,93,94,95,96,97,98,99
```

Let's retrieve the `link:title` column but limit our scan to the rows starting with row key `org.hbase.www`:

```
hbase> scan 'linkshare', {COLUMNS => ['link:title'], STARTROW => 'org.hbase.www'}

ROW                     COLUMN+CELL
 org.hbase.www          column=link:title, timestamp=1453184861236,
 value=Apache HBase
1 row(s) in 0.0250 seconds
```

But the STARTROW and ENDROW values do not require an exact match for the row key. It will match the first row key that is equal to or larger than the given start row and

---

10 See "Data Model: Rows" (*http://hbase.apache.org/book.html#datamodel*) in the Apache HBase Reference Guide.

equal to or less than the end row; because these parameters are inclusive, we do not need to specify the `ENDROW` if it is the same as the `STARTROW` value:

```
hbase> scan 'linkshare', {COLUMNS => ['link:title'], STARTROW => 'org'}

ROW                  COLUMN+CELL
org.hadoop.www       column=link:title, timestamp=1422153262507,
value=Apache Hadoop
org.hbase.www        column=link:title, timestamp=1422145743298,
value=Apache HBase
2 row(s) in 0.0210 seconds
```

Filters

HBase provides a number of filter classes that can be applied to further filter the row data returned from a `get` or `scan` operation. These filters can provide a much more efficient means of limiting the row data returned by HBase and offloading the row-filtering operations from the client to the server. Some of HBase's available filters include:

RowFilter (http://bit.ly/1r1Y7Ez)
Used for data filtering based on row key values

ColumnRangeFilter (http://bit.ly/1r1Yb7m)
Allows efficient intra-row scanning, can be used to get a *slice* of the columns of a very wide row (i.e., you have a million columns in a row but you only want to look at columns bbbb-bbdd)

SingleColumnValueFilter (http://bit.ly/1r1Yf70)
Used to filter cells based on column value

RegexStringComparator (http://bit.ly/1r1Ydft)
Used to test if a given regular expression matches a cell value in the column

The HBase Java API (*https://hbase.apache.org/apidocs/*) provides a Filter (*http://bit.ly/ 1r1YizN*) interface and abstract FilterBase class (*http://bit.ly/1r1YizN*) plus a number of specialized Filter subclasses (*http://bit.ly/1r1YsXP*). Custom filters can also be created by subclassing the FilterBase abstract class and implementing the key abstract methods.

HBase filters are best applied by utilizing the HBase API within a Java program as they generally require importing several dependent filter and comparator classes, but we can demonstrate a simple example of a filter in the shell.

To begin, we need to import the necessary classes, including the `org.apache.hadoop.hbase.util.Bytes` to convert our column family, column, and values into bytes, and the filter and comparator classes:

```
hbase> import org.apache.hadoop.hbase.util.Bytes
hbase> import org.apache.hadoop.hbase.filter.SingleColumnValueFilter
hbase> import org.apache.hadoop.hbase.filter.BinaryComparator
hbase> import org.apache.hadoop.hbase.filter.CompareFilter
```

Next, we'll create a filter that limits the results to rows where the `statistics:like` counter column value is greater than or equal to 10:

```
hbase> likeFilter = SingleColumnValueFilter.new(Bytes.toBytes('statistics'),
    Bytes.toBytes('like'),
    CompareFilter::CompareOp.valueOf('GREATER_OR_EQUAL'),
    BinaryComparator.new(Bytes.toBytes(10)))
```

And because we don't have a value for this column for every row, we need to set a flag that tells this filter to skip any rows without a value in this column:

```
hbase> likeFilter.setFilterIfMissing(true)
```

At this point, we can run our `scan` operation with the filter we configured:

```
hbase> scan 'linkshare', { FILTER => likeFilter }

ROW                   COLUMN+CELL
org.hbase.www         column=link:title, timestamp=1422145743298,
    value=Apache HBase
org.hbase.www         column=statistics:like, timestamp=1422153344211,
    value=\x00\x00\x00\x00\x00\x00\x00\x1F
org.hbase.www         column=statistics:share, timestamp=1422153337498,
    value=\x00\x00\x00\x00\x00\x00\x00\x02
1 row(s) in 0.0470 seconds
```

This should return all rows that contain a column value for `statistics:like` that is greater than or equal to 10; this should include row key `com.oreilly.www` in this example.

Further reading on HBase

HBase is useful when you need to store large volumes of streaming data with a flexible structure, and query that data in small chunks at a time while ensuring that:

- The data is kept "whole" (such as sales or financial data)
- The data may change over time
- Single rows and subsets of rows and columns can be queried and updated

HBase isn't intended to be a one-for-one replacement of an RDBMS, HDFS, or Hive, but does provide the means to leverage Hadoop's data scalability while enabling random access to that data. HBase can then be combined with traditional SQL or Hive to allow snapshots, ranges, or aggregate data to be queried.

For more information and further reading on using and integrating HBase, we recommend consulting the official *Apache HBase Reference Guide* (*http://hbase.apache.org/book.html*) as well as *HBase: The Definitive Guide* by Lars George (O'Reilly).

Conclusion

In this chapter, we introduced Hive, which many consider the de facto standard for SQL querying in Hadoop, and HBase, one of the most popular NoSQL databases that runs on top of Hadoop. However, there are many other Hadoop projects and tools within the data warehousing and data mining space that, while beyond the scope of this book, should be explored as you delve further into data analysis with Hadoop.

In addition to Hive, there are several other query engines that enable SQL querying over HDFS or HBase. Impala (*http://impala.io*) provides low-latency querying by performing local in-memory computations and thus avoiding the overhead of executing MapReduce jobs. Spark SQL (*https://spark.apache.org/sql/*) also enables high-performance SQL querying by running queries as Spark jobs.

The beauty of Hadoop is that we have the flexibility to support and use a myriad of querying and processing engines, choosing whichever tool best fits our particular use case. For more in-depth information on other data warehousing and data mining solutions on Hadoop, including other SQL-on-Hadoop projects, see *Hadoop Application Architectures* by Mark Grover, Ted Malaska, Jonathan Seidman, and Gwen Shapira (O'Reilly).

## CHAPTER 7

Data Ingestion

One of Hadoop's greatest strengths is that it's inherently schemaless and can work with any type or format of data regardless of structure (or lack of structure) from any source, as long as you implement Hadoop's Writable or DBWritable interfaces and write your MapReduce code to parse the data correctly. However, in cases where the input data is already structured because it resides in a relational database, it would be convenient to leverage this known schema to import the data into Hadoop in a more efficient manner than uploading CSVs to HDFS and parsing them manually.

Sqoop is designed to transfer data between relational database management systems (RDBMS) and Hadoop. It automates most of the data transformation process, relying on the RDBMS to provide the schema description for the data to be imported. As we'll see in this chapter, Sqoop can be a very useful link in the analytics pipeline for data infrastructures that involve relational databases as a primary or intermediary data store.

While Sqoop works very well for bulk-loading data that already resides in a relational database into Hadoop, many new applications and systems involve fast-moving data streams like application logs, GPS tracking, social media updates, and sensor-data that we'd like to load directly into HDFS to process in Hadoop. In order to handle and process the high-throughput of event-based data produced by these systems, we need the ability to support continuous ingestion of data from multiple sources into Hadoop.

Apache Flume was designed to efficiently collect, aggregate, and move large amounts of log data from many different sources into a centralized data store. While Flume is most often used to direct streaming log data into Hadoop, usually HDFS or HBase, Flume data sources are actually quite flexible and can be customized to transport many types of event data, including network traffic data, social media–generated data, and sensor data into any Flume-compatible consumer. In this chapter, we'll take a look at how to use Flume to ingest streaming data from a custom log into Hadoop.

Importing Relational Data with Sqoop

Sqoop (SQL-to-Hadoop) is a relational database import and export tool created by Cloudera,[1] and is now an Apache top-level project. Sqoop is designed to transfer data between a relational database like MySQL or Oracle, into a Hadoop data store, including HDFS, Hive, and HBase. It automates most of the data transfer process by reading the schema information directly from the RDBMS. Sqoop then uses Map-Reduce to import and export the data to and from Hadoop.[2]

Sqoop gives us the flexibility to maintain our data in its production state while copying it into Hadoop to make it available for further analysis without modifying the production database. We'll walk through a few ways to use Sqoop to import data from a MySQL database into various Hadoop data stores, including HDFS, Hive, and HBase.

 In the Sqoop examples in this chapter, we assume the existence of a MySQL database that resides on the same machine and is accessible via localhost. To install and configure a local MySQL database, follow the official installation guides on the MySQL site (*http://bit.ly/1r21lba*), or this concise guide (*http://bit.ly/1r21qvx*) on the Linode site (remember that you'll need to use sudo for most of these commands; also, ignore the step of setting up a hostname for "servername" as this will cause conflicts when attempting to connect via localhost).

For this chapter, we assume that you have installed the latest stable version of Sqoop that is compatible with your version of Hadoop, and that Hadoop is configured in pseudo-distributed mode with all HDFS and YARN processes running. We will use MySQL as the source and target RDBMS for the examples in this chapter, so we also assume that a MySQL database resides on the same host as your Hadoop/Sqoop services and is accessible via localhost and the default port, 3306. The steps for installing Sqoop and configuring it with MySQL can be found in Appendix B.

1 Aaron Kimball, "Cloudera—Introducing Sqoop" (*https://blog.cloudera.com/blog/2009/06/introducing-sqoop/*), Cloudera Engineering Blog, June 1, 2009.

2 See the *Sqoop User Guide* (*http://sqoop.apache.org/docs/1.4.6/SqoopUserGuide.html*).

Importing from MySQL to HDFS

When importing data from relational databases like MySQL, Sqoop reads the source database to gather the necessary metadata for the data being imported. Sqoop then submits a map-only Hadoop job to transfer the actual table data based on the metadata that was captured in the previous step. This job produces a set of serialized files, which may be delimited text files, binary format (e.g., Avro), or SequenceFiles containing a copy of the imported table or datasets.[3] By default, the files are saved as comma-separated files to a directory on HDFS with a name that corresponds to the source table name. We'll use these defaults to export data from MySQL to HDFS.

Assuming that you have set up MySQL, let's go ahead and create a sample database with some tables and data. We'll start by creating a database called energydata and a table called average_price_by_state:

```
~$ mysql -uroot -p

mysql> CREATE DATABASE energydata;
Query OK, 1 row affected (0.00 sec)

mysql> GRANT ALL PRIVILEGES ON energydata.* TO '%'@'localhost';
Query OK, 0 rows affected (0.00 sec)

mysql> GRANT ALL PRIVILEGES ON energydata.* TO ''@'localhost';
Query OK, 0 rows affected (0.00 sec)

mysql> USE energydata;

mysql> CREATE TABLE average_price_by_state(
    year INT NOT NULL,
    state VARCHAR(5) NOT NULL,
    sector VARCHAR(255),
    residential DECIMAL(10,2),
    commercial DECIMAL(10,2),
    industrial DECIMAL(10,2),
    transportation DECIMAL(10,2),
    other DECIMAL(10,2),
    total DECIMAL(10,2)
);
Query OK, 0 rows affected (0.02 sec)

mysql> quit;
```

The data that we load into the average_price_by_state table is provided by the US Energy Information Administration (*http://www.eia.gov/electricity/data/state/*) and includes the annual data from 1990–2012 on the average energy price per kilowatt

---

3 See "Basic Usage" (*http://bit.ly/1r23vHN*) in the Sqoop User Guide.

hour (KwH) by state and provider type. You can find the CSV named *avg-price_kwh_state.csv* within the GitHub repo's */data* directory. Download this CSV and load it into the MySQL table we just created:

```
~$ mysql -h localhost -u root -p energydata --local-infile=1

mysql> LOAD DATA LOCAL INFILE
    '/home/hadoop/hadoop-fundamentals/data/avgprice_kwh_state.csv'
    INTO TABLE average_price_by_state
    FIELDS TERMINATED BY ','
    LINES TERMINATED BY '\n' IGNORE 1 LINES;

Query OK, 3272 rows affected, 6 warnings (0.03 sec)
Records: 3272  Deleted: 0  Skipped: 0  Warnings: 6

mysql> quit;
```

Before we proceed to run the sqoop `import` command, verify that HDFS and YARN are started with the `jps` command:

```
~$ sudo su hadoop
hadoop@ubuntu:~$ jps

4051 NodeManager
31134 Jps
3523 DataNode
3709 SecondaryNameNode
3375 NameNode
3921 ResourceManager
```

At this point, we can import the data in table `average_price_by_state` into HDFS by using the `import` command. We can specify the source database's connection string, username, and tablename with the `--connect` option, `--username` option, and `--table` option, respectively. We'll set the optional -m flag to 1 to indicate that this job should use a single map task:

```
/srv/sqoop$ sqoop import --connect jdbc:mysql://localhost:3306/energydata
    --username root --table average_price_by_state -m 1

15/01/20 22:47:35 INFO sqoop.Sqoop: Running Sqoop version: 1.4.6
15/01/20 22:47:35 INFO manager.MySQLManager: Preparing to use a MySQL
    streaming resultset.
15/01/20 22:47:35 INFO tool.CodeGenTool: Beginning code generation
15/01/20 22:47:36 INFO manager.SqlManager: Executing SQL statement:
    SELECT t.* FROM `average_price_by_state` AS t LIMIT 1

(output truncated)

15/01/25 22:47:53 INFO mapreduce.ImportJobBase: Transferred 200.4287 KB in
    15.3718 seconds (13.0387 KB/sec)
15/01/25 22:47:53 INFO mapreduce.ImportJobBase: Retrieved 3272 records.
```

In this particular example, we needed to specify that the `import` command should use a single `map` task, as our table does not contain a primary key, which is required to split and merge multiple map tasks. Because we specified that the import task use 1 map task, we should expect a single file in HDFS:

```
/srv/sqoop$ hadoop fs -head average_price_by_state/part-m-00000 | head

2012,AK,Total Electric Industry,17.88,14.93,16.82,0.00,null,16.33
2012,AL,Total Electric Industry,11.40,10.63,6.22,0.00,null,9.18
2012,AR,Total Electric Industry,9.30,7.71,5.77,11.23,null,7.62
2012,AZ,Total Electric Industry,11.29,9.53,6.53,0.00,null,9.81
2012,CA,Total Electric Industry,15.34,13.41,10.49,7.17,null,13.53
2012,CO,Total Electric Industry,11.46,9.39,6.95,9.69,null,9.39
2012,CT,Total Electric Industry,17.34,14.65,12.67,9.69,null,15.54
2012,DC,Total Electric Industry,12.28,12.02,5.46,9.01,null,11.85
2012,DE,Total Electric Industry,13.58,10.13,8.36,0.00,null,11.06
2012,FL,Total Electric Industry,11.42,9.66,8.04,8.45,null,10.44
```

We have now successfully imported data from MySQL to HDFS! From here, we can now run any further MapReduce processing on the imported data, or load the data into another Hadoop data source such as Hive, HBase, or HCatalog.

Importing from MySQL to Hive

Given that our data is already structured in a relational schema (MySQL, in this case), it makes a lot of sense to import that data into a similar schema within Hive, especially if we intend to run relational queries on the data. Sqoop provides a couple ways to do this, either exporting to HDFS first and then loading the data into Hive using the LOAD DATA HQL command in the Hive shell, or by using Sqoop to directly create the tables and load the relational database data into the corresponding tables in Hive.

Sqoop can generate a Hive table and load data based on the defined schema and table contents from a source database, using the `import` command. However, because Sqoop still actually utilizes MapReduce to implement the data load operation, we must first delete any preexisting data directory with the same output name before running the import tool:

```
/srv/sqoop$ hadoop fs -rm -r /user/hadoop/average_price_by_state
```

We can then run Sqoop's `import` command, passing it the JDBC connection string to the database, the table name, field delimiter, line terminator, and null string value:

```
/srv/sqoop$ sqoop import --connect jdbc:mysql://localhost:3306/energydata
    --username root --table average_price_by_state
    --hive-import --fields-terminated-by ','
    --lines-terminated-by '\n' --null-string 'null' -m 1

(output truncated)

15/01/20 00:14:37 INFO hive.HiveImport: Table default.average_price_by_state stats:
```

```
    [numFiles=2, numRows=0, totalSize=205239, rawDataSize=0]
15/01/20 00:14:37 INFO hive.HiveImport: OK
15/01/20 00:14:37 INFO hive.HiveImport: Time taken: 0.435 seconds
15/01/20 00:14:37 INFO hive.HiveImport: Hive import complete.
15/01/20 00:14:37 INFO hive.HiveImport: Export directory is empty, removing it.
```

Our double columns will be converted by Hive to float types, and any NOT NULL fields will not be enforced, but otherwise the structure will reflect the initial definition of the MySQL table for average_price_by_state using the same table name.

 If you are running HBase on the same machine and the HBASE_HOME environment variable is set, you may encounter the following error after running the preceding command:

```
INFO hive.HiveImport: Exception in thread "main"
    java.lang.NoSuchMethodError:
    org/apache/thrift/EncodingUtils.setBit(BIZ)B
```

This is due to the conflicting versions of Thrift between HBase and Hive. You can get around this error by temporarily setting HBASE_HOME to a nonexistent path and then reloading your bash profile after the import:

```
/srv/sqoop$ export HBASE_HOME=/fake/path

(Sqoop Hive commands)

/srv/sqoop$ source ~/.profile
```

In local mode, Hive will create a *metastore_db* directory within the file system location from which it was run; in the previous example, the *metastore_db* will be created under the *SQOOP_HOME* (*/srv/sqoop*). Open the Hive shell and verify that the table average_price_by_state was created:

```
/srv/sqoop$ hive

hive> DESC average_price_by_state;

OK
year                int
state               string
sector              string
residential         double
commercial          double
industrial          double
transportation      double
other               double
total               double
Time taken: 0.858 seconds, Fetched: 9 row(s)
```

You can also run a COUNT query to verify that 3,272 rows have been imported; alternatively, because this dataset is relatively small, you can run a SELECT * FROM aver age_price_by_state to validate the data. With our data and schema now imported into Hive, we can continue running any further analysis on the data via the Hive command-line interface or other Hive interface.

Importing from MySQL to HBase

HBase is designed to handle large volumes of data for a large number of concurrent clients that need real-time access to row-level data. While relational databases also handle this requirement well in most low-to-modestly high-scale data applications, if the storage requirements of an application start to demand a more scalable solution, we may consider offloading some of the high-scale and heavy-load data components to a distributed database like HBase.

Sqoop's import tool allows us to import data from a relational database to HBase. As with Hive, there are two approaches to importing this data. We can import to HDFS first and then use the HBase CLI or API to load the data into an HBase table, or we can use the --hbase-table option to instruct Sqoop to directly import to a table in HBase.

In this example, the data that we want to offload to HBase is a table of weblog stats where each record contains a primary key composed of the pipe-delimited IP address and year, and a column for each month that contains the number of hits for that IP and year. You can find the CSV named *weblogs.csv* in the GitHub repo's */data* directory. Download this CSV and load it into a MySQL table:

```
~$ mysql -u root -p

mysql> CREATE DATABASE logdata;

mysql> GRANT ALL PRIVILEGES ON logdata.* TO '%'@'localhost';

mysql> GRANT ALL PRIVILEGES ON logdata.* TO ''@'localhost';

mysql> USE logdata;

mysql> CREATE TABLE weblogs (ipyear varchar(255) NOT NULL PRIMARY KEY,
    january int(11) DEFAULT NULL,
    february int(11) DEFAULT NULL,
    march int(11) DEFAULT NULL,
    april int(11) DEFAULT NULL,
    may int(11) DEFAULT NULL,
    june int(11) DEFAULT NULL,
    july int(11) DEFAULT NULL,
    august int(11) DEFAULT NULL,
    september int(11) DEFAULT NULL,
    october int(11) DEFAULT NULL,
```

```
    november int(11) DEFAULT NULL,
    december int(11) DEFAULT NULL);

mysql> quit;

~$ mysql -u root -p logdata --local-infile=1

mysql> LOAD DATA LOCAL INFILE '/home/hadoop/hadoop-fundamentals/data/weblogs.csv'
    INTO TABLE weblogs FIELDS TERMINATED BY ','
    LINES TERMINATED BY '\n' IGNORE 1 LINES;

Query OK, 27300 rows affected (0.20 sec)
Records: 27300  Deleted: 0  Skipped: 0  Warnings: 0

mysql> quit;
```

Again, we need to verify that Hadoop is running, as well as HBase daemons:

```
~$ cd $HBASE_HOME
/srv/hbase$ bin/start-hbase.sh
```

We can then run Sqoop's `import` command, passing it the JDBC connection string to the database, the table name, HBase table name, column family name, and row key name:

```
sqoop import --connect jdbc:mysql://localhost:3306/logdata
    --table weblogs --hbase-table weblogs --column-family traffic
    --hbase-row-key ipyear --hbase-create-table -m 1

(output truncated)

15/01/20 00:33:01 INFO mapreduce.ImportJobBase: Transferred 0 bytes in
19.0716 seconds (0 bytes/sec)
15/01/20 00:33:01 INFO mapreduce.ImportJobBase: Retrieved 27300 records.
```

Once the import MapReduce job has completed, you should see a console message indicating INFO mapreduce.ImportJobBase: Retrieved 27300 records. We can verify that the HBase table and rows have been imported successfully in the HBase shell with the `list` and `scan` commands:

```
/srv/sqoop$ cd $HBASE_HOME
/srv/hbase$ bin/hbase shell

hbase(main):001:0> list

TABLE
linkshare
weblogs
2 row(s) in 1.2900 seconds

=> ["linkshare", "weblogs"]

hbase(main):002:0> scan 'weblogs', {'LIMIT' => 50}
```

```
(output truncated)
```

We have successfully used Sqoop to import relational data from MySQL to HDFS, Hive, and HBase, using the import tool, which actually generates a Java class that encapsulates the schema of each row of the imported table.[4] This class is used during the import process by Sqoop itself, but can also be used in subsequent MapReduce processing of the data. Thus, in addition to automating import/export to and from Hadoop and relational databases, Sqoop allows you to quickly develop processing pipelines across other Hadoop-compatible data sources. We encourage you to read more about Sqoop's features and capabilities on the Apache Sqoop User Guide (*http:// bit.ly/1r2610A*).

Ingesting Streaming Data with Flume

Flume is designed to collect and ingest high volumes of data from multiple data streams into Hadoop. A very common use case for Flume is the collection of log data, such as collecting web server log data emitted from multiple application servers, and aggregating it in HDFS for later search or analysis. However, Flume isn't restricted to simply consuming and ingesting log data sources, but can also be customized to transport massive quantities of event data from any custom event source. In both cases, Flume enables us to incrementally and continuously ingest streaming data *as it is written* into Hadoop, rather than writing custom client applications to batch-load the data into HDFS, HBase, or other Hadoop data sink. Flume provides a unified yet flexible method of pushing data from many fast-moving, disparate data streams into Hadoop.

Flume's flexibility is derived from its inherently extensible data flow architecture. In addition to flexibility, Flume is designed to maintain both fault-tolerance and scalability through its distributed architecture. Flume provides multiple failover and recovery mechanisms, although the default "end-to-end" reliability mode that guarantees that accepted events will eventually be delivered is generally the recommended setting.[5]

We've covered the very high-level overview of Flume's features, but in order to understand how a Flume data flow is constructed we'll need to review the basic building block of a Flume data flow: a Flume agent.

---

4 See "Basic Usage" (*http://bit.ly/1r25bkq*) in the Sqoop User Guide.

5 See the *Flume User Guide* (*https://flume.apache.org/FlumeUserGuide.html#reliability*).

Flume Data Flows

Flume expresses the data ingestion pathway from origin to destination as a *data flow*. In a data flow, a unit of data or *event* (e.g., a single log statement) travels from a source to the next destination via a sequence of hops (*https://flume.apache.org/ FlumeUserGuide.html#data-flow-model*). This concept of data flow is expressed even in the simplest entity in a Flume flow, a Flume *agent*. A Flume agent is a single unit within a Flume data flow (actually, a JVM process), through which events propagate once initiated at an external source. Agents consist of three configurable components: the *source*, *channel*, and *sink*, as shown in Figure 7-1.

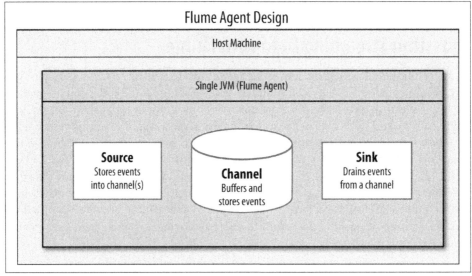

Figure 7-1. Flume agent design

A Flume source is configured to listen for and consume events from one or more external data sources (not to be confused with a Flume source), which are configured by setting a name, type, and additional optional parameters for each data source. For example, we could configure up a Flume agent's source to accept events from an Apache access log by running a `tail -f /etc/httpd/logs/access_log` command. This type of source is called an `exec` source because it requires Flume to execute a Unix command to retrieve events.

When the agent consumes an event, the Flume source writes it to a channel, which acts as a storage queue that stores and buffers events until they are ready to be read. Events are written to channels transactionally, meaning that a channel keeps all events queued until they have been consumed and the corresponding transactions are explicitly closed. This enables Flume to maintain durability of data events even if an agent goes down.

Flume sinks eventually read and remove events from the channel and forward them to their next hop or final destination.[6] Sinks can thus be configured to write its output as a streaming source for another Flume agent, or to a data store like HDFS or HBase. Flume supports many types of built-in sink types, which are documented in the Apache Flume User Guide (*https://flume.apache.org/FlumeUserGuide.html#flume-sinks*).

Using this source-channel-sink paradigm, we can easily construct a simple single-agent Flume data flow to consume events from an Apache access log and write the log events to HDFS, as shown in Figure 7-2.

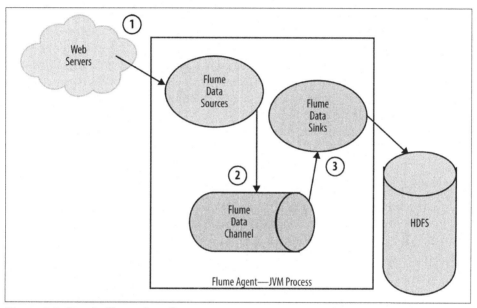

Figure 7-2. Simple Flume data flow

But because Flume agents are so adaptable and can even be configured to have multiple sources, channels, and sinks, we can actually construct multi-agent data flows by chaining several Flume agents together, as shown in Figure 7-3.

---

6 Hari Shreedharan, *Using Flume, 1e* (O'Reilly).

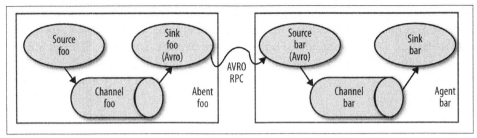

Figure 7-3. Multi-agent Flume data flow

There's almost no boundaries around how Flume agents can be organized into these complex data flows, although certain patterns and topologies of Flume data flows have emerged to handle common scenarios when dealing with a streaming data-processing architecture. For instance, a common scenario in log collection is when a large number of log producing clients are writing events to several Flume agents, which we call "first-tier" agents, as they are consuming data at the layer of the external data source(s).[7] If we want to write these events to HDFS, we can set up each of the first-tier agents' sinks to write to HDFS, but this could present several problems as the first-tier scales out. Because several disparate agents are writing to HDFS independently, this data flow wouldn't be able to handle periodic bursts of data writes to the storage system and could thus introduce spikes in load and latency.

We could achieve better isolation between the first-tier agents and data sink (HDFS) by adding a second-tier agent that will consolidate and buffer the events from the first-tier. This allows the second-tier agent(s) to both aggregate the received events, which provides an additional benefit of easier debugging, and control the rate of writes to the storage system so that the overall flow can absorb longer and larger spikes in load.[8] This topology pattern is called the *fan-in flow*, as shown in Figure 7-4.

---

7 Hari Shreedharan, *Using Flume, 1e* (O'Reilly).

8 Ibid.

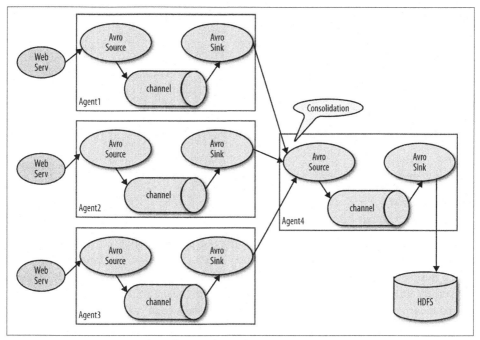

Figure 7-4. Fan-in Flume data flow

As you might guess, as the number of servers producing data increases and the number of first-tier agents correspondingly increases, the number of subsequent agents and tiers will also often need to increase. While tuning and designing such complex Flume architectures is outside the scope of this book, if you are interested in reading further on Flume design principles, we recommend reading Hari Shreedharan's excellent book *Using Flume* (O'Reilly). In the next section, we will configure a simple single-agent Flume data flow to ingest a custom log.

Ingesting Product Impression Data with Flume

Examples of single-agent Flume data flows that ingest standard log data like Apache access logs (*http://bit.ly/1r278NW*), or streaming data from the Twitter firehose (*http://bit.ly/1r27c04*) are fairly ubiquitous, but Flume is also a great fit for ingesting custom data streams such as real-time analytics data generated by a custom application.

In this example, we will use Flume to consume the streaming user-interaction data generated by a hypothetical online store. Many ecommerce companies seek to measure micro-conversion rates within their online stores that track online marketing performance. These metrics can be useful for measuring the overall effectiveness of the online store, and may include:[9]

Look-to-click rate
> How many product impressions are converted to *clickthroughs*, or the action of a visitor clicking a link/image to navigate to a product detail page

Add-to-cart rate
> How many clickthroughs are converted to cart placements

Cart-to-buy rate
> How many cart-additions are converted to purchases

Look-to-buy rate
> What percentage of product impressions are eventually converted to purchases

In general, the data requirements for deriving these metrics involve capturing granular *product impressions*, where the ecommerce web application is instrumented to log every interaction a visitor has with a product. These interactions can include viewing a product link, clicking through to the product details, adding/removing a product to/from cart, and purchasing the product. This data is then extracted and analyzed at some interval after being written to generate reports, tune features, drive personalized experiences, and so on.

We will simulate an ecommerce impressions log that records user-product interactions in the following JSON format:

```
{
    "sku": "T9921-5",
    "timestamp": 1453167527737,
    "cid": "51761",
    "action": "add_cart",
    "ip": "226.43.51.25"
}
```

The types of actions can include "view", "click", "add_cart", "remove_cart", and "purchase". A script that generates a sample impressions log can be found in the GitHub repository within the */flume* directory, and can be run by executing:

```
$ ./impression_tracker.py
```

This will both output and create a file named *impressions.log* and place it at the path */tmp/impressions/*. To create the necessary directories in the local file system and HDFS, run the *setup.sh* script as a user with sudo privileges:

```
$ ./setup.sh
```

---

9 Ron Kohavi and Foster Provost, "Applications of Data Mining to Electronic Commerce," Data Mining and Knowledge Discovery 5:1–2 (2001): 5–10.

This example simulates a simple two-agent Flume flow, where we establish a single *client* agent that will run on a web server and ingest the *impression.log* records and send those events to a single Avro sink. Avro is a lightweight RPC protocol that also provides easy data serialization. Avro allows us to easily set up an RPC protocol to transmit data between the client agent's sink to a *collector* agent's source. The collector agent will then write those events to HDFS. The final workflow is configured as shown in Figure 7-5.

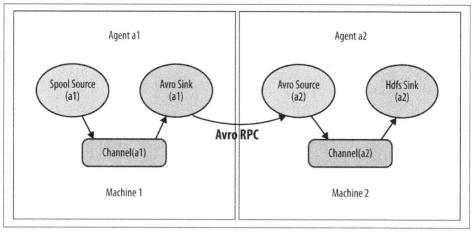

Figure 7-5. Log ingestion into HDFS

Setting up a Flume agent starts with writing a configuration file. As we noted earlier, all Flume agents are composed of a source, channel, and one or more sinks. Let's start by configuring our client agent's source to the location of our impression log:

```
# Define spooling directory source:
client.sources=r1
client.sources.r1.channels=ch1
client.sources.r1.type=spooldir
client.sources.r1.spoolDir=/tmp/impressions
```

We have established the source name, r1, which we will use to reference and set the other properties for this source. We need to specify a named channel for the source, which we've named ch1. In addition, we've configured the r1 source with type spool dir, which is used to ingest data from a specified "spooling" directory on disk. This source will watch the specified directory for new files, and parses events out of new files as they appear. After a given file has been fully read into the channel, it is renamed to indicate that the file has been fully ingested by Flume (*http://bit.ly/flume-spool*).

Next, we'll configure the client agent's channel, which buffers the data from the source to the sink. We've set up a channel named ch1 and and set its type to FILE. By default, the File Channel buffers data by writing to files to a path within the user's home directory, named *checkpoint* and *data*. These filepaths can be overridden for a given channel by configuring its `checkpointDir` and `dataDirs` values:

```
# Define a file channel:
client.channels=ch1
client.channels.ch1.type=FILE
```

Finally, we need to configure our sink for the client agent. In this example, our client agent will write its data out to an Avro sink. We name it k1 and configure it to ingest from ch1 channel. Avro sinks require a `hostname` and `port`:

```
# Define an Avro sink:
client.sinks=k1
client.sinks.k1.type=avro
client.sinks.k1.hostname=localhost
client.sinks.k1.port=4141
client.sinks.k1.channel=ch1
```

Next, we configure the collector agent, which consumes events from the Avro source we configured earlier and writes those events to HDFS. The source, channel, and sink configurations look like this:

```
# Define an Avro source:
collector.sources=r1
collector.sources.r1.type=avro
collector.sources.r1.bind=0.0.0.0
collector.sources.r1.port=4141
collector.sources.r1.channels=ch1

# Define a file channel using multiple disks for reliability:
collector.channels=ch1
collector.channels.ch1.type=FILE
collector.channels.ch1.checkpointDir=/tmp/flume/checkpoint
collector.channels.ch1.dataDirs=/tmp/flume/data

# Define HDFS sinks to persist events as text.
collector.sinks=k1
collector.sinks.k1.type=hdfs
collector.sinks.k1.channel=ch1
```

Note that the source name does not need to match the sink name from the client agent, as long as the type, `bind` host, and `port` configurations are consistent. We also configure a `FILE` channel for this agent, but override the checkpoint and data directories so that there are no conflicts with the client agent's channel. We also declare a single sink called k1 of type hdfs, which consumes from the ch1 channel that we configured for this agent.

HDFS sinks require a `path` configuration that specifies the location on HDFS where this agent will write its data. In addition, we specify some other optional configuration parameters for the expected filename prefix and suffix, file format, and maximum number of events to write per batch:

```
# HDFS sink configurations
collector.sinks.k1.hdfs.path=/user/hadoop/impressions
collector.sinks.k1.hdfs.filePrefix=impressions
collector.sinks.k1.hdfs.fileSuffix=.log
collector.sinks.k1.hdfs.fileType=DataStream
collector.sinks.k1.hdfs.writeFormat=Text
collector.sinks.k1.hdfs.batchSize=1000
```

With our client and collector agent now fully configured, we can run the Flume agents to execute the full flow. First, ensure that you have run the *setup.sh* script and generated the *impressions.log* file under */tmp/impressions*. Then open three tabs in your terminal. In the first tab, navigate to the location of the Flume configuration files and run the command:

```
$ flume-ng agent -n collector --conf . -f collector.conf
```

This should start the collector agent, which is waiting to receive events from the client agent. Now in the second tab we'll start the client agent:

```
$ flume-ng agent -n client --conf . -f client.conf
```

Once the client agent has fully processed the *impressions.log* file, you should see a console message indicating that the *impressions.log* file has been completely processed and renamed to *impressions.log.COMPLETED*:

```
INFO avro.ReliableSpoolingFileEventReader: Preparing to move file
/tmp/impressions/impressions.log to
/tmp/impressions/impressions.log.COMPLETED
```

You can then check the first tab to verify that the collector agent has processed all events and written them to HDFS. Confirm that the logs have been written to the HDFS source directory that we specified in our configuration:

```
$ hadoop fs -ls /user/hadoop/impressions/
$ hadoop fs -cat /user/hadoop/impressions/impressions.1453085307781.log | head
```

Although your file should be prefixed with *impressions* and suffixed with the *.log* extension, the intermediary timestamp will vary based on the date and time that you ran the Flume flow. This two-agent flow demonstrated a very simple example of a multi-agent Flume data flow, but Flume provides rich support for many other types and configurations of agent sources, channels, and sinks to enable more complex and scalable data flows, which can be found in Flume's User Documentation (*https:// flume.apache.org/FlumeUserGuide.html*).

Conclusion

In this chapter, we learned how to use Sqoop to efficiently transfer bulk data from a relational database into various Hadoop data stores. For further information on integrating Sqoop, we recommend the *Apache Sqoop Cookbook* by Kathleen Ting and Jarek Jarcec Cecho (O'Reilly). We also learned how Flume enables us to ingest streaming data into Hadoop in a reliable and scalable manner. If you are interested in learning more about configuring and architecting Flume flows, we recommend Hari Shreedharan's excellent book *Using Flume* (O'Reilly).

While Sqoop and Flume are among the most commonly used data ingestion tools for Hadoop, there are many other Hadoop ecosystem projects within the space of data ingestion and streaming processing that we didn't cover in this chapter. Apache Kafka is another such project that, while not specifically designed for Hadoop, allows for high-throughput, parallel data loading into Hadoop. In addition to Flume and Kafka, there has been a lot of recent emphasis on developing tools and patterns for real-time streaming data ingestion and processing in Hadoop and Spark. For more information on the practical use cases for data ingestion with these and other tools, we recommend the "Data Movement" chapter in *Hadoop Application Architectures*.

## CHAPTER 8

Analytics with Higher-Level APIs

In Chapter 6, we touched upon some of the motivations for working in a higher-level language such as Hive as opposed to native MapReduce, which can be difficult, unwieldy, and verbose even for relatively simple operations. Even experienced Java and MapReduce programmers find that most non-trivial Hadoop applications can entail a long development cycle, writing and chaining several mappers and reducers to form a complex job-chain or data processing workflow.

Furthermore, because MapReduce is designed to run in a batch-oriented fashion, it presents a number of limitations when performing data analysis that entails iterative processing (including many machine learning algorithms) or interactive data mining that requires responsive feedback. These criticisms of native MapReduce regarding development efficiency, maintenance, and runtime performance provide much of the motivation for both higher-level abstractions of Hadoop, and even a new processing engine that extends the MapReduce paradigm.

In this chapter, we introduce Pig, a programming abstraction of MapReduce that facilitates building MapReduce-based data flows. We also introduce some newer Spark APIs that extend the core RDD APIs by making it easier for developers to compute over structured data using familiar SQL-based concepts and syntax. These projects seek to boost developer productivity in programming MapReduce and Spark applications by providing expressive APIs that allow analysts to build complex applications in a few lines of code.

Pig

Pig, like Hive, is an abstraction of MapReduce, allowing users to express their data processing and analysis operations in a higher-level language that then compiles into a MapReduce job. Pig was developed at Yahoo as a tool for researchers and engineers to more easily write their data mining Hadoop scripts by representing them as data flows[1]. Pig (*http://pig.apache.org*) is now a top-level Apache Project that includes two main platform components:

- Pig Latin, a procedural scripting language used to express data flows.
- The Pig execution environment to run Pig Latin programs, which can be run in local or MapReduce mode and includes the Grunt command-line interface.

Unlike Hive's HQL, which draws heavily from SQL's declarative style, Pig Latin is procedural in nature and designed to enable programmers to easily implement a series of data operations and transformations that are applied to datasets to form a data pipeline.[2] While Hive is great for use cases that translate well to SQL-based scripts, SQL can become unwieldy when multiple complex data transformations are required. Pig Latin is ideal for implementing these types of multistage data flows, particularly in cases where we need to aggregate data from multiple sources and perform subsequent transformations at each stage of the data processing flow.

Pig Latin scripts start with data, apply transformations to the data until the script describes the desired results, and execute the entire data processing flow as an optimized MapReduce job. Additionally, Pig supports the ability to integrate custom code with user-defined functions (UDFs) that can be written in Java, Python, or JavaScript, among other supported languages.[3] Pig thus enables us to perform near arbitrary transformations and ad hoc analysis on our big data using comparatively simple constructs.

It is important to remember the earlier point that Pig, like Hive, ultimately compiles into MapReduce and cannot transcend the limitations of Hadoop's batch-processing approach. However, Pig does provide us with powerful tools to easily and succinctly write complex data processing flows, with the fine-grained controls that we need to build real business applications on Hadoop. In the next section, we'll review some of the basic components of Pig and implement both native Pig Latin operators and custom-defined functions to perform some simple sentiment analysis on Twitter data. We assume that you have installed Pig to run on Hadoop in pseudo-distributed mode. The steps for installing Pig can be found in Appendix B.

---

1 Tom White, *Hadoop: The Definitive Guide, 4th Edition* (O'Reilly).

2 Alan Gates, "Comparing Pig Latin and SQL for Constructing Data Processing Pipelines" (*http://yhoo.it/1r2bK6I*), Yahoo Developer Network's Hadoop Blog, January 29, 2010.

3 See the documentation for Apache Pig (*http://pig.apache.org/docs/r0.12.0/start.html*).

Pig Latin

Now that we have Pig and the Grunt shell set up, let's examine a sample Pig script and explore some of the commands and expressions that Pig Latin provides. The following script loads Twitter tweets with the hashtag #unitedairlines over the course of a single week.

 You can find this script and the corresponding data in the GitHub repo under the *data/sentiment_analysis/* folder.

The data file, *united_airlines_tweets.tsv*, provides the tweet ID, permalink, date posted, tweet text, and Twitter username. The script loads a dictionary, *dictionary.tsv*, of known "positive" and "negative" words along with sentiment scores (1 and -1, respectively) associated to each word. The script then performs a series of Pig transformations to generate a sentiment score and classification, either POSITIVE or NEGATIVE, for each computed tweet:

```
grunt> tweets = LOAD 'united_airlines_tweets.tsv' USING PigStorage('\t')
    AS (id_str:chararray, tweet_url:chararray, created_at:chararray,
    text:chararray, lang:chararray, retweet_count:int, favorite_count:int,
    screen_name:chararray);
grunt> dictionary = LOAD 'dictionary.tsv' USING PigStorage('\t')
    AS (word:chararray, score:int);
grunt> english_tweets = FILTER tweets BY lang == 'en';
grunt> tokenized = FOREACH english_tweets GENERATE id_str,
    FLATTEN( TOKENIZE(text) ) AS word;
grunt> clean_tokens = FOREACH tokenized GENERATE id_str,
    LOWER(REGEX_EXTRACT(word, '[#@]{0,1}(.*)', 1)) AS word;
grunt> token_sentiment = JOIN clean_tokens BY word, dictionary BY word;
grunt> sentiment_group = GROUP token_sentiment BY id_str;
grunt> sentiment_score = FOREACH sentiment_group
    GENERATE group AS id, SUM(token_sentiment.score) AS final;
grunt> classified = FOREACH sentiment_score
    GENERATE id, ( (final >= 0)? 'POSITIVE' : 'NEGATIVE' ) AS classification,
    final AS score;
grunt> final = ORDER classified BY score DESC;
grunt> STORE final INTO 'sentiment_analysis';
```

Let's break down this script at each step of the data processing flow.

Relations and tuples

The first two lines in the script loads data from the file system into relations called tweets and dictionary:

```
tweets = LOAD 'united_airlines_tweets.tsv' USING PigStorage('\t')
    AS (id_str:chararray, tweet_url:chararray, created_at:chararray,
```

```
            text:chararray, lang:chararray, retweet_count:int, favorite_count:int,
            screen_name:chararray);

        dictionary = LOAD 'dictionary.tsv' USING PigStorage('\t') AS (word:chararray,
            score:int);
```

In Pig, a *relation* is conceptually similar to a table in a relational database, but instead of an ordered collection or rows, a relation consists of an unordered set of tuples. *Tuples* are an ordered set of fields. It is important to note that although a relation declaration is on the left side of an assignment, much like a variable in a typical programming language, relations are not variables. Relations are given aliases for reference purposes, but they actually represent a checkpoint dataset within the data processing flow.

We used the LOAD operator to specify the filename of the file (either on the local file system or HDFS) to load into the tweets and dictionary relations. We also use the USING clause with the PigStorage load function to specify that the file is tab-delimited. Although not required, we also defined a schema for each relation using the AS clause and specifying column aliases for each field, along with the corresponding data type. If a schema is not defined, we can still reference the fields for each tuple in our relation by using Pig's positional columns ($0 for the first field, $1 for the second, etc.). This may be preferable if we are loading data with many columns, but are only interested in referencing a few of them.

Filtering

The next line performs a simple FILTER data transformation on the tweets relation to filter out any tuples that are not in English:

```
        english_tweets = FILTER tweets BY lang == 'en';
```

The FILTER operator selects tuples from a relation based on some condition, and is commonly used to select the data that you want; or, conversely, to filter out (remove) the data you don't want. Because the "lang" field is typed as a chararray, the Pig equivalent of the Java String data type, we used the == comparison operator to retain values that equal *en* for English. The result is stored into a new relation called english_tweets.

Projection

Now that we've filtered the data to retain only English tweets (our dictionary after all, is in English) we need to split the tweet text into word tokens, which we can match against our dictionary, and perform some additional data cleanup on the words to remove hashtags, preceded by #, and user handle tags, preceded by @:

```
        tokenized = FOREACH english_tweets GENERATE id_str,
            FLATTEN( TOKENIZE(text) ) AS word;
```

```
clean_tokens = FOREACH tokenized GENERATE id_str,
  LOWER(REGEX_EXTRACT(word, '[#@]{0,1}(.*)', 1)) AS word;
```

Pig provides the FOREACH...GENERATE operation to work with columns of data in relations or collections and apply a set of expressions to every tuple in the collection. The GENERATE clause contains the values and/or evaluation expression that will derive a new collection of tuples to pass onto the next step of the pipeline. In our example, we project the id_str key from the english_tweets relation, and use the TOKENIZE function to split the text field into word tokens (splitting on whitespace). The FLATTEN function extracts the resulting collection of tuples into a single collection.

The collection of tuples we generate is actually a special data type in Pig, called a *bag*, and represents an unordered collection of tuples, similar to a relation although relations are called the "outer bag" because they cannot be nested within another bag. In our FOREACH command, the result produces a new relation called tokenized where the first field is the stock_tweet ID (id_str) and the second field is a bag composed of single-word tuples.

We then perform another projection based on the tokenized relation to project the id_str and lowercased word without any leading hashtag or handle tag. We've performed quite a few transformations on our data, so it would be a good time to verify that our relations are well structured. We can use the ILLUSTRATE operator at any time to view the schemas of each relation generated based on a concise sample dataset (output truncated due to size):

```
grunt> ILLUSTRATE clean_tokens;
-------------------------------------------------------------------
| tweets | id_str:chararray | tweet_url:chararray |
-------------------------------------------------------------------
|        | 474415416874250240 | https://.../474415416874250240   |
-------------------------------------------------------------------
```

The ILLUSTRATE command is helpful to use periodically as we design our Pig flows to help us understand what our queries are doing and validate each checkpoint in the pipeline.

Grouping and joining

Now that we've tokenized the selected tweets and cleaned the word tokens, we would like to JOIN the resulting tokens against the dictionary, matching against the word if found:

```
token_sentiment = JOIN clean_tokens BY word, dictionary BY word;
```

Pig provides the JOIN command to perform a join on two or more relations based on a common field value. Both inner joins and outer joins are enabled, although inner joins are used by default. In our example, we perform an inner join between the clean_tokens relation and dictionary relation based on the word field, which will generate a new relation called token_sentiment that contains the fields from both relations:

```
----------------------------------------------------------------
| token_sentiment | clean_tokens::id_str:chararray |
clean_tokens::word:chararray |
dictionary::word:chararray | dictionary::score:int |
----------------------------------------------------------------
|                 | 473233757961723904 | delayedflight | delayedflight | -1 |
----------------------------------------------------------------
```

Now we need to GROUP those rows by the Tweet ID, id_str, so we can later compute an aggregated SUM of the score for each tweet:

```
sentiment_group = GROUP token_sentiment BY id_str;
```

The GROUP operator groups together tuples that have the same group key (id_str). The result of a GROUP operation is a relation that includes one tuple per group, where the tuple contains two fields:

- The first field is named "group" (do not confuse this with the GROUP operator) and is the same type as the group key.

- The second field takes the name of the original relation (token_sentiment) and is of type bag.

We can now perform the final aggregation of our data, by computing the sum score for each tweet, grouped by ID:

```
sentiment_score = FOREACH sentiment_group GENERATE group AS id,
  SUM(token_sentiment.score) AS final;
```

And then classify each tweet as POSITIVE or NEGATIVE based on the score:

```
classified = FOREACH sentiment_score GENERATE id,
( (final >= 0)? 'POSITIVE' : 'NEGATIVE' )
    AS classification, final AS score;
```

Finally, let's sort the results by score in descending order:

```
final = ORDER classified BY score DESC;
```

We've now defined all the operations and projections needed for our sentiment analysis. In the next section, we'll save this data to a file on HDFS where we can later view and analyze the results.

Storing and outputting data

Now that we've applied all the necessary transformations on our data, we would like to write out the results somewhere. For this purpose, Pig provides the STORE statement, which takes a relation and writes the results into the specified location. By

default, the STORE command will write data to HDFS in tab-delimited files using Pig-
Storage. In our example, we dump the results of the final relation into our Hadoop
user directory (*/user/hadoop/*) in a folder called *sentiment_analysis*:

```
STORE final INTO 'sentiment_analysis';
```

The contents of that directory will include one or more part files:

```
$ hadoop fs -ls sentiment_analysis
Found 2 items
-rw-r--r--   1 hadoop supergroup          0 2015-02-19 00:10
sentiment_analysis/_SUCCESS
-rw-r--r--   1 hadoop supergroup       7492 2015-02-19 00:10
sentiment_analysis/part-r-00000
```

In local mode, only one part file is created, but in MapReduce mode the number of
part files depends on the parallelism of the last job before the store. Pig provides a
couple features to set the number of reducers for the MapReduce jobs generated; you
can read more about Pig's parallel features in the Apache Pig documentation (*http://
pig.apache.org*).

When working with smaller datasets, it's convenient to quickly output the results
from the grunt shell to the screen rather than having to store it. The DUMP command
takes the name of a relation and prints the contents to the console:

```
grunt> DUMP sentiment_analysis;
```

The DUMP command is convenient for quickly testing and verifying the output of your
Pig script, but generally for large dataset outputs, you will STORE the results to the file
system for later analysis.

Data Types

We covered some of the nested data structures available in Pig, including fields,
tuples, and bags. Pig also provides a *map* structure, which contains a set of key/value
pairs. The key should always be of type chararray, but the values do not have to be of
the same data type. We saw some of the native scalar types that Pig supports when we
defined the schema for the stock data.

Table 8-1 shows the full list of scalar types that Pig supports.

Table 8-1. Pig scalar types

Category	Type	Description	Example
Numeric	int	32-bit signed integer	12
	long	64-bit signed integer	34L
	float	32-bit floating-point number	2.18F
	double	64-bit floating-point number	3e-17

Category	Type	Description	Example
Text	`chararray`	String or array of characters	hello world
Binary	`bytearray`	Blob or array of bytes	N/A

Relational Operators

Pig provides data manipulation commands via the relational operators in Pig Latin. We used several of these to load, filter, group, project, and store data earlier in our example. In addition, Table 8-2 shows the relational operators that Pig supports.

Table 8-2. Pig relational operators

Category	Operator	Description
Loading and storing	LOAD	Loads data from the file system or other storage source
	STORE	Saves a relation to the file system or other storage
	DUMP	Prints a relation to the console
Filtering and projection	FILTER	Selects tuples from a relation based on some condition
	DISTINCT	Removes duplicate tuples in a relation
	FOREACH...GENERATE	Generates data transformations based on columns of data.
	MAPREDUCE	Executes native MapReduce jobs inside a Pig script
	STREAM	Sends data to an external script or program
	SAMPLE	Selects a random sample of data based on the specified sample size
Grouping and joining	JOIN	Joins two or more relations
	COGROUP	Groups the data from two or more relations
	GROUP	Groups the data in a single relation
	CROSS	Creates the cross-product of two or more relations
Sorting	ORDER	Sorts the relation by one or more fields
	LIMIT	Limits the number of tuples returned from a relation
Combining and splitting	UNION	Computes the union of two or more relations
	SPLIT	Partitions a relation into two or more relations

The complete usage syntax for Pig's relational operators and arithmetic, boolean, and comparison operators can be found in Pig's User Documentation (*http://pig.apache.org/docs/r0.14.0/*).

User-Defined Functions

One of Pig's most powerful features lies in its ability to let users combine Pig's native relational operators with their own custom processing. Pig provides extensive support for such user-defined functions (UDFs) (*http://pig.apache.org/docs/r0.14.0/udf.html*), and currently provides integration libraries for six languages: Java, Jython,

Python, JavaScript, Ruby, and Groovy. However, Java is still the most extensively supported language for writing Pig UDFs, and generally more efficient, as it is the same language as Pig and can thus integrate with Pig interfaces such as the Algebraic Interface and the Accumulator Interface.

Let's demonstrate a simple UDF for the script we wrote earlier. In this scenario, we would like to write a custom eval UDF that will allow us to convert the score classification evaluation into a function, so that instead of:

```
classified = FOREACH sentiment_score GENERATE id,
    ( (final >= 0)? 'POSITIVE' : 'NEGATIVE' )
    AS classification, final AS score;
```

We can write something like:

```
classified = FOREACH sentiment_score GENERATE id,
    classify(final) AS classification, final AS score;
```

In Java, we need to extend Pig's EvalFunc class and implement the exec() method, which takes a tuple and will return a String:

```java
package com.statistics.pig;

import java.io.IOException;

import org.apache.pig.EvalFunc;
import org.apache.pig.backend.executionengine.ExecException;
import org.apache.pig.data.Tuple;

public class Classify extends EvalFunc {

    @Override
    public String exec(Tuple input) throws IOException {
        if (args == null || args.size() == 0) {
            return false;
        }
        try {
            Object object = args.get(0);
            if (object == null) {
                return false;
            }
            int i = (Integer) object;
            if (i >= 0) {
                return new String("POSITIVE");
            } else {
                return new String("NEGATIVE");
            }
        } catch (ExecException e) {
            throw new IOException(e);
        }
    }
}
```

To use this function, we need to compile it, package it into a JAR file, and then register the JAR with Pig by using the `REGISTER` operator:

```
grunt> REGISTER statistics-pig.jar;
```

We can then invoke the function in a command:

```
grunt> classified = FOREACH sentiment_score GENERATE id,
        com.statistics.pig.Classify(final) AS classification, final AS score;
```

We encourage you to read the documentation on UDFs, which contains a list of supported UDF interfaces and provides example scripts to perform tasks for evaluation, loading and storing data, and aggregating/filtering data. Pig also provides a collection of user-contributed UDFs called Piggybank, which is distributed with Pig but you must be registered to use it. See the Apache documentation on Piggybank (*https:// cwiki.apache.org/confluence/display/PIG/PiggyBank*) for more information.

Wrapping Up

Pig can be a powerful tool for users who prefer a procedural programming model. It provides the ability to control data checkpoints in the pipeline, as well as fine-grained controls over how the data is processed at each step. This makes Pig a great choice when you require more flexibility in controlling the sequence of operations in a data flow (e.g., an extract, form, and load, or ETL, process), or when you are working with semi-structured data that may not lend itself well to Hive's SQL syntax.

Spark's Higher-Level APIs

There are now numerous projects and tools that have been built around MapReduce and Hadoop to enable common data tasks and provide a more productive developer experience. For instance, we've seen how we can use frameworks like Hadoop Streaming to write and submit MapReduce jobs in a non-Java language such as Python. We also introduced tools that provide higher-level abstractions to Map-Reduce including Hive, which provides both a relational interface and declarative SQL-based language for querying structured data, and Pig, which offers a procedural interface for writing data flow-oriented programs in Hadoop.

But in practice, a typical analytic workflow will entail some combination of relational queries, procedural programming, and custom processing, which means that most end-to-end Hadoop workflows involve integrating several disparate components and switching between different programming APIs. Spark, in contrast, provides two major programming advantages over the MapReduce-centric Hadoop stack:

- Built-in expressive APIs in standard, general-purpose languages like Scala, Java, Python, and R

- A unified programming interface that includes several built-in higher-level libraries to support a broad range of data processing tasks, including complex interactive analysis, structured querying, stream processing, and machine learning

In Chapter 4, we used Spark's Python-based RDD API to write a program that loaded, cleansed, joined, filtered, and sorted a dataset within a single Python program of approximately 10 lines of non-helper code. As we've seen, Spark's RDD API provides a much richer set of functional operations that can greatly reduce the amount of code needed to write a similar program in MapReduce. However, because RDDs are a general-purpose and type-agnostic data abstraction, working with structured data can be tedious because that fixed schema is known only to you; this often leads to a lot of boilerplate code to access the internal data types and translating simple query operations to the functional semantics of RDD operations. Consider the operation shown in Figure 8-1, which attempts to compute the average age of professors grouped by department.

dept	age	name
Bio	48	H Smith
CS	54	A Turing
Bio	42	B Jones
Chem	61	M Kennedy

RDD API

```
pdata.map(lambda x: (x.dept, [x.age, 1])) \
    .reduceBy Key(lambda x, y: [x[0] + y[0], x[1] + y[1]]) \
    .map(lambda x: [x[0], x[1][0] / x[1][1]]) \
    .collect()
```

Figure 8-1. Aggregation with Spark's RDD API

In practice, it's much more natural to manipulate structured, tabular data like this using the lingua franca of relational data: SQL. Fortunately, Spark provides an integrated module that allows us to express the preceding aggregation into the simple one-liner shown in Figure 8-2.

dept	age	name
Bio	48	H Smith
CS	54	A Turing
Bio	42	B Jones
Chem	61	M Kennedy

DataFrame API

```
data.groupBy("dept").avg("age")
```

Figure 8-2. Aggregation with Spark's DataFrames API

Spark SQL

Spark SQL is a module in Apache Spark that provides a relational interface to work with structured data using familiar SQL-based operations in Spark. It can be accessed through JDBC/ODBC connectors, a built-in interactive Hive console, or via its built-in APIs. The last method of access is the most interesting and powerful aspect of Spark SQL; because Spark SQL actually runs as a library on top of Spark's Core engine and APIs, we can access the Spark SQL API using the same programming interface that we use for Spark's RDD APIs, as shown in Figure 8-3.

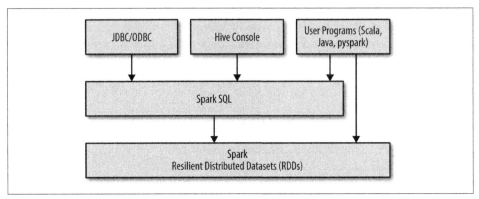

Figure 8-3. Spark SQL interface

This allows us to seamlessly combine and leverage the benefits of relational queries with the flexibility of Spark's procedural processing and the power of Python's analytic libraries, all in one programming environment.[4]

Let's write a simple program that uses the Spark SQL API to load JSON data and query it. You can enter these commands directly in a running `pyspark` shell or in a Jupyter notebook that is using a `pyspark` kernel; in either case, ensure that you have a running SparkContext, which we'll assume is referenced by the variable `sc`.

> The following examples use a Jupyter notebook that is running from the */sparksql* directory. Make sure you have extracted the *sf_parking.zip* file within the GitHub repo's */data* directory. You can view the *sf_parking.ipynb* file from our GitHub repository under the */sparksql* directory.

---

4 Michael Armbrust et al., "Spark SQL: Relational Data Processing in Spark," ACM SIGMOD Conference 2015.

To begin, we'll need to import the `SQLContext` class from the *pyspark.sql* package. The `SQLContext` class is the entry point into the Spark SQL API and is created by wrapping an active SparkContext:

```
from pyspark.sql import SQLContext
sqlContext = SQLContext(sc)
```

In this example, we'll load a JSON-formatted dataset from SF Open Data (*https://data.sfgov.org*) that lists publicly available off-street parking in San Francisco as of September 2011.[5]

Spark SQL, like Hadoop, requires that JSON data be formatted so that the first and last curly brace or square bracket is removed, and each JSON object is contained in a single line followed by a newline (i.e., no multiline JSON objects). We have provided a cleaned data file called *sf_parking_clean.json* for you, using the provided utility *clean_json.py*.

However, for extremely large datasets, you can use Spark itself to perform the formatting. For example, if we manually remove the first and last square bracket from the JSON file, we could load and format the file as follows:

```
input = sc.wholeTextFiles(input_path).map \
(lambda (x,y): y)
data = input.flatMap(lambda x: json.loads(x))
data.map(lambda x: json.dumps(x)) \
.saveAsTextFile(output_path)
```

The `wholeTextFiles` function creates a `PairRDD` with the key being the filename with a fully qualified path (e.g., "hdfs://localhost:9000/user/hadoop/sf_parking/sf_parking.json"). The value is the entire contents of the file as a String. We use a `map` operation to extract just the contents as `input` and then use `flatMap` to read the String contents into a JSON format.

With the file properly formatted, we can easily load its contents by calling `sqlContext.read.json` and passing it the path to the file:

```
parking = sqlContext.read.json('../data/sf_parking/sf_parking_clean.json')
```

Alternatively, we can pass the `sqlContext` a path to a directory and it will load all files found within into the parking object. Spark SQL automatically infers the schema of a JSON dataset, which we can visualize in a nice tree-format with the `printSchema` method:

---

5 SF Open Data, "Off-Street Parking Lots and Parking Garages" (*http://bit.ly/1r2n9Do*).

```
parking.printSchema()

root
 |-- address: string (nullable = true)
 |-- garorlot: string (nullable = true)
 |-- landusetyp: string (nullable = true)
 |-- location_1: struct (nullable = true)
 |    |-- latitude: string (nullable = true)
 |    |-- longitude: string (nullable = true)
 |    |-- needs_recoding: boolean (nullable = true)
 |-- mccap: string (nullable = true)
 |-- owner: string (nullable = true)
 |-- primetype: string (nullable = true)
 |-- regcap: string (nullable = true)
 |-- secondtype: string (nullable = true)
 |-- valetcap: string (nullable = true)
```

We can also view a sample of the first row of data:

```
parking.first()

Row(address=u'2110 Market St', garorlot=u'L', landusetyp=u'restaurant',
location_1=Row(latitude=u'37.767378', longitude=u'-122.429344',
needs_recoding=False), mccap=u'0', owner=u'Private', primetype=u'PPA',
regcap=u'13', secondtype=u' ', valetcap=u'0')
```

In order to run a SQL statement against our dataset, we must first register it as a temporary named table:

```
parking.registerTempTable("parking")
```

This allows us to run additional table and SQL methods, including show, which will display the first 20 rows of data in a tabular format:

```
parking.show()

...output truncated...
```

To execute a SQL statement on the parking table, we use the sql method, passing it the full query. Let's run an aggregation, grouping the parking by primary and secondary types and getting the count as well as average number of spaces for general parking spaces available. We'll store it in aggr_by_type and call show() to view the full results:

```
aggr_by_type = sqlContext.sql("SELECT primetype, secondtype,
                               count(1) AS count,
                               round(avg(regcap), 0) AS avg_spaces " +
                       "FROM parking " +
                       "GROUP BY primetype, secondtype " +
                       "HAVING trim(primetype) != '' " +
                       "ORDER BY count DESC")

aggr_by_type.show()
```

In addition to JSON, Spark SQL supports several other data sources, including files (such as text, parquet, or CSV, which can be parsed with Databricks's CSV-reader utility (*https://github.com/databricks/spark-csv*), etc.) from the local file system, HDFS, or S3, JDBC sources like MySQL, and Hive. Additionally, Spark can even be used as the underlying execution engine in Hive, simply by setting `hive.execu tion.engine=spark` in your active Hive session.

However, the Spark SQL module is much more than just a SQL interface, and the power of Spark SQL comes down to its underlying data abstraction, the DataFrame.

DataFrames

DataFrames are the underlying data abstraction in Spark SQL. The data frame concept should be very familiar to users of Python's Pandas (*http://pandas.pydata.org*) or R (*https://www.r-project.org*), and in fact, Spark's DataFrames are interoperable with native Pandas (using `pyspark`) and R data frames (using SparkR (*https://spark.apache.org/docs/1.6.0/sparkr.html*)). In Spark, a DataFrame also represents a tabular collection of data with a defined schema. The key difference between a Spark DataFrame and a dataframe in Pandas or R is that a Spark DataFrame is a distributed collection that actually wraps an RDD; you can think of it as an RDD of row objects.

Additionally, DataFrame operations entail many optimizations under the hood that not only compile the query plan into executable code, but substantially improve the performance and memory-footprint over comparable handcoded RDD operations. In fact, in a benchmark test that compared the runtimes between DataFrames code that aggregated 10 million integer pairs against equivalent RDD code, DataFrames were not only found to be up to 4–5x faster for these workloads, but they also close the performance gap between Python and JVM implementations (*http://bit.ly/1r2vMhm*), as shown in Figure 8-4.

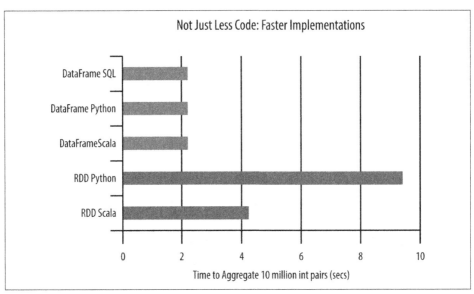

Figure 8-4. DataFrames optimization

The concise and intuitive semantics of the DataFrames API coupled with the performance optimizations provided by its computational engine was the impetus to make DataFrames the main interface for all of Spark's modules, including Spark SQL, RDDs, MLlib, and GraphX. In this way, the DataFrames API provides a unified engine across all of Spark's data sources, workloads, and environments, as shown in Figure 8-5.

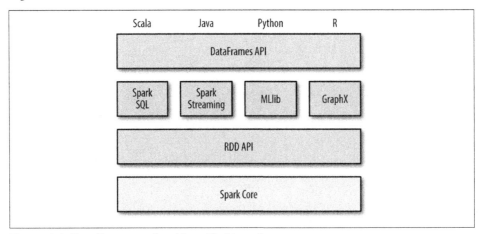

Figure 8-5. DataFrames as Spark's unified interface

When we loaded the SF parking data in the last example using Spark SQL's `read` interface, we actually created a DataFrame called `parking`. While in that example we registered the DataFrame as a temporary table to execute raw SQL queries, there are a multitude of relational operators and window functions that can be called on the parking DataFrame itself. In fact, we can rewrite the SQL query in the previous example by chaining several simple DataFrame operations:

```
from pyspark.sql import functions as F

aggr_by_type = parking.select("primetype", "secondtype", "regcap") \
                    .where("trim(primetype) != ''") \
                    .groupBy("primetype", "secondtype") \
                    .agg(
                      F.count("*").alias("count"),
                      F.round(F.avg("regcap"), 0).alias("avg_spaces")
                    ) \
                    .sort("count", ascending=False)
```

The advantage of this approach over raw SQL is that we can easily iterate on a complex query by successively chaining and testing operations. Additionally, we have access to a rich collection of built-in functions from the DataFrames API, including the `count`, `round`, and `avg` aggregation functions that we used previously. The `pyspark.sql.functions` module also contains several mathematical and statistical utilities that include functions for:

- Random data generation
- Summary and descriptive statistics
- Sample covariance and correlation
- Cross tabulation (a.k.a. contingency table)
- Frequency computation
- Mathematical functions

Let's use one such function to compute some descriptive summary statistics to get a better sense of the distribution and frequency of the parking availability data. The function `describe` returns a DataFrame containing the count of non-null entries, mean, standard deviation, and minimum and maximum values for each numerical column specified:

```
parking.describe("regcap", "valetcap", "mccap").show()
```

```
+-------+------------------+------------------+------------------+
|summary|            regcap|          valetcap|             mccap|
+-------+------------------+------------------+------------------+
|  count|              1000|              1000|              1000|
|   mean|           137.294|             3.297|             0.184|
| stddev|361.05120902655824|22.624824279398823|1.9015151221485882|
|    min|                 0|                 0|                 0|
|    max|               998|                96|                 8|
+-------+------------------+------------------+------------------+
```

Perhaps we want to determine what the joint frequency distribution is between the parking owner and the parking's primary type, or "primetype". This is commonly done in statistics by computing a *contingency table* or *cross-tabulation* that displays the co-occurrence frequencies between two variables in a matrix format. We can easily compute this for a Spark DataFrame by using the `crosstab` method from the `stat` interface:

```
parking.stat.crosstab("owner", "primetype").show()
```

```
+--------------------+---+---+---+---+---+
|    owner_primetype|PPA|PHO|CPO|CGO|   |
+--------------------+---+---+---+---+---+
|         Port of SF|  7|  7|  0|  4|  0|
|               SFPD|  0|  3|  0|  6|  0|
|              SFMTA| 42| 14|  0|  0|  0|
|GG Bridge Authority|  2|  0|  0|  0|  0|
|               SFSU|  2|  6|  0|  0|  0|
|               SFRA|  2|  0|  0|  0|  0|
..output truncated..
```

Data wrangling DataFrames

Note that because the "owner" column seems to be a high-cardinality dimension, the results are truncated to the first 20 rows of data. While many of the operations and functions in Spark's DataFrames API should translate well to Pandas and R users, there are some important differences due to the immutable and distributed nature of DataFrames that Pandas/R programmers should be aware of. For instance, while Spark does its best to infer data types on load, the default fallback type is a string, as can be observed in our SF parking example for the "regcap" column. In Pandas, we could easily cast the values in this column by selecting the columns and using `astype` to cast the values:

```
parking['regcap'].astype(int)
```

However, because DataFrames are actually just a wrapper for RDDs, which are immutable collections, we need to perform a few steps in order to convert this column into an `int` type. This workaround involves creating a new column based off the existing column, casting its values to the correct type, and finally dropping the old column. In order to retain the column name, we'll first use the `withColumnRenamed` method to rename the existing column to "regcap_old", then use the `withColumn` method to add the new column "regcap", which will contain the values of the cast values from `regcap_old`:[6]

---

6 We use Spark's cast method here, but as of Spark 1.4, you can use `astype` as a Pandas-friendly alias to the cast method.

```
parking = parking.withColumnRenamed('regcap', 'regcap_old')
parking = parking.withColumn('regcap', parking['regcap_old'].cast('int'))
parking = parking.drop('regcap_old')
parking.printSchema()
```

We'll also want to do this for other numerical columns, so in the spirit of DRY ("don't repeat yourself"), let's define a utility function that will perform this conversion for any arbitrary column and data type:

```
def convert_column(df, col, new_type):
    old_col = '%s_old' % col
    df = df.withColumnRenamed(col, old_col)
    df = df.withColumn(col, df[old_col].cast(new_type))
    df.drop(old_col)
    return df

parking = convert_column(parking, 'valetcap', 'int')
parking = convert_column(parking, 'mccap', 'int')
parking.printSchema()
```

Unfortunately, this function doesn't work with "latitude" and "longitude," because they're actually fields in the "location_1" struct. However, we can do even better and define another function that will take a "location_1" struct type and use Google's Geocoding API (*http://bit.ly/1r2xH5F*) to perform a lookup on the latitude and longitude to return the neighborhood name. We'll use the requests (*http://docs.python-requests.org/en/master/*) library to make request:

```
import requests

def to_neighborhood(location):
    """
    Uses Google's Geocoding API to perform a reverse-lookup on latitude and
    longitude
    https://developers.google.com/maps/documentation/geocoding/
    intro#reverse-example
    """
    name = 'N/A'
    lat = location.latitude
    long = location.longitude

    r = requests.get(
    'https://maps.googleapis.com/maps/api/geocode/json?latlng=%s,%s' %
    (lat, long))

    if r.status_code == 200:
        content = r.json()
        # results is a list of matching places
        places = content['results']
        neighborhoods = [p['formatted_address'] for p in places if
        'neighborhood' in p['types']]

        if neighborhoods:
```

```
                    # Addresses are formatted as Japantown, San Francisco, CA
                    # so split on comma and just return neighborhood name
                    name = neighborhoods[0].split(',')[0]

            return name
```

The to_neighborhood function accepts a location struct and returns a string type, but how can we use this function in the context of a column expression? The pyspark.sql.functions module provides the udf function to register a user-defined function (UDF). We declare an inline UDF by passing UDF a callable Python function and the Spark SQL data type that corresponds to the return type; in this case, we are returning a string so we will use the StringType data type from pyspark.sql.types. Once registered, we can use the UDF to reformat the "location_1" column with a withColumn expression:

```
from pyspark.sql.functions import udf
from pyspark.sql.types import StringType

location_to_neighborhood=udf(to_neighborhood, StringType())

sfmta_parking = parking.filter(parking.owner == 'SFMTA') \
                    .select("location_1", "primetype", "landusetyp",
                    "garorlot", "regcap", "valetcap", "mccap") \
                    .withColumn("location_1",
                    location_to_neighborhood("location_1")) \
                    .sort("regcap", ascending=False)

sfmta_parking.show()
```

```
+------------------+---------+----------+--------+------+--------+-----+
|        location_1|primetype|landusetyp|garorlot|regcap|valetcap|mccap|
+------------------+---------+----------+--------+------+--------+-----+
|    South of Market|      PPA|          |      G|  2585|       0|   47|
|               N/A|      PPA|          |      G|  1865|       0|    0|
|Financial District|      PPA|          |      G|  1095|       0|    0|
|      Union Square|      PPA|          |      G|   985|       0|    0|
.. output truncated ..
```

 In Spark local mode, we're unable to take advantage of parallelizing the HTTP requests to the API due to the threading limitations of Python's *global interpreter lock*, or GIL (*https://wiki.python.org/moin/GlobalInterpreterLock*). As such, using this utility in local mode would require running through the entire RDD serially, which can take a considerable amount of time. We have thus filtered the DataFrame in this example to a modest size to allow the operation to complete in a reasonable amount of time.

As you can see, the process of defining and registering a UDF in Spark's DataFrame API is much easier than in Pig or Hive. Once registered, UDFs can be used by other programs on the same Spark cluster and even by BI tools that are connected to Spark SQL via JDBC/ODBC interface. This makes the udf function easily the most powerful function provided by the DataFrames API, as it exposes endless possibilities for applying advanced computations or operations to SQL users. But there are a multitude of other built-in capabilities and functions that we haven't covered in this book and the list continues to grow with each Spark release.

To see the latest list of supported classes and functions in pyspark's Spark SQL and DataFrames APIs, refer to the official API docs. Another great source of Spark development news is from Databricks (*https://databricks.com/*), a company founded by Spark's creators. Databricks often publishes blog posts that describe any major new features that are added to the APIs, such as "Statistical and Mathematical Functions with DataFrames in Spark" (*http://bit.ly/26B8HDd*).

Conclusion

In this chapter, we learned how Pig can greatly ease the process of building a Map-Reduce data pipeline. Traditional ETL data pipeline processes probably form the large majority of use cases for Pig. However, Pig can also be an excellent tool for performing ad hoc analysis and building iterative processing or predictive models from large batches of data, especially as the analysis grows more complex.

We also introduced the Spark SQL module and the DataFrames API, which provide a built-in integration in Spark to support relational processing over structured datasets and allow users to mix relational and complex analytics within a single programming environment. DataFrames open a wide range of analytic possibilities that were not previously possible for Python programmers in Hadoop or Spark. We encourage you to explore Spark's DataFrames APIs further by reading Spark's official DataFrames API docs (*http://spark.apache.org/docs/latest/sql-programming-guide.html*) in your preferred language stack, and keeping an eye on future developments from Spark's News updates (*http://spark.apache.org/news/*).

## CHAPTER 9

Machine Learning

Machine learning computations aim to derive predictive models from current and historical data. The inherent premise is that a learned algorithm will improve with more training or experience, and in particular, machine learning algorithms can achieve extremely effective results for very narrow domains using models trained from large datasets.

As a result, computations of scale are implicated in most machine learning algorithms. For this reason, machine learning computations are well suited to a distributed computing paradigm, like Spark, in order to leverage large training sets to produce meaningful results. This chapter introduces the built-in Spark machine learning library, Spark MLlib (*http://spark.apache.org/docs/1.5.0/mllib-guide.html*), which consists of many common learning algorithms and utilities, including classification, regression, clustering, collaborative filtering, dimensionality reduction, as well as a new "ML-pipeline" framework, spark.ml, which provides a uniform set of high-level APIs that help users create and tune practical machine learning pipelines.[1]

Scalable Machine Learning with Spark

In Chapter 4, we introduced Spark as an in-memory distributed computing engine that can run on a Hadoop cluster. But additionally, the Spark platform ships with several built-in components that utilize Spark's processing engine to enable other types of analytical workloads, which benefit from Spark's computational optimizations. In this chapter, we'll take a closer look at Spark's built-in machine learning library,

---

1 See Spark's Machine Learning Library (MLlib) Guide (*http://spark.apache.org/docs/1.5.0/mllib-guide.html*).

MLlib, which includes a suite of common statistical and machine learning algorithms and utilities, all of which are designed to scale out across a cluster.[2]

Some of you may already be familiar with programming libraries for data mining and machine learning, such as Python's Weka (*http://www.cs.waikato.ac.nz/ml/weka/*) or Scikit-Learn (*http://scikit-learn.org*). These libraries work well for small to medium-sized datasets that can be processed on a single machine, but for large datasets that require distributed storage and the power of parallel processing, we not only need a computational engine that can process a distributed dataset but we also need algorithms that are designed for parallel platforms. Spark MLlib only contains parallel algorithms, in which operations can be applied in parallel across nodes using Spark's RDD operations. Fortunately, there are a number of machine learning techniques and algorithms that are well suited to parallelization. But it's important to remember that when using Spark MLlib, as with the Spark API, we need to be mindful of creating data (as RDDs) and operating on data in a distributed, parallelizable manner—for example, calling `parallelize()` on a small primitive dataset like a Python dictionary or list, so that it can be made available to all nodes in the cluster.

While Spark MLlib includes a number of statistical and machine learning techniques, including sampling, correlation calculation, hypothesis testing, and more, we will specifically focus on MLlib's machine learning algorithms. This class of algorithms attempts to make predictions or decisions based on training data, often maximizing a mathematical objective about how the algorithm should behave.[3] Spark MLlib learning algorithms focus on three key areas of machine learning, often referred to as the three Cs of machine learning:

Collaborative filtering
> Also known as recommender engines, which produce recommendations based on past behavior, preferences, or similarities to known entities/users

Classification
> Also known as supervised learning, which learns from a supervised training set and assigns a category to unclassified items based on that training set

Clustering
> Also known as unsupervised learning, which groups data into clusters based on similar characteristics

In general, the implementation of these algorithms begins with defining and extracting a set of features from the data as numerical representations of features. For exam-

---

2 Holden Karau et al., *Learning Spark* (O'Reilly).

3 SNN Adaptive Intelligence, "What Is Machine Learning?" (*http://www.mlplatform.nl/what-is-machine-learning/*)

ple, if we were to design a recommendation system that suggests products with similar attributes (price, color, brand, etc.), we could define feature vectors consisting of weighted number values for each product attribute. Or, in the case of extracting features from unstructured text (i.e., filtering emails based on spam detection), we might represent each word as a vector of its *term frequency-inverse document frequency (TF-IDF)* per classification category (i.e., spam, not spam).

Once we have extracted the feature vectors from the data, we can feed them as training data into a machine learning algorithm that will return a trained model representing the predictions. When training supervised learning models, we'll generally hold back a segment of the training data as "test data," apply the model to the test data, and quantify the accuracy of the model by comparing the test data predictions to the actual results. This allows us to assess the accuracy of the model and tune its precision. The high-level stages of the machine learning pipeline are shown in Figure 9-1.

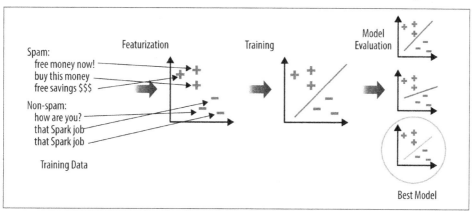

Figure 9-1. The machine learning pipeline

We will apply this common machine learning pipeline in the next few examples, and use some of MLlib's built-in evaluation tools to assess our learning models. We will assume that you have installed Spark and met the requirements to run Spark MLlib, as outlined in Appendix B.

Collaborative Filtering

Collaborative filtering, or *recommendation systems*, are perhaps most commonly recognized in the ecommerce space, where companies like Amazon and Netflix mine user-behavior data such as views, ratings, clicks, and purchases to generate and suggest other product recommendations. Broadly, there are two types of collaborative filtering algorithms:

User-based recommenders
   Finds users that are similar to the target user, and uses their collaborative ratings to make recommendations for the target user

Item-based recommenders
   Finds and recommends items that are similar or related to items associated with the target user

MLlib's collaborative filtering library focuses on user-based recommendations, using an implementation of the Alternating Least Squares (ALS) algorithm.[4] MLlib's collaborative filtering approach represents a user's preferences as a user-item association matrix, where each dot-product of user and item is a value derived from the preference-score (or rating) multiplied by a weighted factor. This allows us to accept users' explicit (i.e., positive ratings, purchases) and implicit (i.e., views, clicks) feedback and incorporate them into our model as a combination of binary preferences and confidence values. The model then tries to find latent factors that can be used to predict the expected preference for an item.

User-based recommender: An example

Let's use MLlib's ALS algorithm to generate recommendations or potential matches for an online dating service. We'll generate the recommendations for a given user based on a dataset consisting of profile ratings from an existing dating site.

In the GitHub repo under the *data/mllib/dating* directory, you'll find two CSVs containing datasets: user-ratings data containing 1+ million anonymous ratings (*ratings.dat*) for 168,791 user profiles (*gender.dat*). The data is available from Occam's Lab (*http://www.occamslab.com/petricek/data*).

The ratings data is formatted in the following format: UserID, ProfileID, Rating. UserID is the user who provided the rating, ProfileID is the user who has been rated, and Rating is a score on a 1–10 scale where 10 is the highest rating.

UserIDs range between 1 and 135,359 and ProfileIDs range between 1 and 220,970 (not every profile has been rated). Only users who have provided at least 20 ratings were included. Users who provided constant ratings were excluded.

User gender information is in the following format: UserID, Gender. Gender is denoted by a "M" for male and "F" for female and "U" for unknown.

The full program to the working dating recommender can be found in the GitHub repository under:

---

4 Koren Yehuda et al., "Matrix Factorization Techniques For Recommender Systems" (*http://dl.acm.org/citation.cfm?id=1608614*), *Computer* 14.8 (2009): 30–37.

```
hadoop-fundamentals/mllib/collaborative_filtering/als/matchmaker.py
```

This program can be run on Spark using the `spark-submit` command and passing it two arguments: the UserID of the user who we should generate matches for and the gender preference (M or F) for partner matches. We recommend piping this output to a file, too:

```
$ $SPARK_HOME/bin/spark-submit \
~/hadoop-fundamentals/mllib/collaborative_filtering/als/matchmaker.py 1 M \
> ~/matchmaking_recs.txt
```

We'll examine each major step of the program. First, we need to configure our Spark-Context with the name of the application and set the amount of memory to use per executor to 2 GB, as the ALS algorithm on this amount of data will require a lot of memory:

```
# Configure Spark
conf = SparkConf().setMaster("local") \
                .setAppName("Dating Recommender") \
                .set("spark.executor.memory", "2g")
sc = SparkContext(conf=conf)
```

Next, we'll read the argument for the User ID as well as the user's gender preference for matches, and call a custom-defined `parse_rating` method against each record in the ratings file:

```
def parse_rating(line, sep=','):
    """
    Parses a rating line
    Returns: tuple of (random integer, (user_id, profile_id, rating))
    """
    fields = line.strip().split(sep)
    user_id = int(fields[0])      # convert user_id to int
    profile_id = int(fields[1])   # convert profile_id to int
    rating = float(fields[2])     # convert rated_id to int
    return random.randint(1, 10), (user_id, profile_id, rating)
```

Given a rating row, the `parse_rating` method returns a tuple where the first item is a random integer and the second item is another tuple of (`user_id`, `profile_id`, `rating`):

```
matchseeker = int(sys.argv[1])
gender_filter = sys.argv[2]

# Create ratings RDD of (randint, (user_id, profile_id, rating))
ratings = sc.textFile(
    "/home/hadoop/hadoop-fundamentals/data/dating/ratings.dat")\
    .map(parse_rating)
```

We generate a random number for the first item in the tuple to use later as a key on which we can split this RDD into training and test sets. ALS requires that we represent Rating objects as these (UserId, ItemId, Rating) tuples. In this case, the ItemId will actually be mapped to the user IDs of other user profiles.

Next, we read the user profile data from *gender.dat* by mapping the custom-defined parse_user method to each row of the file:

```
def parse_user(line, sep=','):
    """
    Parses a user line
    Returns: tuple of (user_id, gender)
    """
    fields = line.strip().split(sep)
    user_id = int(fields[0])  # convert user_id to int
    gender = fields[1]
    return user_id, gender
```

Given a user row, the parse_user method returns a tuple of (user_id, gender). Once we've generated the RDD of user tuples, we'll call collect() to convert the RDD to a list:

```
# Create users RDD
users = dict(sc.textFile(
"/home/hadoop/hadoop-fundamentals/data/dating/gender.dat")\
.map(parse_user).collect())
```

Now let's split our ratings data into a training set that we'll use to train the model, and a validation set that we'll use to evaluate our model. We'll try to reserve 60% of the data for training and 40% for validation, by filtering on the random integer key we added to each tuple. We'll increase the parallelism of these RDDs by setting the number of partitions to 4 (or whatever number of cores your machine supports), and caching the result:

```
# Create the training (60%) and validation (40%) set, based on last digit
# of timestamp
num_partitions = 4
training = ratings.filter(lambda x: x[0] < 6) \
                    .values() \
                    .repartition(num_partitions) \
                    .cache()

validation = ratings.filter(lambda x: x[0] >= 6) \
                    .values() \
                    .repartition(num_partitions) \
                    .cache()

num_training = training.count()
num_validation = validation.count()

print "Training: %d and validation: %d\n" % (num_training, num_validation)
```

ALS provides us with the following training parameters that we can set and adjust to tune the model:

rank

> Size of feature vectors to use, where size is determined by the number of latent factors; larger ranks can lead to better models, but are more expensive to compute (default: 10)

num_iterations

> Number of iterations to run (default: 10)

lambda

> Regularization parameter (default: 0.01)

alpha

> A constant used for computing confidence in implicit ALS (default: 1.0)

Because we are just capturing explicit ratings here, we will ignore alpha and use the default value. For the other parameters, we'll use a rank of 8, and set the number of iterations to 8, and a lambda of 0.1. These initial training parameters are somewhat arbitrary, considering we don't know enough about the data to determine the number of latent factors or appropriate regularization value; however, we can start with this combination and later evaluate the results against other models with different combinations of training parameters to determine the best-fitting model:

```
# rank is the number of latent factors in the model
# num_iterations is the number of iterations to run.
# lambda specifies the regularization parameter in ALS
rank = 8
num_iterations = 8
lambda = 0.1
```

We can now create the model using the ALS.train() method, which accepts the training RDD of ratings tuples and our training parameters:

```
# Train model with training data and configured rank and iterations
model = ALS.train(training, rank, num_iterations, lambda)

# evaluate the trained model on the validation set
print "The model was trained with rank = %d, lambda = %.1f, and %d iterations.
\n" % \
    (rank, lambda, num_iterations)
```

> A word of warning when running the train() method in verbose logging mode: this operation requires several RDD projections and operations, so be prepared for up to several minutes of log-scrolling.

Once the model is created, we'll use the root mean squared error (RMSE) to compute the error of each model. The RMSE is the *square root of the average value of (actual rating – predicted rating)^2* for all users that have an actual rating.[5]

$$RMS = \left(\frac{1}{n} \sum_{i=1}^{n} \left(\text{model}_i - \text{observed}_i \right)^2 \right)^{\frac{1}{2}}$$

In our recommender program, we can implement the RMSE computation accordingly:

```
def compute_rmse(model, data, n):
    """
    Compute Root Mean Squared Error (RMSE), or square root of the average value
        of (actual rating - predicted rating)^2
    """
    predictions = model.predictAll(data.map(lambda x: (x[0], x[1])))
    predictions_ratings = predictions.map(lambda x: ((x[0], x[1]), x[2])) \
        .join(data.map(lambda x: ((x[0], x[1]), x[2]))) \
        .values()
    return sqrt(predictions_ratings.map(lambda x: (x[0] - x[1]) ** 2). \
    reduce(add) / float(n))
```

The RMSE indicates the absolute fit of the model to the data (how close the observed data points are to the model's predicted values) and has the useful property of being in the same units as the rating value. Lower values of RMSE indicate better fit, but because it's relative to the rating value, we should evaluate it on a scale of 1–10. Depending on the result, we may decide to tune our model by adjusting the training parameters or by providing more or better training data:

```
# Print RMSE of model
validation_rmse = compute_rmse(model, validation, num_validation)

print "The model was trained with rank=%d, lambda=%.1f, and %d iterations." % \
(rank, lambda, num_iterations)
print "Its RMSE on the validation set is %f.\n" % validation_rmse
```

Assuming that we are fine with our model's fit as indicated by the RMSE value, we can now apply it to generate recommendations for the given user. We'll first generate a set of eligible users by filtering on the given user's preferred gender. This will form our recommendation candidates, RDD:

```
# Filter on preferred gender
partners = sc.parallelize([u[0] for u in filter(lambda u: u[1] ==
  gender_filter, users.items())])
```

5 See Kaggle's "Root Mean Squared Error" (*https://www.kaggle.com/wiki/RootMeanSquaredError*).

Now we'll use the model's `predictAll()` method, passing it a pair RDD with key=user_id where the user_id is the given matchseeker. This allows the model to generate its recommendations. We'll collect the results into a list, and sort them by reverse rating value, taking the top 10 recommended users:

```
# run predictions with trained model
predictions = model.predictAll(partners.map(lambda x: (matchseeker, x))) \
.collect()

# sort the recommendations
recommendations = sorted(predictions, key=lambda x: x[2], reverse=True)[:10]
```

Finally, we'll print the full list of recommendations and stop the SparkContext:

```
print "Eligible partners recommended for User ID: %d" % matchseeker
for i in xrange(len(recommendations)):
    print ("%2d: %s" % (i + 1, recommendations[i][1])).encode('ascii', 'ignore')

# clean up
sc.stop()
```

If you submitted this job to Spark using this command to save the output to a results file, you should see output similar to the following:

```
$ cat matchmaking_recs.txt

Training: 542953 and validation: 542279

The model was trained with rank = 8, lambda = 0.1, and 8 iterations.

Its RMSE on the validation set is 3.580347.

Eligible partners recommended for User ID: 1
 1: 100939
 2: 70020
 3: 109013
 4: 54998
 5: 132170
 6: 3843
 7: 170778
 8: 51378
 9: 8849
10: 118595
```

Computing the RMSE gives us a useful metric to evaluate the performance of our model, but with collaborative filtering models, as with most ML-algorithms, the model will perform better with more data and iterations. For ALS, it's recommended to try a combination of rank, iterations, and regularization (lambda) parameters and compare their respective RMSEs to find the best fit. You can read more about tuning these parameters and also find another example of the ALS algorithm that implements a movie recommender in the "Collaborative Filtering" section (*http://bit.ly/26BoKB4*) of the Spark MLlib documentation.

Classification

Classification attempts to categorize data, usually text or documents, based on supervised training methods that utilize annotated training sets to discover patterns that will allow the machine learner to quickly label new records. For example, a simple classification algorithm might keep track of the features and words associated with a category, as well as the number of times those words are seen for a given category. Once the machine learner has extracted the features from the training data, it can generate a feature vector and apply a statistical model to build a predictive model, which can then be applied to new data.

MLlib provides several algorithms for binary and multiclass classification, as well as algorithms for regression analysis. In binary classification, we want to classify entities into one of two distinct categories or labels (e.g., determining whether or not emails are spam). In multiclass classification, we want to classify entities into one of more than two categories (e.g., determining what category a news article appears to most belong to). The goal of regression analysis algorithms is to estimate the relationships and dependencies between a dependent variable (e.g., physical activity level) and one or more independent variables (e.g., risk of heart disease) as a continuous function.

In each of these types of algorithms, the MLlib implementation involves applying the algorithm on a set of *labeled* examples. These are represented as `LabeledPoint` objects, which include a numerical value (for binary classification) or feature vector (for multiclass) along with the category label. The training data of already categorized `LabeledPoints` are used to train the model, which can then be used to predict the category for new entities.

You can view MLlib's official documentation (*http://bit.ly/26Bp4zE*) to see the full list of supported classification algorithms grouped by type. In this section, we'll create a simple binary classifier by applying a logistic regression procedure using stochastic gradient descent, also known as `LogisticRegressionWithSGD`.

Logistic regression classification: An example

In this example, we'll build a simple spam classifier that we'll train with email data that we've categorized as spam and not spam (or ham). Our spam classifier will utilize two MLlib algorithms, *HashingTF*, which we'll use to extract the feature vectors as term frequency vectors from the training text, and `LogisticRegressionWithSGD`, which implements a logistic regression using stochastic gradient descent (*http://bit.ly/26Bp7vf*).

The training data, *spam.txt* and *ham.txt,* can be found within the GitHub repo's */data* directory as *spam_classifier.zip.* This data is a subset of the SpamAssassin public corpus (*http://spamassassin.apache.org/publiccorpus/*). The full spam classifier program can be found under the *mllib/classification* directory; you can run the program using the command:

```
$ $SPARK_HOME/bin/spark-submit \
/home/hadoop/hadoop-fundamentals/mllib/classification/spam_classifier.py \
/home/hadoop/hadoop-fundamentals/data/spam_classifier/spam.txt \
/home/hadoop/hadoop-fundamentals/data/spam_classifier/ham.txt
```

We'll examine each of the major steps.

We first configure our SparkContext, again setting the application name and increasing the executor memory to 2 GB:

```
# Configure Spark
conf = SparkConf().setMaster("local") \
                  .setAppName("Spam Classifier") \
                  .set("spark.executor.memory", "2g")
sc = SparkContext(conf=conf)
```

Next, we'll read the command-line arguments to get the paths to the spam and ham training data files. We'll read those in to create the spam and ham RDDs:

```
spam_file = sys.argv[1]
ham_file = sys.argv[2]

spam = sc.textFile(spam_file)
ham = sc.textFile(ham_file)
```

Now we'll instantiate the HashingTF object, setting the number of features to extract at 10,000:

```
tf = HashingTF(numFeatures=10000)
```

We'll apply HashingTF's `transform()` method to our spam and ham data, first splitting the contents into word tokens. This will extract the term frequency vectors from the spam and ham RDDs, and project them as new RDDs of feature vectors:

```
spam_features = spam.map(lambda email: tf.transform(email. \
  split(" ")))
ham_features = ham.map(lambda email: tf.transform(email. \
  split(" ")))
```

We'll now convert each feature vector in our RDDs into a `LabeledPoint`. This is a binary classifier, so we'll represent spam as 1 and ham as a 0. The second value in the `LabeledPoint` object will consist of the feature. We'll take the union of these RDDs as our training dataset, and cache it because logistic regression is an iterative algorithm:

```
positive_examples = spam_features.map(lambda features: LabeledPoint(1, features))
negative_examples = ham_features.map(lambda features: LabeledPoint(0, features))
```

```
training = positive_examples.union(negative_examples)
training.cache()
```

Now we'll run the logistic regression using the SGD algorithm and our training data:

```
model = LogisticRegressionWithSGD.train(training)
```

We can now create test data, consisting of text content that should be classified as positive for spam, as well as content that should classified as negative (ham). We'll use our trained model to predict whether the test data is considered spam or ham. Recall from our discussion of LabeledPoints that 1 is considered spam, and 0 is considered ham:

```
# Create test data and test the model
positive_test = tf.transform("Guaranteed to Lose 20 lbs in 10 days
Try FREE!".split(" "))
negative_test = tf.transform("Hi, Mom, I'm learning all about Hadoop
and Spark!".split(" "))

print "Prediction for positive test example: %g" % model.predict(positive_test)
print "Prediction for negative test example: %g" % model.predict(negative_test)
```

From here, we can evaluate the accuracy of our classifier model by comparing the predicted results against a holdout of categorized data, or apply the model on an unlabeled set of data. MLlib's classification algorithms are optimized for large sets of supervised training data, so in general, more data will yield better results than small, but higher-precision data. However, it's still important to consider the data and apply the most appropriate algorithm and evaluation methods. For the full list of supported classification algorithms and evaluation metrics, refer to the official Spark MLlib documentation (*http://bit.ly/26Bp4zE*) and pay particular attention to what APIs (Scala, Java, Python) are supported for each.

Clustering

Unlike collaborative filtering and classification algorithms, clustering utilizes unsupervised learning techniques to build a model. Clustering algorithms attempt to organize a collection of data into groups of similar items. Examples of clustering might include finding groups of customers with similar characteristics or interests, or grouping animals/plants into common species. The goal of clustering is to partition data into a number of clusters such that the data within each cluster is more similar to each other than to data in other clusters.[6]

Spark MLlib offers a handful of popular clustering models, but perhaps the simplest and most popular clustering algorithm included is *k-means*. The *k*-means algorithm

---

6 Alex Holmes, *Hadoop In Practice* (Manning Publications).

requires that we represent all objects as a set of numerical features, and that we specify the target number of clusters (k clusters) we want up front.

MLlib's implementation of k-means clustering starts again with vectorizing the dataset, and representing each object within a feature vector in n-dimensional space, where n is the number of all features used to describe the objects to be clustered. The algorithm randomly chooses k points in that vector space, which serve as the initial centers, or *centroids*, of the clusters. The algorithm then assigns each object to the centroid that it's closest to, recalculating the centroid point using the average of the coordinates of all the points in the cluster and reassigning objects to their closest cluster, as necessary. The process of assigning objects and re-computing centers is repeated until the process converges, as shown in Figure 9-2.[7]

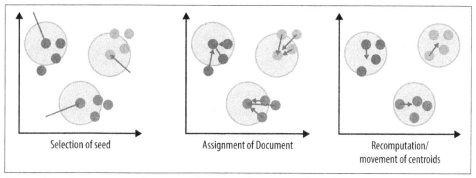

| Selection of seed | Assignment of Document | Recomputation/ movement of centroids |

Figure 9-2. Computational stages of k-means clustering algorithm

The most important issue in clustering is to determine how to quantify the similarity of the objects being clustered. The weighting method may be derived from TF-IDF (term frequency-inverse document frequency), which is particularly useful for text-documents, or it may be determined by a function of other custom properties in our data (i.e., segmenting customers based on total purchase amount in dollars) based on average engagement as measured by some computed metric. For MLlib's k-means clustering input, we need to express whatever weighting method we use as a feature vector. For example, if we determined that we want to cluster all customers by three features: total purchase amount, average purchase frequency, and average per/ purchase amount, then a sample of our customers might be represented as shown in Table 9-1.

---

7 Holden Karau et al., *Learning Spark* (O'Reilly).

Table 9-1. Customer feature vectorization

Name	Total purchase amount (in $)	Average # purchases per-month	Average per-purchase amount	Feature vector
Jane	825	5	115	[825,5,115]
Bob	201	1	45	[201,1,45]
Emma	649	2	65	[649,2,65]

With multiple features, we must be mindful of dimension values that are expressed in different units, or are not normalized with respect to each other. If we applied a simple distance-based metric to determine similarity between these vectors, total purchase amounts would dominate the results. Weighting the different dimensions solves this problem.[8]

k-means clustering: An example

In this example, we'll apply the *k*-means clustering algorithm to determine which areas in the United States. have been most hit by earthquakes so far this year.[9] This information can be found within the GitHub repo's */data* directory, as *earthquakes.csv*. The columns for this CSV file are as follows:

- time
- latitude
- longitude
- depth
- magnitude
- magnitudeType
- nst
- gap
- dmin
- rms
- net
- id
- updated
- place

---

8 Sean Owen, Robin Anil, Ted Dunning, and Ellen Friedman, *Mahout in Action* (Manning Publications)

9 See "USGS Earthquakes Hazard Program" (*http://earthquake.usgs.gov/earthquakes/feed/v1.0/csv.php*).

We'll extract the latitude and longitude from these records, and use that as the input for training our model. In this iteration, we'll attempt to generate 6 clusters. The full program can be run using the command:

```
$ $SPARK_HOME/bin/spark-submit \
/home/hadoop/hadoop-fundamentals/mllib/clustering/earthquakes_clustering.py \
/home/hadoop/hadoop-fundamentals/data/earthquakes.csv \
6 > clusters.txt
```

First, we'll configure Spark and create our SparkContext:

```
# Configure Spark
conf = SparkConf().setMaster("local") \
                  .setAppName("Earthquake Clustering") \
                  .set("spark.executor.memory", "2g")
sc = SparkContext(conf=conf)
```

Next, we'll create our training RDD from the earthquakes file, parsing the latitude and longitude from each line and converting it into a NumPy array:

```
# Create training RDD of (lat, long) vectors
earthquakes_file = sys.argv[1]
training = sc.textFile(earthquakes_file).map(parse_vector)
```

We'll set k-clusters based on the second argument passed—in this case, 6:

```
k = int(sys.argv[2])
```

Now we can call KMeans.train() and pass it our training set and k (set to 6). This will generate the model and allow us to access the cluster centers:

```
# train model based on training data and k-clusters
model = KMeans.train(training, k)

print "Earthquake cluster centers: " + str(model.clusterCenters)
sc.stop()
```

If you inspect the output, *clusters.txt*, you should see output similar to the following:

```
Earthquake cluster centers: [array([  38.63343185, -119.22434212]),
array([  13.9684592 ,  142.97677391]),
array([  61.00245376, -152.27632577]),
array([ 35.74366346,   27.33590769]),
array([  10.8458037 , -158.656725  ]),
array([ 23.48432962, -82.3864285 ])]
```

From here, we can plot the resulting output against the training data to perform an "eyeball" evaluation of the results, and tune the number of clusters (k) and number of iterations to adjust the cluster centers. For a more precise evaluation metric, we could also compute the "Within Set Sum of Squared Errors", which measures the compactness of cluster points around each center point:

```
def error(point):
    center = model.centers[model.predict(point)]
```

```
        return sqrt(sum([x**2 for x in (point - center)]))

    WSSSE = training.map(lambda point: error(point)).reduce(lambda x, y: x + y)
    print("Within Set Sum of Squared Error = " + str(WSSSE))
```

Conclusion

In this chapter, we implemented a simple user-based recommender, categorized emails using a binary classifier that implements a logistic regression, clustered a collection of documents using a k-means clustering algorithm, and learned a bit about vector representation of input data. But we have only just scratched the surface of MLlib's predictive analytics capabilities.

In addition to other algorithms and data preparation tools, MLlib also offers tools to evaluate the quality and performance of our algorithms. We hope that this short introduction has demonstrated the potential of using MLlib to apply powerful statistical learning techniques to large datasets, and we encourage you to learn more about Spark MLlib's statistical and machine learning offerings and upcoming developments as it continues to evolve into a broader distributed machine learning framework. The data types, algorithms, and utilities can all be found in the official Spark MLlib guide (*http://spark.apache.org/docs/latest/mllib-guide.html*). We also recommend the excellent, example-driven book *Advanced Analytics with Spark* by Sandy Ryza, Uri Laserson, Sean Owen, and Josh Wills (O'Reilly).

## CHAPTER 10

Summary: Doing Distributed Data Science

Throughout this book, we've looked at specific pieces of the Hadoop ecosystem. Part I discussed how to interact with and utilize a cluster. As we've discussed, Hadoop is an operating system for distributed computing; like an operating system on a local computer that provides a file system and process management, Hadoop provides distributed data storage and access through HDFS as well as a resource and scheduling framework in the form of YARN. Together, HDFS and YARN provide a mechanism to do distributed analysis on extremely large datasets.

The original method to program distributed jobs was to use the MapReduce framework, which allowed you to specify mapper and reducer tasks that could be chained together for larger computations. Because Python is one of the most popular tools for data science, we looked specifically at how you might use Hadoop Streaming to execute MapReduce jobs with Python scripts. We also explored a more native solution: the use of Spark's Python API to execute Spark jobs in a Hadoop cluster using YARN. Finally, we wrapped up our discussion of lower-level tools with a look at distributed analyses and design patterns that are routinely employed on a cluster.

Part II shifted away completely from the lower-level programming details to the higher-level tools for data mining, data ingestion, data flows, and machine learning. This section oriented itself toward the more day-to-day aspects of performing distributed data analysis with Hadoop with the various tools that exist, and did so by framing the tools in the context of the big data pipeline: ingestion, wrangling/staging, computation and analysis, and workflow management.

Hopefully this left you with the question, "How do all these tools and components in Hadoop and Spark come together?"

In the very first chapter, we discussed why big data has become important, primarily because of the rise of *data products*—applications that derive their value from data and generate new data through their applied use in prediction or pattern recognition. Data products necessarily have to be self-adaptable and broadly applicable (generalizable); as a result, machine learning and reinforcement techniques have become more and more prominent in the successful deployment of a data product. The self-adapting behavior of data products requires that they are not static and that they are constantly learning. The generalizability of data products requires a lot of data reference points to fit a model to. As a result, distributed computation is required for data products to handle both the variety and velocity of data that is characteristic of modern machine learning.

 Data products are built consumables (not necessarily wholly software) that derive their value from data and generate new data in return. This definition therefore necessarily requires the application of machine learning techniques. Data-driven applications are simply applications that use data (which encompasses every software product)—for example, blogs, online banking, ecommerce, and so on. Data-driven applications do not necessarily generate new data even if they derive their value from data.

In this chapter, we will specifically look at how to build a data product using all the tools we've discussed in the book and in so doing, answer the question of how low-level operations of distributed computing and higher-level ecosystem tools fit together. If this book is meant to be a low-barrier introduction to Hadoop and distributed computing, we also want to conclude by offering advice on what to do next and where to go from here. We hope that by contextualizing the entire data product and machine learning lifecycle, you will more easily be able to identify and understand the tools and techniques that are critical for your workflow.

Data Product Lifecycle

Building data products requires the construction and maintenance of an active data engineering pipeline. The pipeline itself involves multiple steps of ingestion, wrangling, warehousing, computation, and exploratory analysis that when taken as a whole, form a data workflow management system. The primary goal of the data workflow is to build and operationalize fitted (trained) models. At its heart, this involves extract, transform, and load (ETL) processes that extract data from an application context and load it into Hadoop, process the data in the Hadoop cluster, then ETL the data back to the application. As shown in Figure 10-1, this simple wrapping can be viewed as an active or regular lifecycle where new data and interaction is used to adapt and engage machine learning models for users.

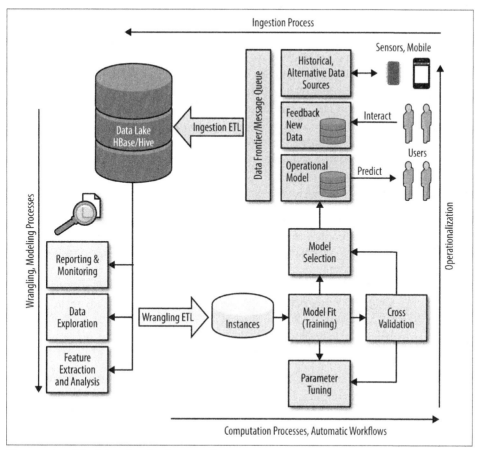

Figure 10-1. The lifecycle of a data product

The data product lifecycle requires big data analytics and Hadoop to fully engage machine learning algorithms. An application with a non-trivial amount of users is going to necessarily generate a lot of data, but processing a large amount of data *volume* could be handled through effective sampling and analysis on a beefy server with 128 GB of memory and multiple cores. Instead, it is primarily the *variety* and *velocity* of data that requires the flexibility of Hadoop and cluster-based approaches.

Flexibility is really the key word when it comes to cluster-based systems. Input data sources in the form of web log records (for clickstream data), user interactions, and streaming datasets like sensor data are constantly feeding into applications. These data sources are written to a variety of locations, including logfiles, NoSQL databases, and relational database backends to web APIs. Additionally, augmenting information, like data from web crawls, data services and APIs, surveys, and other business sources are also being generated. This additional data must also be analyzed with and against existing application data to determine if there are features that might improve the data product models.

As a result, the data product lifecycle usually revolves around a central data store (or stores) that provides extreme flexibility with no constraints (as in a relational database) but with a high degree of durability. Such central data stores are WORM systems, "write once, read many," a critical part of providing reliable data to downstream analytics, allowing for historical analyses and reproducible ETL generation (which is vital for science). WORM storage systems have become so critical to data science, they've taken on a new name: *data lakes*.

Data Lakes

Traditionally, in order to perform routine, aggregate analyses in a business context we would use the data warehouse model. Data warehouses are extended relational databases that typically normalize data into a star schema; schemas of this type have multiple dimensions joined to one central fact table (which causes a diagram of the relations to look like a star). Transactions normally occur on the dimension tables; their decoupling giving some performance benefit to writes and reads from individual aspects of the organization. ETL processes then load the fact table via one massive join that constructs a "data (hyper)cube" upon which pivots and other analytical mechanisms can be applied.

In order to effectively employ a traditional data warehouse, a clear schema must be designed up front, necessitating lengthy cycles of database administration, data transformation, and loading via ETLs before data can even be accessed for analysis. Unfortunately, this traditional model of data analytics can become both time consuming and restricting when you view data products as living, active engines that require new data and new data sources. Simple changes to an application, new historical data sources, or new log records and extraction techniques would require the restructuring and renormalization of the data cube and star schema. This restructuring takes time and effort but also forces a business decision: will this data be valuable enough that it will be worthwhile to scale machines to handle the new volume?

As data scientists, we know that all data can at least be potentially valuable, and it's hard to answer questions about data value and their relative benefit against costs. So instead of spending money solely on a data warehouse, many companies have instead opted to develop *data lakes* as their primary data collection and sync strategy.

Data lakes allow the inflow of raw, unprocessed data from a variety of sources in both structured and unstructured forms, storing the entire collection of data together without much organization, as shown in Figure 10-2. Structured data can be ingested from relational databases, structured files such as XML or JSON, or delimited files such as logfiles, and is usually added to the system in a text-based format or some sort of serialized binary format like SequenceFiles, Avro, or Parquet. Semi and unstructured data can include sensor data, binary data such as images, or text files that are not record-oriented but rather document-oriented, such as emails. The data lake pattern allows any type of data to flow freely into storage, and then flow out via ETL processes that impose the required schema at processing time. Once extracted and transformed as required by the analytical requirements, the data can then be loaded into one or more *data warehouses* for routine or critical analysis. By providing online access to the entire set of "full fidelity" data in its raw, source form and deferring schema definition at processing time, the data lake pattern can provide organizations with the agility to perform new processing and analysis as requirements change.

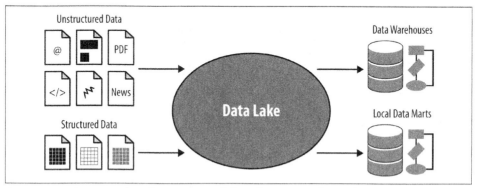

Figure 10-2. Structured and unstructured data flow into a data lake, which is then queried against using ETL processes to produce a data warehouse that can be analyzed

Although we specifically focused on HDFS in this book, there are many other distributed data storage solutions, including GlusterFS, EMC's Isilon OneFS, and Amazon's Simple Storage Service (S3), among others. However, HDFS is the default file system for Hadoop and actually a very effective way of constructing a data lake. HDFS distributes data across many machines, allowing for more, smaller hard disks to store the data while also making the data available for computation in a distributed framework without network traffic from storage area networks (SANs). Additionally, HDFS replicates data blocks, providing durability and fault tolerance so that data is never lost. Moreover, NameNodes provide immediate data namespace organization in the form of a hierarchical file system without the cost of designing per-field data schemas.

Instead of having a single master data warehouse that is susceptible to excessive load and capacity limitations, data can be stored in an HDFS data lake, analyzed flexibly by MapReduce or Spark jobs, and extracted from the data lake to be loaded into target systems such as an enterprise data warehouse for a business unit that requires a particular type of analysis. Additionally, older historical data that would typically be archived onto tape and made inaccessible for analysis can be offloaded to Hadoop and made available for exploratory analysis. Seen this way, Hadoop can alleviate much of the maintenance burdens and scalability limitations of traditional data warehouses, and even complement an existing data warehouse architecture, as shown in Figure 10-3.

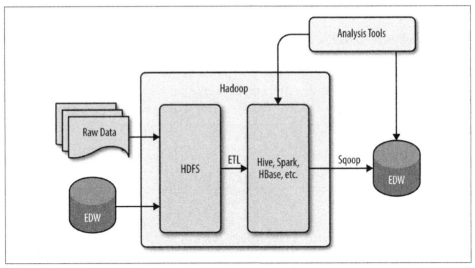

Figure 10-3. A hybrid data warehouse architecture with Hadoop

Data Ingestion

With a better understanding of the central object of the data product lifecycle, the data lake, we can now turn our attention to data ingestion and data warehousing, and how data scientists typically view these processes. We will start with data ingestion.

Generally speaking, most data ingestion acquires data from an application context. That is, a business unit that has some software product that users interact with, or a logical unit that collects information in a real-time basis. For example, for an ecommerce platform of significant size, one software application may be written to solely deal with customer reviews, while another unit collects network traffic information for security and logging. Both of these data sources are extremely valuable for data products like anomaly detection (for fraud) or recommendation systems, but have to be ingested separately into the data lake. We have proposed two tools to aid in the ingestion for both of these contexts: Sqoop and Flume.

Sqoop makes use of the JDBC (Java database connector) library to generally connect to any relational database system and export it to HDFS. Relational databases are the backend servers for almost every single web application that exists right now, as well as where most sequential (non-distributed) analyses currently happen. Because relational databases are the focus of smaller-scale analytics and are ubiquitous in web applications, Sqoop is an essential tool for extracting data from most large sources into HDFS. Moreover, because Sqoop is extracting data from a relational context, Hive and SparkSQL are almost immediately able to leverage the data ingested from these sources after some wrangling to ensure that primary keys are consistent across databases. In our example, Sqoop would be the ideal tool to extract customer review data that is stored in a relational database.

Flume, on the other hand, is a tool for ingesting log records, but also can ingest from any HTTP source. Whereas Sqoop is for structured data, Flume can be used primarily for unstructured data such as logs containing network traffic data. Log records are typically considered semi-structured because they are text that requires parsing, but usually the line entries are in the same standard format. Flume can also ingest HTML, XML, CSV, or JSON data from web requests, which makes it useful for dealing with specific semi-structured data, or wrappers for unstructured data like comments, reviews, or other text data. Because Flume is more general than Sqoop, it doesn't necessarily have parity with a downstream data warehousing product, and as a general rule requires ETL mechanisms between the ingestion process and analysis.

Other tools that we have not discussed in this book are message queue *services*. For example, Kafka is a distributed queue system that can be used to create a data frontier between the real world, the applications in your data system, and the data lake. Instead of having a user send a request to an application, which will then be ingested to Hadoop, the request is queued in Kafka, which can then be ingested on demand. Message queues essentially make the data ingestion process a bit more real-time, or at least piece-at-a-time rather than having to do big batch jobs as with Sqoop.

However, in order to get into real-time data sources, other tools for dealing with *streaming data* are required. Streaming data refers to unbounded and possibly unordered data that is coming in constantly to a system in an online fashion. Tools like Storm (now Heron) by Twitter as well as MillWheel and Timely allow distributed, fault-tolerant processing of real-time datasets. These tools can be run on YARN and use HDFS as a storage tool at the end of their processing. Similarly, Spark Streaming provides micro-batch analysis of streaming datasets, allowing you to collect and batch records together at a regular interval (e.g., on a per-second basis) and analyze or work with them all at once.

Many modern analytic architectures utilize some combination of these various ingestion and processing tools to support both batch and streaming workloads, also known as a *lambda architecture*, as shown in Figure 10-4.

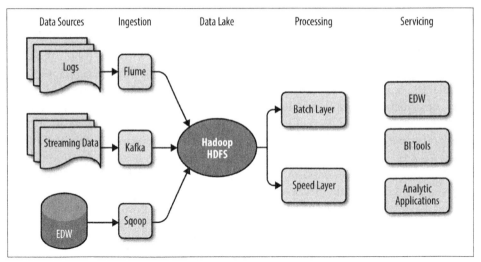

Figure 10-4. A lambda architecture

When you consider these tools together, you can clearly see that there is a continuum —from large-scale batches that feed directly into data warehousing for analysis to real-time streaming, which requires ETL and processing before large-scale analyses can be made. The choice of what to use is largely a function of the specific velocity of the data and the trade-off between timeliness (analyses are available immediately or within a specific time limit) and completeness (approximations versus exactness).

Computational Data Stores

As we move toward the more formal warehousing and analysis phase of the data product lifecycle, we once again need to consider the requirements for our distributed storage. As we discussed, by using Hadoop as a data lake to store raw, unprocessed data we can gain considerable flexibility and agility in our analytic capabilities. However, there are many use cases where some structure and order is necessary. This is especially true in the case of data warehousing, where data is expected to reside in a shared repository and a dimensional schema provides easier and optimized querying for analytical tasks. For these types of applications, it's not sufficient to merely interact with our data as a collection of files using the file system interface of HDFS; we instead require a higher-level interface that natively understands structured table semantics of SQL.

Relational approaches: Hive

In this book we have proposed Hive as the primary method for performing data warehousing tasks in Hadoop. The Hive project includes many components, including the Hive Metastore, which acts as a storage manager on top of HDFS to store metadata (database/table entities, column names, types, etc.), Hive driver and execution engine to compile SQL queries into MapReduce or Spark jobs, and the Hive Metastore Service and HCatalog to allow other Hadoop ecosystem tools to interact with the Hive Metastore. There are many other distributed SQL or SQL-on-Hadoop technologies that we did not discuss—Impala, Presto, and Hive on Tez, to name a few. All of these alternatives actually interact with the Hive Metastore either directly or via HCatalog. Which solution you choose should be driven by your data warehousing and performance requirements, but Hive is often a good choice for long-running queries where fault tolerance is required.

One important consideration when storing data in HDFS and Hive is figuring out how to partition data in a meaningful but efficient way. For Hive, the partitioning strategy should take into account the predicates that will be most commonly applied when querying your dataset. For example, if analyses have `WHERE` clauses in the form of `WHERE year = 2015` or `WHERE updated > 2016-03-15`, then clearly filtering the records by date will be an important access pattern and we may want to partition our data on day (e.g., 2016-03-01) accordingly. This allows Hive to read only the specific partitions that are required, thus reducing the amount of I/O and improving query times significantly.[1]

Unfortunately, most SQL queries are necessarily complex, and you can end up with a lot of different partitions for the various predicates that are applied for analysis. This can cause either extreme data fragmentation or reduced flexibility of your data stores. Instead of executing complex queries over the distributed data, a second option is to use Sqoop to digest your data out from Hadoop, after some primary transformations and filters are applied, and stick it back into a relational database such that normal reporting or Tableau visualizations can be applied more directly. Understanding the flow of data from many smaller systems to a larger lake system and back out to a smaller system therefore is the most critical part of the warehousing.

NoSQL approaches: HBase

The non-relational option for data warehousing we have discussed is HBase, a columnar NoSQL database. Columnar databases are workhorses for OLAP (online analytical processing) style database access. These types of accesses usually scan most or all of various database tables, selecting only a portion of the columns available. Consider questions like, "How many orders are there per region, per week?" This query on an orders table requires two columns, region and order date. Columnar databases stream only these two columns in a compact and compressed format to computation, rather than taking a row-oriented approach, which requires a row-by-row scan of every row in every table, including joins and columns that are not required. As a

---

1 Mark Grover et al., *Hadoop Application Architectures* (O'Reilly).

result, columnar (also called vertex-centric) computations give a huge performance boost to these types of aggregations.

When considering non-relational tools and NoSQL databases, there are usually specific requirements that lead to their choice. For example, if queries require a single fast lookup of a value, then a key/value store should be considered. If the data access requirements involve row-level writes for sparse data and the analysis is primarily aggregation focused, HBase could be a good candidate. If data is in a graph form with many relationships (edges) between entities (vertices), then a graph database like Titan should be considered. If you're working with sensor or time-series data, then a database that natively understands time-series data like InfluxDB should be considered. There are a surprising number of NoSQL databases, precisely because they all typically constrain themselves to optimizing for a very specific use case. In most cases, these data storage backends are part of a larger and more complex distributed storage and computing architecture.

Machine Learning Lifecycle

In Chapter 5, we explored sampling techniques to decompose a dataset, placing it on a single computer and then using Scikit-Learn to generate the model. This model can then be pickled and cross-validated against the entire dataset using a distributed approach. Generally speaking this is a very effective technique called "last-mile computing" that uses MapReduce or Spark to filter, aggregate, or summarize data down to a domain that can fit in the memory of a single computer (say 64 GB) and be computed upon using more readily available tools. Additionally, this is the only way to perform computations or analyses that do not have distributed implementations.

In Chapter 9, we explored using the SparkML library to perform classification, regression, and clustering in a distributed context. Big data machine learning has relied on the Mahout library and graph analytics libraries like Pregel in the past, and now the SparkML and GraphX libraries are being even more widely used in an analytical context. To some extent, there has been a land rush for converting powerful tools to a distributed format, but in other cases the distributed algorithm has come before the single process version.

As we have defined a data product, hopefully it is clear that all of the data management techniques discussed in this book drive toward machine learning, primarily in the form of feature engineering. Feature engineering is the process of analyzing the creation of a *decision space*—that is, what dimensions (columns or fields) do you need in order to create an effective model? In fact, this process is the primary work of the data scientist; it is the employment of the tools discussed in the earlier chapters, not their design or development that is the ultimate data product objective.

As a result, it's probably most useful not to discuss machine learning directly but rather to have a clear understanding of what it is that a machine learning algorithm expects.

 This book has focused on equipping data scientists with the ability to do feature engineering for machine learning on large datasets. Almost all machine learning algorithms operate on a single instance table, where each row is a single instance to learn on and each column is a dimension in the decision space. This has a large effect on how you choose tools in the data product lifecycle.

In a relational context, this means that datasets must be *denormalized* before they can be analyzed (e.g., joined from multiple tables into a single one). This might cause redundant data to be entered in the system, but this is what is required to feed into the algorithms. Almost all machine learning systems are iterative, which means the system will make multiple passes over the data. In a big data context, this can be very expensive, and is the reason that we might use Spark over MapReduce to do machine learning—Spark keeps the data in memory, making each pass much faster.

Denormalization, redundancy, and iterative algorithms have implications for the data lifecycle as well. If we are constantly generating single tables, then we must ask ourselves why are we normalizing our data in the first place from the data lake. Can't we simply send denormalized data directly into machine learning models? In practice, schema design in Hadoop is highly dependent on the specific analytic process or ML model's input requirements. In many cases, there may be multiple similar data schema requirements with small differences, such as the required partitioning or bucketing scheme. While storing the same datasets using different physical organizations is generally considered an anti-pattern in traditional data warehouses, this approach can make sense in Hadoop, where data is optimized for being written once and there is little overhead in storing duplicate data.[2]

After considering data storage for the build phase of machine learning, the second thing to consider is how to get the model out of the data product lifecycle and into production so that it can actually be used to recognize patterns, make predictions, or adapt to user behavior! Models are fitted to data such that they can be applied generally to new input data. The fitting process often creates some expression of the model that can be used for prediction. For example, if you are using a Naive Bayes model family, then the fitted model is actually a set of probabilities. These probabilities are used to compute the conditional probability of a class given the probabilities of the features that exist in the instance. If you're using linear models, then the fitted model

---

2 Mark Grover et al., *Hadoop Application Architectures* (O'Reilly).

is expressed as a set of coefficients and an intercept whose linear combination with independent variables (features) produces a a dependent variable (the target).

Somehow this expression must be exported from the system for operationalization and evaluation. In the case of a linear model, the expression can be very small—it's just a set of coefficients. In the case of a Bayesian model, the fitted model may be bigger; it's a set of probabilities for every feature and class that exists in the system, therefore the size of the model expression is directly related to how many features there are. Random forests are the collection of multiple decision trees that partition the decision space using rule-based approaches. While each decision tree is a small tree-like data structure, in a big data context where the decision space might be huge and complex, the number of trees in the forest might start to present a storage problem. The expression of the model gets bigger and bigger all the way to k-nearest neighbor approaches that require storage of every single instance trained on for distance computation to make a decision.

So far we've seen two primary mechanisms of exporting fitted models: pickling data with Python and Scikit-Learn and writing Spark models back to HDFS. But if the model expression management process is part of the data product lifecycle, you will notice other analytical tasks become strong requirements: canonicalization, deduplication, and sampling, to name a few.

Conclusion

Doing big data science is equivalent to conducting both descriptive and inferential analyses using distributed computing techniques, with the hopes that the volume, variety, and velocity of data that makes distributed computing necessary will lead to deeper or more targeted insights. Furthermore, the outcomes of doing data science are *data products*—products that derive their value from data and generate new data in return. As a result, the integration of the various ecosystem tools is usually architected around the data product lifecycle.

The data product lifecycle wraps an inner machine learning lifecycle that contains two primary phases: a *build* phase and an *operational* phase. The build phase requires feature analysis and data exploration; the operational phase is meant to expose the data-generating aspects of the products to real users who interact meaningfully with the data product, generating data that can be used to adapt models to make them more accurate or generalizable. The data product lifecycle provides workflows to build and operationalize models by providing ingestion, data wrangling, exploration, and computational frameworks. Most production architectures are a combination of hands-on, steered (data scientists drive the computation) analyses and automatic data processing workflows. These workflows are provided and managed by the ecosystem of Hadoop technologies.

The ecosystem of Hadoop and distributed computing technologies is vast and ever-expanding, but throughout the course of this book we've discussed the essential underlying concepts, as well as some of the considerations and tradeoffs to be made when evaluating and choosing Hadoop-based tools and algorithms to implement the data product workflow as it pertains to your requirements. Where you choose to go from here, whether that be experimenting and applying some of these tools and patterns on your own cluster, or investigating Hadoop or its related projects more deeply, is up to you. But we hope that the concepts, tools, and techniques that we've introduced in this book have provided a well-informed starting point, and can continue to serve as a touchstone for you to refer back to throughout your distributed data analysis journey.

If you're reading this, congratulations! You've finally reached the end of what we hope was a broad yet practical guide to performing distributed data analysis with Hadoop. Our goal with this book was to equip you with enough of the fundamentals and context to understand how distributed computing with Hadoop can be used to perform powerful data analysis at scale, and to prepare you to dive deeper into some of the subtopics and technologies that we introduced.

Creating a Hadoop Pseudo-Distributed Development Environment

In order to execute the code in this book, you'll need to set up a development environment. Hadoop developers usually test their scripts and code on a *pseudo-distributed environment* (also known as a *single node setup*), which is a virtual machine that runs all of the Hadoop daemons simultaneously on a single machine.

These instructions will help you install a pseudo-distributed environment with Hadoop 2.5.0 on Ubuntu 14.04.

Quick Start

There are a couple of options if you are not familiar with systems administration on Linux, or do not wish to work through the process of installing Hadoop yourself. We have provided a VMDK for you to use in the virtualization software of your choice (e.g., VirtualBox or VMWare Fusion). Alternatively, both Hortonworks and Cloudera supply virtual machines for quick download.

To get up and started quickly, simply download the VM and run it in your favorite virtualization software. Be aware that if you do use Cloudera or Hortonworks distributions, the environment may be subtly different than the one we use. To get everything set up, either download the preconfigured machine or follow the steps described here.

If you are using the VMDK supplied by us, to log in to the machine use the username and password as follows:

```
username: student
password: password
```

If you're brave enough to set up the environment yourself, go ahead and move to the next section!

Setting Up Linux

Before you can get started installing Hadoop, you'll need to have a Linux environment configured and ready to use. These instructions assume that you can get an Ubuntu 14.04 distribution installed on the machine of your choice, either in a dual booted configuration or using a virtual machine. Using Ubuntu Server or Ubuntu Desktop is left to your preference, as you'll also need to be familiar working with the command line.

Our base environment is Ubuntu x64 Desktop 14.04 LTS.

Make sure your system is fully up to date by running the following commands:

```
$ sudo apt-get update && sudo apt-get upgrade
$ sudo apt-get install build-essential ssh lzop git rsync curl
$ sudo apt-get install python-dev python-setuptools
$ sudo apt-get install libcurl4-openssl-dev
$ sudo easy_install pip
$ sudo pip install virtualenv virtualenvwrapper python-dateutil
```

Creating a Hadoop User

In order to secure our Hadoop services, we will make sure that Hadoop is run as a Hadoop-specific user and group. This user would be able to initiate SSH connections to other nodes in a cluster, but not have administrative access to do damage to the operating system upon which the service was running. Implementing Linux permissions also helps secure HDFS and is the start of preparing a secure computing cluster.

This tutorial is not meant for operational implementation; however, as a data scientist these permissions may save you some headache in the long run, so it is helpful to have the permissions in place in your development environment. Needless to say, this will also ensure that the Hadoop installation is separate from other software applications and will help organize the maintenance of the machine.

Create the hadoop user and group, then add the student user to the Hadoop group:

```
$ sudo addgroup hadoop
$ sudo adduser --ingroup hadoop hadoop
$ sudo usermod -a -G hadoop student
```

Once you have logged out and logged back in (or restarted the machine) you should be able to see that you've been added to the Hadoop group by issuing the groups command.

Configuring SSH

SSH is required and must be installed on your system to use Hadoop (and to better manage the virtual environment, especially if you're using a headless Ubuntu). Generate some `ssh` keys for the `hadoop` user by issuing the following commands:

```
$ sudo su hadoop
$ ssh-keygen
Generating public/private rsa key pair.
Enter file in which to save the key (/home/student/.ssh/id_rsa):
Created directory '/home/student/.ssh'.
Enter passphrase (empty for no passphrase):
Enter same passphrase again:
Your identification has been saved in /home/student/.ssh/id_rsa.
Your public key has been saved in /home/student/.ssh/id_rsa.pub.
[... snip ...]
```

Simply press Enter at all the prompts to accept the default and to create a key that does not require a password to authenticate (this is required for Hadoop). It is good practice to keep an administrative user separate from the Hadoop user because of the password-less SSH requirement; however, because this is a developer cluster, we'll take the shortcut of making the student user the Hadoop user.

In order to allow the key to be used to SSH into the box, copy the public key to the *authorized_keys* file with the following command:

```
$ cat ~/.ssh/id_rsa.pub >> ~/.ssh/authorized_keys
$ chmod 600 ~/.ssh/authorized_keys
```

You should be able to download this key and use it to SSH into the Ubuntu environment. To test the SSH key, issue the following command:

```
$ ssh -l hadoop localhost
```

If this completes without asking you for a password, then you have successfully configured SSH for Hadoop.

Installing Java

Hadoop and most of the Hadoop ecosystem require Java to run. Hadoop requires a minimum of Oracle Java 1.6.x or greater, and used to recommend particular versions of Java to use with Hadoop. However, now Hadoop maintains a reporting of the various JDKs that work well with Hadoop. Ubuntu does not maintain an Oracle JDK in Ubuntu repositories because it is proprietary code, so instead we will install OpenJDK. For more information on supported Java versions, see Hadoop Java Versions (*http://wiki.apache.org/hadoop/HadoopJavaVersions*) and for information about installing different versions on Ubuntu, see Installing Java on Ubuntu (*https:// help.ubuntu.com/community/Java*).

```
$ sudo apt-get install openjdk-7-*
```

Do a quick check to ensure the right version of Java is installed:

```
$ java -version
java version "1.7.0_55"
OpenJDK Runtime Environment (IcedTea 2.4.7) (7u55-2.4.7-1ubuntu1)
OpenJDK 64-Bit Server VM (build 24.51-b03, mixed mode)
```

Hadoop is currently built and tested on both OpenJDK and Oracle's JDK/JRE.

Disabling IPv6

It has been reported for a while now that Hadoop running on Ubuntu has a conflict with IPv6, and ever since Hadoop 0.20, Ubuntu users have been disabling IPv6 on their clustered boxes. It is unclear whether this is still a bug in the latest versions of Hadoop, but in a single node or pseudo-distributed environment we will have no need for IPv6, so it is best to simply disable it and not worry about any potential problems.

Edit the */etc/sysctl.conf* file by executing the following lines of code:

```
$ gksu gedit /etc/sysctl.conf
```

Then add the following lines to the end of the file:

```
# disable ipv6
net.ipv6.conf.all.disable_ipv6 = 1
net.ipv6.conf.default.disable_ipv6 = 1
net.ipv6.conf.lo.disable_ipv6 = 1
```

For this change to take effect, reboot your computer. Once it has rebooted, check the status with the following command:

```
$ cat /proc/sys/net/ipv6/conf/all/disable_ipv6
```

If the output is 0 then IPv6 is enabled, if it is 1 then we have successfully disabled IPv6.

Installing Hadoop

To get Hadoop, you'll need to download the release of your choice from one of the Apache Download Mirrors (*http://www.apache.org/dyn/closer.cgi/hadoop/common/*). These instructions will download the current stable vesion of Hadoop with YARN at the time of this writing, Hadoop 2.5.0.

After you've selected a mirror, type the following commands into a Terminal window, replacing http://apache.mirror.com/hadoop-2.5.0/ with the mirror URL that you selected and that is best for your region:

```
$ curl -O http://apache.mirror.com/hadoop-2.5.0/hadoop-2.5.0.tar.gz
```

You can verify the download by ensuring that the `md5sum` matches the `md5sum`, which should also be available at the mirror:

```
$ md5sum hadoop-2.5.0.tar.gz
5d5f0c8969075f8c0a15dc616ad36b8a  hadoop-2.5.0.tar.gz
```

Of course, you can use any mechanism you wish to download Hadoop—`wget` or a browser will work just fine.

Unpacking

After obtaining the compressed tarball, the next step is to unpack it. You can use an Archive Manager or simply follow the instructions that follow. The most significant decision that you have to make is where to unpack Hadoop.

The Linux operating system depends upon a hierarchical directory structure to function. At the root, many directories that you've heard of have specific purposes: */etc* is used to store configuration files and */home* is used to store user specific files. Most applications find themselves in a variety of locations; for example, */bin* and */sbin* include programs that are vital for the OS and */usr/bin* and */usr/sbin* are for programs that are not vital but are system-wide. The directory */usr/local* is for locally installed programs and */var* is used for program data including caches and logs. You can read more about these directories in this Stack Exchange post (*http://bit.ly/1Tr6QuW*).

A good choice to move Hadoop to is the */opt* and */srv* directories; */opt* contains non-packaged programs, usually source; a lot of developers stick their code there for deployments. The */srv* directory stands for services; Hadoop, HBase, Hive and others run as services on your machine, so this seems like a great place to put things—and it's a standard location that's easy to get to—so let's stick everything there. Enter the following commands:

```
$ tar -xzf hadoop-2.5.0.tar.gz
$ sudo mv hadoop-2.5.0 /srv/
$ sudo chown -R hadoop:hadoop /srv/hadoop-2.5.0
$ sudo chmod g+w -R /srv/hadoop-2.5.0
$ sudo ln -s /srv/hadoop-2.5.0 /srv/hadoop
```

These commands unpack Hadoop, move it to the service directory where we will keep all of our Hadoop and cluster services, then set permissions. Finally, we create a symlink to the version of Hadoop that we would like to use, which makes it easy to upgrade our Hadoop distribution in the future.

Environment

In order to ensure everything executes correctly, we are going to set some environment variables so that Hadoop executes in its correct context. Enter the following command on the command line to open up a text editor with the profile of the hadoop user to change the environment variables:

```
$ gksu gedit /home/hadoop/.bashrc
```

Add the following lines to this file:

```
# Set the Hadoop-related environment variables
export HADOOP_HOME=/srv/hadoop
export PATH=$PATH:$HADOOP_HOME/bin

# Set the JAVA_HOME
export JAVA_HOME=/usr/lib/jvm/java-7-openjdk-amd64
```

We'll also add some convenience functionality to the student user environment. Open the student user bash aliases file with the following command:

```
$ gedit ~/.bash_aliases
```

Add the following contents to that file:

```
# Set the Hadoop-related environment variables
export HADOOP_HOME=/srv/hadoop
export HADOOP_STREAMING=$HADOOP_HOME/share/hadoop/tools/lib/
hadoop-streaming-2.5.0.jar
export PATH=$PATH:$HADOOP_HOME/bin

# Set the JAVA_HOME
export JAVA_HOME=/usr/lib/jvm/java-7-openjdk-amd64

# Helpful aliases
alias ..="cd .."
alias ...="cd ../.."
alias hfs="hadoop fs"
alias hls="hfs -ls"
```

These simple aliases may save you a lot of typing in the long run! Feel free to add any other helpers that you think might be useful in your development work.

Check that your environment configuration has worked by running a Hadoop command:

```
$ hadoop version
Hadoop 2.5.0
Subversion http://svn.apache.org/repos/asf/hadoop/common -r 1616291
Compiled by jenkins on 2014-08-06T17:31Z
Compiled with protoc 2.5.0
From source with checksum 423dcd5a752eddd8e45ead6fd5ff9a24
This command was run using /srv/hadoop-2.5.0/share/hadoop/common/
hadoop-common-2.5.0.jar
```

If that ran with no errors and displayed output similar to what is shown here, then everything has been configured correctly up to this point.

Hadoop Configuration

The penultimate step to setting up Hadoop as a pseudo-distributed node is to edit configuration files for the Hadoop environment, the MapReduce site, the HDFS site, and the YARN site. This will mostly entail configuration file editing.

Edit the *hadoop-env.sh* file by entering the following on the command line:

```
$ gedit $HADOOP_HOME/etc/hadoop/hadoop-env.sh
```

The most important part of this configuration is to change the following line:

```
# The Java implementation to use
export JAVA_HOME=/usr/lib/jvm/java-7-openjdk-amd64
```

Next, edit the core site configuration file:

```
$ gedit $HADOOP_HOME/etc/hadoop/core-site.xml
```

Replace the <configuration></configuration> with the following:

```
<configuration>
    <property>
        <name>fs.default.name</name>
        <value>hdfs://localhost:9000</value>
    </property>
    <property>
        <name>hadoop.tmp.dir</name>
        <value>/var/app/hadoop/data</value>
    </property>
</configuration>
```

Edit the mapreduce site configuration following by copying the template then opening the file for editing:

```
$ cp $HADOOP_HOME/etc/hadoop/mapred-site.xml.template \
     $HADOOP_HOME/etc/hadoop/mapred-site.xml
$ gedit $HADOOP_HOME/etc/hadoop/mapred-site.xml
```

Replace the <configuration></configuration> with the following:

```
<configuration>
    <property>
        <name>mapreduce.framework.name</name>
        <value>yarn</value>
    </property>
</configuration>
```

Now edit the hdfs site configuration by editing the following file:

```
$ gedit $HADOOP_HOME/etc/hadoop/hdfs-site.xml
```

Replace the <configuration></configuration> with the following:

```
<configuration>
    <property>
```

```
        <name>dfs.replication</name>
        <value>1</value>
    </property>
</configuration>
```

Finally, edit the yarn site configuration file:

```
$ gedit $HADOOP_HOME/etc/hadoop/yarn-site.xml
```

And update the configuration as follows:

```
<configuration>
    <property>
        <name>yarn.nodemanager.aux-services</name>
        <value>mapreduce_shuffle</value>
    </property>
    <property>
        <name>yarn.nodemanager.aux-services.mapreduce_shuffle.class</name>
        <value>org.apache.hadoop.mapred.ShuffleHandler</value>
    </property>
    <property>
        <name>yarn.resourcemanager.resource-tracker.address</name>
        <value>localhost:8025</value>
    </property>
    <property>
        <name>yarn.resourcemanager.scheduler.address</name>
        <value>localhost:8030</value>
    </property>
    <property>
        <name>yarn.resourcemanager.address</name>
        <value>localhost:8050</value>
    </property>
</configuration>
```

With these files edited, Hadoop should be fully configured as a pseudo-distributed environment.

Formatting the Namenode

The final step before we can turn Hadoop on is to format the Namenode. The Namenode is in charge of HDFS—the distributed file system. The Namenode on this machine is going to keep its files in the */var/app/hadoop/data* directory. We need to initialize this directory, then format the Namenode to properly use it:

```
$ sudo mkdir -p /var/app/hadoop/data
$ sudo chown hadoop:hadoop -R /var/app/hadoop
$ sudo su hadoop
$ hadoop namenode -format
```

You should see a bunch of Java messages scrolling down the page. If the namenode command has executed successfully (there should be directories inside of the */var/app/hadoop/data* directory including a *dfs* directory) then Hadoop is set up and ready to use!

Starting Hadoop

At this point, we can start and run our Hadoop daemons. When you formatted the Namenode, you switched to being the `hadoop` user with the `sudo su hadoop` command. If you're still that user, go ahead and execute the following commands:

```
$ $HADOOP_HOME/sbin/start-dfs.sh
$ $HADOOP_HOME/sbin/start-yarn.sh
```

The daemons should start up and issue messages about where they are logging to and other important information. If you get asked about your SSH key, just type y at the prompt. You can see the processes that are running via the `jps` command:

```
$ jps
5298 Jps
4690 ResourceManager
4541 SecondaryNameNode
4813 NodeManager
4227 NameNode
```

If the processes are not running, then something has gone wrong. You can also access the Hadoop cluster administration site by opening a browser and pointing it to *http://localhost:8088*; this should bring up a page with the Hadoop logo and a table of applications.

To wrap up the configuration, prepare a space on HDFS for our student account to store data and to run analytical jobs on:

```
$ hadoop fs -mkdir -p /user/student
$ hadoop fs -chown student:student /user/student
```

You can now exit from the `hadoop` user's shell with the `exit` command.

Restarting Hadoop

If you reboot your machine, the Hadoop daemons will stop running and will not automatically be restarted. If you are attempting to run a Hadoop command and you get a "Connection refused" message, it is likely because the daemons are not running. You can check this by issuing the `jps` command as `sudo`:

```
$ sudo jps
```

To restart Hadoop in the case that it shuts down, issue the following commands:

```
$ sudo -H -u hadoop $HADOOP_HOME/sbin/start-dfs.sh
$ sudo -H -u hadoop $HADOOP_HOME/sbin/start-yarn.sh
```

The processes should start up again as the dedicated hadoop user and you'll be back on your way!

Installing Hadoop Ecosystem Products

In addition to the core functionality provided in Hadoop, this book covers several other Hadoop ecosystem projects that are built on top of Hadoop. In a typical setting, these products are often installed either on the same cluster that hosts Hadoop and YARN, or are configured to connect to the Hadoop cluster. In this book, we will assume that you have setup and configured Apache Hadoop in a single node, pseudo-distributed mode. However, there are several other options to get up and running with a single node Hadoop cluster along with the Hadoop ecosystem products that we will discuss in this book.

Packaged Hadoop Distributions

The easiest way to get up and running with a single-machine configuration of Hadoop is to install one of the virtualized Hadoop distributions provided by the major Hadoop vendors. These include Cloudera's Quickstart VM (*http://bit.ly/ 1YWtzPC*), Hortonworks Sandbox (*http://bit.ly/1YWtyLy*), or MapR's sandbox for Hadoop (*http://bit.ly/1YWtz27*). These virtual machines contain a single-node Hadoop cluster in addition to the popular Apache Hadoop ecosystem projects as well as proprietary applications and tools that are included in a simple turn-key bundle. You can use your preferred virtualization software such as VMWare Player (*https:// www.vmware.com/products/player*) or Virtualbox (*https://www.virtualbox.org/wiki/ Downloads*) to run these VMs.

Self-Installation of Apache Hadoop Ecosystem Products

If you are not using a packaged distribution of Hadoop, but instead installing Apache Hadoop manually, then you will also need to manually install and configure the various Hadoop ecosystem projects that we discuss in this book to work with your Hadoop installation.

For the most part, installing services (e.g., Hive, HBase, or others) in the Hadoop environment we have set up will consist of the following:

1. Download the release tarball of the service
2. Unpack the release to the */srv/* directory (where we have been installing our Hadoop services) and create a symlink from the release to a simple name
3. Configure environment variables with the paths to the service
4. Configure the service to run in pseudo-distributed mode

In this appendix, we'll walk through the steps to install Sqoop to work with our pseudo-distributed Hadoop cluster. These steps can be reproduced for nearly all the other Hadoop ecosystem projects that we discuss in this book.

Basic Installation and Configuration Steps

Let's start by downloading the latest stable release of Sqoop from the Apache Sqoop Download Mirrors (*http://www.apache.org/dyn/closer.cgi/sqoop/1.4.6*), which as of this writing is currently at version 1.4.6. Make sure you are a user with admin (sudo) privileges and grab the version of Sqoop that is compatible with your version of Hadoop (in this example, Hadoop 2.5.1):

```
~$ wget http://apache.arvixe.com/sqoop/1.4.6/sqoop-1.4.6.bin__
hadoop-2.0.4-alpha.tar.gz
~$ sudo mv sqoop-1.4.6.bin__hadoop-2.0.4-alpha.tar.gz /srv/
~$ cd /srv
/srv$ sudo tar -xvf sqoop-1.4.6.bin__hadoop-2.0.4-alpha.tar.gz
/srv$ sudo chown -R hadoop:hadoop sqoop-1.4.6.bin__hadoop-2.0.4-alpha
/srv$ sudo ln -s $(pwd)/sqoop-1.4.6.bin__hadoop-2.0.4-alpha $(pwd)/sqoop
```

Now switch to the hadoop user using the sudo su command and edit your Bash configuration to add some environment variables for convenience:

```
/srv$ sudo su hadoop
$ vim ~/.bashrc
```

Add the following environment variables to your bashrc profile:

```
# Sqoop aliases
export SQOOP_HOME=/srv/sqoop
export PATH=$PATH:$SQOOP_HOME/bin
```

Then source the profile to add the new variables to the current shell environment:

```
~$ $ source ~/.bashrc
```

We can verify that Sqoop is successfully installed by running `sqoop help` from $SQOOP_HOME:

```
/srv$ cd $SQOOP_HOME
/srv/sqoop$ sqoop help

15/06/04 21:57:40 INFO sqoop.Sqoop: Running Sqoop version: 1.4.6
usage: sqoop COMMAND [ARGS]

Available commands:
  codegen            Generate code to interact with database records
  create-hive-table  Import a table definition into Hive
  eval               Evaluate a SQL statement and display the results
  export             Export an HDFS directory to a database table
  help               List available commands
  import             Import a table from a database to HDFS
  import-all-tables  Import tables from a database to HDFS
  job                Work with saved jobs
  list-databases     List available databases on a server
  list-tables        List available tables in a database
  merge              Merge results of incremental imports
  metastore          Run a standalone Sqoop metastore
  version            Display version information

See 'sqoop help COMMAND' for information on a specific command.
```

If you see any warnings displayed pertaining to HCatalog, you can safely ignore them for now. As you can see, Sqoop provides a list of import- and export-specific commands and tools that expect to connect with either a database or Hadoop data source.

Sqoop processes are executed either manually, by running a Sqoop command, or by an upstream system that either schedules or triggers a Sqoop operation. However, some of the other products that we'll install include commands to start daemonized processes. These running processes, like all Java processes, can be listed by using the `jps` command. The `jps` command is very useful in verifying that all expected Hadoop processes are running; for example, if you followed the instructions to start Hadoop as outlined in Appendix A, you should see the following processes:

```
~$ jps
10029 NameNode
10670 NodeManager
21694 Jps
10187 DataNode
10373 SecondaryNameNode
11034 JobHistoryServer
10541 ResourceManager
```

If you do not see these processes, review how to start and stop Hadoop services, discussed in Appendix A and Chapter 2.

Sqoop-Specific Configurations

Before we can import our MySQL table data into HDFS, we will need to download the MySQL JDBC connector driver and add it to Sqoop's *lib* folder:

```
~$ wget http://dev.mysql.com/get/Downloads/Connector-J/mysql-connector-java-5.1.
30.tar.gz
~$ tar -xvf mysql-connector-java-5.1.30.tar.gz
~$ cd mysql-connector-java-5.1.30
$ sudo cp mysql-connector-java-5.1.30-bin.jar /srv/sqoop/lib/
$ cd $SQOOP_HOME
```

This allows Sqoop to connect to our MySQL database. You should now have successfully installed Sqoop and MySQL server and client in your local development environment, and configured Sqoop to successfully import from and export to MySQL.

Hive-Specific Configuration

Hive is installed similarly to Sqoop, but once we've installed Hive we need to configure it to run on our Hadoop single node cluster. Specifically, Hive requires us to configure the Hive warehouse (which will contain Hive's data files) and the metastore database (which will contain the metadata for Hive's schemas and tables).

Hive warehouse directory

By default, Hive data is stored in HDFS, in a warehouse directory located under */user/hive/warehouse*. We'll need to make sure this location exists in HDFS and is writable by all Hive users. If you want to change this location, you can modify the value for the *hive.metastore.warehouse.dir* property by overriding the configuration in *$HIVE_HOME/conf/hive-site.xml*.

For our single node configuration, let's assume we'll use the default warehouse directory and create the necessary directories in HDFS. We'll create a */tmp* directory, a *hive* user directory, and the default warehouse directory:

```
$ hadoop fs -mkdir /tmp
$ hadoop fs -mkdir -p /user/hive
$ hadoop fs -mkdir /user/hive/warehouse
```

We also need to set the permissions for these directories so they can be written to by Hive:

```
$ hadoop fs -chmod g+w /tmp
$ hadoop fs -chmod g+w /user/hive/warehouse
```

Additionally, Hive will write a temporary directory where you configured your local Hadoop temporary data directory. You'll need to make sure the hadoop group has write permissions to create directories in that path as well:

```
$ chmod g+w /var/app/hadoop/data
```

Hive metastore database

Hive requires a metastore service backend, which Hive uses to store table schema definitions, partitions, and related metadata. The Hive metastore service also provides clients (including Hive) with access to the metastore info via the metastore service API.

The metastore can be configured in a few different ways, with the default Hive configuration using an embedded metastore called the Derby SQL Server that provides single-process storage where the Hive driver, metastore interface, and Derby database all share the same JVM. This is a convenient configuration for development and unit testing, but will not support true cluster-configurations because only a single user can connect to the Derby database at any given time. Production-ready candidates would include databases like MySQL or PostgreSQL.

For the purposes of this chapter, we will use the embedded Derby server as our metastore service. But we encourage you to refer to the Apache Hive manual for installing a local or remote metastore server for production-level configurations.

By default, Derby will create a *metastore_db* subdirectory under the current working directory from which you started your Hive session. However, if you change your working directory, Derby will fail to find the previous metastore and will re-create it. To avoid this behavior, we need to configure a permanent location for the metastore database by updating the metastore configuration:

```
~$ cd $HIVE_HOME/conf
/srv/hive/conf$ sudo cp hive-default.xml.template hive-site.xml
/srv/hive/conf$ vim hive-site.xml
```

Find the property with the name `javax.jdo.option.ConnectionURL` and update it to an absolute path:

```
<property>
    <name>javax.jdo.option.ConnectionURL</name>
    <value>jdbc:derby:;databaseName=/home/hadoop/metastore_db;create=true</value>
    <description>JDBC connect string for a JDBC metastore</description>
</property>
```

Once you've updated the `ConnectionURL` databaseName, save and close the file.

Verifying Hive is running

We can now verify that Hive is configured properly and able to run on our pseudo-distributed Hadoop cluster by starting the pre-packaged Hive command-line interface (CLI) from Hive's installation directory.

To start the Hive CLI from the `$HIVE_HOME` directory:

```
~$ cd $HIVE_HOME
/srv/hive$ bin/hive
```

If Hive is properly configured, this command will initiate the CLI and display a Hive CLI prompt:

```
hive>
```

You may see a warning related to a deprecated Hive metastore configuration:

```
WARN conf.HiveConf: DEPRECATED: hive.metastore.ds.retry.* no longer has any
effect.
Use hive.hmshandler.retry.* instead
```

But if you see any errors, check your configuration based on the previous recommendations and try again. At any time, you can exit the Hive CLI using the following command:

```
hive> exit;
```

You are now ready to use Hive in local and pseudo-distributed mode to run Hive scripts.

HBase-Specific Configurations

HBase requires some additional configuration after installation, and unlike Sqoop and Hive, requires daemon processes to be started so that we can interact with HBase.

Once you have unpacked and installed HBase, within the HBase directory is a /conf directory that includes the configuration files for HBase. We'll edit the config file conf/hbase-site.xml, to configure HBase to run in pseudo-distributed mode with HDFS and write ZooKeeper files to a local directory. Edit the HBase configuration with vim:

```
$ vim $HBASE_HOME/conf/hbase-site.xml
```

Then add three overrides to the configuration as follows:

```
<configuration>
    <property>
        <name>hbase.rootdir</name>
        <value>hdfs://localhost:9000/hbase</value>
    </property>
    <property>
        <name>hbase.cluster.distributed</name>
        <value>true</value>
    </property>
    <property>
        <name>hbase.zookeeper.property.dataDir</name>
        <value>/home/hadoop/zookeeper</value>
    </property>
</configuration>
```

With this configuration, HBase will start up an HBase Master process, a ZooKeeper server, and a RegionServer process. By default, HBase configures all directories to a */tmp* path, which means you'll lose all your data whenever your server reboots unless you change it as most operating systems clear */tmp* on restart. By updating the `hbase.zookeeper.property.dataDir` property, HBase will now write to a reliable data path under the `hadoop` home directory.

 HBase requires write permission to the local directory to maintain ZooKeeper files. Because we'll be running HBase as the `hadoop` user (or whichever user you've set up to start HDFS and YARN), make sure that the `dataDir` is configured to a path that the Hadoop user can write to (e.g., */home/hadoop*).

We also need to update our HBase `env` settings with the `JAVA_HOME` path. To do this, uncomment and modify the following settings in *conf/hbase-env.sh*:

```
export JAVA_HOME=/usr/lib/jvm/java-7-oracle
```

HBase should now be configured properly to run in pseudo-distributed mode on our single node cluster.

Starting HBase

We're now ready to start the HBase processes. But before we start HBase, we should ensure that Hadoop is running:

```
/srv/hbase$ jps
4051 NodeManager
3523 DataNode
3709 SecondaryNameNode
3375 NameNode
9436 Jps
3921 ResourceManager
```

If the HDFS and YARN processes are not running, make sure you start them first with the scripts under *$HADOOP_HOME/sbin*.

Now we can start up HBase!

```
/srv/hbase$ bin/start-hbase.sh
localhost: starting zookeeper, logging to /srv/hbase/bin/../logs/
hbase-hadoop-zookeeper-ubuntu.out
starting master, logging to /srv/hbase/logs/
hbase-hadoop-master-ubuntu.out
localhost: starting regionserver, logging to
/srv/hbase/bin/../logs/hbase-hadoop-regionserver-ubuntu.out
```

We can verify which processes are running by using the `jps` command, which should display the running Hadoop processes as well as the HBase and ZooKeeper processes, HMaster, HQuorumPeer, and HRegionServer:

```
/srv/hbase$
4051 NodeManager
10225 Jps
3523 DataNode
3709 SecondaryNameNode
3375 NameNode
3921 ResourceManager
9708 HQuorumPeer
9778 HMaster
9949 HRegionServer
```

You can stop HBase and ZooKeeper at any time with the *stop-hbase.sh* script:

```
/srv/hbase$ bin/stop-hbase.sh
stopping hbase.................
HBase Shell
```

With HBase started, we can connect to the running instance with the HBase shell:

```
/srv/hbase$ bin/start-hbase.sh
/srv/hbase$ bin/hbase shell
```

You will be presented with a prompt:

```
HBase Shell; enter 'help<RETURN>' for list of supported commands.
Type "exit<RETURN>" to leave the HBase Shell
Version 0.98.9-hadoop2, r96878ece501b0643e879254645d7f3a40eaf101f,
Mon Dec 15 23:00:20 PST 2014

hbase(main):001:0>
```

For documentation on the commands that the HBase shell supports, use help to get a listing of commands:

```
hbase(main):001:0>  help
```

We can also check the status of our HBase cluster by using the status command:

```
hbase(main):002:0> status
1 servers, 0 dead, 3.0000 average load
```

To exit the shell, simply use the exit command:

```
hbase(main):003:0> exit
```

You are now ready to start using HBase in pseudo-distributed mode. It is important to remember that before you can interact with the HBase shell, Hadoop processes and HBase processes must be started and running.

Installing Spark

Spark is very simple to get set up and running on your local machine, and generally follows the pattern that we've seen for our other Hadoop ecosystem installations. Given the instructions for a pseudo-distributed Ubuntu machine, we already have the

---

primary requirements for Spark, namely Java 7+ and Python 2.6+. Ensure that the `java` and `python` programs are on your path and that the `$JAVA_HOME` environment variable is set (as configured previously).

In previous installation instructions, we used `wget` or `curl` to fetch tarballs directly from Apache mirrors. However, for Spark, things are a bit more nuanced. Open a browser and follow these steps to download the correct version of Spark:

1. Navigate to the Spark downloads page (*http://spark.apache.org/downloads.html*).
2. Select the latest Spark release (1.5.2 at the time of this writing) and ensure to select a prebuilt package for Hadoop 2.4 or later and download directly.

Spark releases tend to be frequent, so to ensure we have a system where we can download new versions of Spark and immediately use them, we will unpack the Spark bundle to our services directory, but then symlink the version to a generic *spark* directory. When we want to update the version, we simply download the latest release, and redirect the symlink to the new version. In this manner, all of our environment variables and configurations will be maintained for the new version as well!

First follow our standard convention to install the Hadoop ecosystem service:

```
$ tar -xzf spark-1.5.2-bin-hadoop2.4.tgz
$ mv spark-1.5.2-bin-hadoop2.4 /srv/spark-1.5.2
```

Then create the symlink version of Spark:

```
$ ln -s /srv/spark-1.5.2 /srv/spark
```

Edit your Bash profile to add Spark to your `$PATH` and to set the `$SPARK_HOME` environment variable. As before, we will switch to the Hadoop user, but you can also add this to the `student` user profile as well:

```
$ sudo su hadoop
$ vim ~/.bashrc
```

Add the following lines to the profile:

```
export SPARK_HOME=/srv/spark
export PATH=$SPARK_HOME/bin:$PATH
```

Then source the profile (or restart the terminal) to add these new variables to the environment. Once this is done, you should be able to run a local `pyspark` interpreter:

```
$ pyspark
Python 2.7.10 (default, Jun 23 2015, 21:58:51)
[GCC 4.2.1 Compatible Apple LLVM 6.1.0 (clang-602.0.53)] on darwin
Type "help", "copyright", "credits" or "license" for more information.
Using Spark's default log4j profile: org/apache/spark/log4j-defaults.properties
[... snip ...]
Welcome to
```

```
       ___              __
   / __/__  ___ _____/ /__
  _\ \/ _ \/ _ `/ __/  '_/
 /__ / .__/\_,_/_/ /_/\_\   version 1.5.2
    /_/

Using Python version 2.7.10 (default, Jun 23 2015 21:58:51)
SparkContext available as sc, HiveContext available as sqlContext.
>>>
```

At this point, Spark is installed and ready to use on your local machine in *standalone mode*. For our purposes, this is enough to run the examples on the book. You can also use `spark-submit` to submit jobs directly to the YARN resource manager that is running in pseudo-distributed mode if you wish to test the Spark/Hadoop connection. For more on this and other topics including using Spark on EC2, or setting Spark up with iPython notebooks, see "Getting Started with Spark (in Python)" by Benjamin Bengfort (*http://bit.ly/1YWurDY*).

Minimizing the verbosity of Spark

The execution of Spark (and PySpark) can be extremely verbose, with many INFO log messages printed out to the screen. This is particularly annoying during development, as Python stack traces or the output of `print` statements can be lost. In order to reduce the verbosity of Spark, you can configure the *log4j* settings in *$SPARK_HOME/conf* as follows:

```
$ cp $SPARK_HOME/conf/log4j.properties.template \
      $SPARK_HOME/conf/log4j.properties
$ vim $SPARK_HOME/conf/log4j.properties
```

Edit the *log4j.properties* file and replace INFO with WARN at every line in the code, similar to:

```
# Set everything to be logged to the console
log4j.rootCategory=WARN, console
log4j.appender.console=org.apache.log4j.ConsoleAppender
log4j.appender.console.target=System.err
log4j.appender.console.layout=org.apache.log4j.PatternLayout
log4j.appender.console.layout.ConversionPattern=%d{yy/MM/dd HH:mm:ss} %p %c{1}:
%m%n

# Settings to quiet third-party logs that are too verbose
log4j.logger.org.eclipse.jetty=WARN
log4j.logger.org.eclipse.jetty.util.component.AbstractLifeCycle=ERROR
log4j.logger.org.apache.spark.repl.SparkIMain$exprTyper=WARN
log4j.logger.org.apache.spark.repl.SparkILoop$SparkILoopInterpreter=WARN
```

Now when you run PySpark you should get much simpler output messages!

Glossary

accessible

In the context of a computing cluster, a node is accessible if it is reachable through the network. In other contexts, a tool or library is accessible if it easily accessed and understandable to particular groups.

accumulator

A shared variable to which only associative operations might be applied, like addition (particularly in Spark, called counters in MapReduce). Because associative operations are order independent, accumulators can stay consistent in a distributed environment, no matter the order of operations.

actions and transformations

See transformations and actions.

agent

Services, usually background processes, that run routinely on the behalf of a user, performing tasks independently. Flume agents are the building blocks of data flows, which ingest and wrangle data from a source to a channel and eventually a sink.

anonymous functions

A function that is not specified by an identifier (variable name). These functions are typically constructed at runtime and passed as arguments to higher-order functions. They can also be used to easily create closures. Anonymous functions are

passed to Spark operations to define their behavior. See also closure and lambda function.

application programming interface (API)

A collection of routines, protocols, or interfaces that specify how software components should interact. The MapReduce API specifies interfaces for constructing `Mapper`, `Reducer`, and `Job` subclasses that define MapReduce behavior. Similarly, Spark has an API of transformations and actions that can be applied to an RDD.

ApplicationMaster

In YARN, an ApplicationMaster is an instance of a framework-specific library (e.g. MapReduce, Spark, or Hive in this book). The ApplicationMaster negotiates for resources from the ResourceManager, executes processes on NodeManagers, tracks the job status, and monitors progress.

associative

In mathematics, associative operations give the same result, however grouped, so long as the order remains the same. Associative operations are important in a distributed context, because it allows you to allow multiple processors to simultaneously compute grouped suboperations, before computing the final whole.

Avro

Apache Avro, developed within Apache Hadoop, is a remote procedure call (RPC) data serialization framework that uses JSON for defining schema and types, then serializes data in a compact binary format.

bag of words

In text processing, a model that encodes documents by the frequency or presence of their most important tokens or words without taking order into account.

bias

In machine learning, the error due to bias is the difference between the expected average prediction of our model and correct values. Bias measures how incorrect, generally, a model will be. As bias increases, variance decreases. See also variance.

big data

Computational methodologies that leverages extremely large datasets to discover patterns, trends, and relationships especially relating to human behavior and interaction. Big data specifically refers to data that is too large, cumbersome, or ephemeral for a single machine to reliably compute upon. Therefore big data techniques largely make use of distributed computing and database technology in order to compute results.

bigrams

A sequence of two consecutive tokens in a string or array. Tokens are typically letters, syllables, or words. Bigrams are a specific form of n-grams, where $n=2$.

block

Blocks are a method of storing large files in HDFS, by splitting the large file into individual chunks (blocks) of data of the same size (usually 128 MB). Blocks are replicated across DataNodes (with a default replication factor of 3) to provide data durability via redundancy and to allow data local computing.

bloom filter

A compact probabilistic data structure that can be used to test whether some data is a member of a set. False positives (indicating an element is a member of a set, when in fact it is not) are possible, but with a probability that can be set by allocating the size of the filter. False negatives (saying an element is is not a member of the set, when in fact it is) are not possible, giving Bloom filters a 100% recall.

broadcast variable

In Spark, a broadcast variable is a mechanism to create a read-only data structure that is transmitted on demand to every node in the cluster. Broadcast variables can be used to include extra information required for computation, the results of previous transformations, or lookup tables. They are cluster safe because they are read-only. See also distributed cache.

build phase

In machine learning, the build phase fits a model form to existing data, usually through some iterative optimization process. The build phase can include feature extraction, feature transformation, and regularization or hyperparameter tuning. The output of the build phase is a fitted model that can be used to make predictions.

byte array

A data structure composed of a fixed-length array of single bytes. This structure can store any type of information (numbers, strings, the contents of a file) and is very general; as a result, it is for row keys in HBase. See also row key.

Cascading

A scale-free data application development framework by Driven, Inc. that provides a high-level abstraction for MapReduce. It is typically used to define data flows or multi-part jobs as a directed acyclic graph.

centrally managed cluster

A computing cluster that contains nodes that serve in two distinct roles: manager (master) and worker. By having one or more coordinating management nodes in the cluster, decision making is centralized, and there is no need for consensus. Management nodes are responsible for data integrity, coordination, consistency, and handling client requests. See also peer-to-peer cluster.

centroids

In unsupervised machine learning (clustering), a centroid is a point in feature space that defines the center of a cluster. Although not all clustering algorithms are centroidal (generate centers), those that are define the center as the mean distance from every other point in the cluster.

channel

In computer science, a pathway through which information flows. Here we refer to channels in Apache Flume, which are passive stores or buffers that keep event information before they are collected by a downstream sink.

clickthroughs

A measurement of the effectiveness of an email, web page, or advertisement whose goal is to direct the user through to additional information. This metric is captured when a user clicks on a hyperlink, an action which causes a log record to be written on the server that handles the hyperlink request. For example, in a shopping cart application, we may measure the clickthroughs of the "buy" button.

client

Generally, the requestor of some computing service or resource, often a human user. In this book, we refer to the client as someone making a web request, submitting a MapReduce job, or the computer of the driver program in a Spark application. Clients can also have routine work done on their behalf by agents.

closure

A function that is bound to its own, closed execution environment such that in this environment there are bound variables. Because the environment maps variables that are assigned to the enclosing function, they cannot be modified by external processes, making closures useful for passing to a distributed context.

cloud computing

The use of shared computing resources in a remote data center (rather than utilizing local servers or personal devices). Often the shared computing resources are elastic, meaning that you can expand and contract usage and resource allocation on demand.

cluster

Generally, a collection of devices that perform collective or related computations. In Hadoop, a set of servers or computers that are running the HDFS and YARN daemons.

coefficients

In linear models, the coefficients are a vector of numeric quantities that define a hyperplane through the dependent variable space. You can use coefficients to predict a target value of some vector of dependent values by taking the dot product (or linear combination) of the variables with the coefficients.

collaborative filtering

A method of making automatic recommendations (filtering a large list of possible items) based on collective preferences from many users (collaboration). Collaborative filtering techniques are usually models developed using machine learning algorithms to make predictions that influence a user's behavior.

collector

A specialized type of Flume agent that listens to data from multiple upstream agents, aggregates their outputs, then collects the output to a log file, HDFS, or HBase.

column families

A set of related columns in HBase that share the same prefix and are logically and physically stored together.

column-oriented/columnar database

A database system that internally stores data as columns rather than rows, which can be more efficient for OLAP use cases that perform aggregations on select columns.

commutative

In mathematics, commutative operations return the same result no matter the order in which they are applied. Commutative operations are important in distributed computing, because they allow data to come in any order and still return the same result.

comparable

Specifically, that two objects are able to be compared using inequalities (e.g., greater than). Both Java and Python provide a data model allowing objects to be compared by defining methods that must return the result of the inequation.

complex key

A key (as in key/value pair) that is not a simple or primitive type like an integer or string. Most complex keys are in the form of compound keys; others can be nested data types (like dictionaries) or byte arrays that can represent any arbitrary data. See also compound key.

compound key

A key (as in key/value pair) that consists of two or more simple keys, usually stored in a tuple. Compound keys are important for data organization between map and reduce phases and between jobs.

computation

In this book, the use of computer processors to perform calculations upon some data. Here, computation is distinct from

"storage", computation acts on data inputs and produces data outputs.

conflict-free replicated data type (CRDT)

A specialized data structure that can be mutated concurrently through the application of associative and commutative operations. CRDTs provide eventual consistency and monotonicity (cannot be rolled back) in distributed systems. See also accumulator and counter.

consistency

The property of distributed computing wherein the failure of a single task does not affect the final result. Alternatively, that all nodes in the distributed system see the same view of the data.

contingency table

A table with two dimensions that allows the examination of the relationship between categorical variables. The table intersection of the table's dimensions (at each cell) contains the co-occurring frequency of the categorical values for each dimension.

counter

In MapReduce, a counter is a shared variable that can only be incremented by a fixed amount. Because summation is associative, the order of the incrementing doesn't matter and therefore can be used safely in a distributed context. See also accumulator.

daemon

A piece of computer software that runs in the background, independent of user input, usually as a service that listens to incoming information on the network and responds appropriately (a server).

data analyst

Data scientists whose primary focus involves the descriptive and inferential aspects of data product development, usually related to modeling, feature engineering, and exploration. See also data modeler.

data application

A software application whose purpose is to deal with large amounts of domain specific data. For example, Microsoft Excel is a data application meant to deal with spreadsheet or financially oriented data. See also data products.

data engineer

Data scientists whose primary focus involves the technical aspects of data, usually related to software development, database tools, and computing infrastructure.

data flow

In a data flow, a unit of data or event (e.g., a single log statement) travels from a source to the next destination via a sequence of hops.

data lakes

A storage system designed to hold vast amounts of *raw* data in its native (ingested) format, usually in a flat or semi-structured format. Extract, transform, and load (ETL) operations are usually applied to data lakes to extract local data marts for downstream computation.

data local computation

A distributed computation concept meant to reduce the amount of network traffic required. Nodes compute upon the data that they store locally, rather than attempt to fetch data from elsewhere in the cluster.

data mining

The process of analyzing data from different sources in order to generate new information or derive deeper insights.

data modeler

Data scientists whose primary focus is the exploration and explanation of data according to statistical and machine learning models.

data parallel

A method of computing across multiple processors wherein data is distributed across different nodes that apply the same or similar computations to it simultaneously.

data products

Self-adapting, broadly applicable economic engines that derive their value from data and generate more data by influencing human behavior or by making inferences or predictions upon new data.

data science

The workflows and processes involved in the creation and development of data products.

data science pipeline

A pedagogical model that describes the analytical process of data science. The pipeline prescribes a linear process wherein data is ingested, wrangled, computed, modeled, and finally visualized.

data scientist

A programmer with a strong statistical background, an analyst with a strong programming background, a designer with a strong understanding of how data affects visualization, or a domain expert with innovative ideas about building data products. In all cases, data scientists are jack-of-all trades generalists with the ability to easily learn new methodologies to handle data.

data warehouse

A large data store, usually in a relational format, that contains data from multiple dimensions or facets of an organization. Data warehouses are typically organized with "star schema" in order to efficiently trade-off transactional costs as well as online asynchronous processing. See also enterprise data warehouse (EDW).

database

Simply, a collection of data stored in an electronic format. However, this is usually shorthand for "database management system," a software application that organizes, manages, and provides access to data stored on disk.

DataFrame

A data structure referring to tabular data structured in rows (cases or instances) and columns (features or measurements). DataFrames were popularized in the R programming language, and have been implemented in Python via the Pandas library and in SparkSQL (now Spark DataFrames).

DataNode

In HDFS, the service that runs on every storage node in the cluster providing data replication. The DataNode connects to the NameNode to give information about the status of the distributed storage and responds to client requests for filesystem operations.

decision space

In machine learning, a region of the space defined by dimensions given as instance features to which decision making is local. The larger the decision space, the more generalizable the model. See also feature space.

declarative language

In programming, a non-imperative language where programmers describe the desired results without explicitly listing the steps that should be taken to get from input to output. SQL is a declarative language, Python is not.

denormalized

The process of describing data that has been normalized into multiple tables by separation of concerns into a single table, usually by using a JOIN function. Denormalized data centralizes single, complete records at the cost of redundancy in the data.

deserialization

The process of loading or transforming a string or byte representation of data, usually software objects, back to an operational representation that can be used by the program.

distributed cache

A MapReduce utility similar to Spark's broadcast variable, wherein files that are required by all nodes for computation (e.g. stopwords lists, lookup tables, etc.) are copied from HDFS to every worker node before any tasks are executed.

distributed computing

A software or computing system where processing components are located on multiple computers which communicate over a network and coordinate the computation by message passing. Distributed computing gives a performance advantage by allowing many computers to work in parallel to complete work, but often requires algorithms structured specifically for distribution due to the coordination requirements.

distributed storage

Data is stored on multiple disks that are mounted on multiple hosts. In order to access the data, network traffic is required to locate and fetch the requested data. Distributed storage ensures that data local computation can take place, because the data is already located where the processing will occur. Additionally, most distributed storage systems also replicate the data, where multiple hosts store redundant copies of the data, to prevent data loss.

domain expert

A member of a data team that has deep knowledge about the field or domain being modeled. Domain experts are required for the feature engineering process in order to provide human intuition about what is predictive or what systems might be in place that guide how models operate. Domain experts usually also serve as customers to agile development, providing guidance about the engineering and analytical processes.

enterprise data warehouse (EDW)

A central data repository used to support enterprise-wide data reporting and analysis, and considered a core component of most business intelligence environments.

executable

A program that can be executed on a computer. Hadoop Streaming can use an executable program that can be located via the $PATH variable as either a mapper or a reducer. For example, Python executables (Python scripts that have execution permissions and a shebang specifying the interpreter) can be used for programming MapReduce

execution plan

A graph or tree describing the order and data flow of executable processes or functions. Spark applications define an execution plan through a series of transformations and a final applied action. SQL and HiveQL are declarative languages that must be translated to an execution plan by the underlying system.

executor

In Spark, an executor is a process that runs on every worker node and manages tasks and data services on behalf of both the cluster manager (the Spark ApplicationMaster on YARN) and by the SparkContext in the driver program.

fault tolerance

If a component fails, it should not result in the failure of the entire system. The system should gracefully degrade into a lower performing state. If a failed component recovers, it should be able to rejoin the system.

feature space

In machine learning, the space defined by the properties or attributes of instances, also called features. Feature space also includes mappings to higher dimensions where functions are applied to features to create new values. For example, given a general linear model with 6 dependent variables, there are 6 dimensions in feature space to fit the hyperplane. However, the feature space would have 12 dimen-

sions for a polynomial regression of degree 2 because the square mapping would be applied to the original 6 dependent variables. See also decision space.

filtering

In functional programming, a filter is a function that accepts another function and a collection and returns a new collection containing only the elements when mapped to the filtering function returned True. Said another way, the filtering function is a test to determine if an element should belong to a new, smaller collection or not.

first normal form

A property of a relation (table) in a normalized database such that each column contains only atomic values and that for each row, the column contains only a single value. E.g. in this normal form, an attribute cannot be a list.

fitted model

The result of fitting a hyperparamaterized model form to data, usually through an optimization function, such that the model parameters are able to make predictions based on new data. The fitted model is the product of training in machine learning.

functional programming

A style of programming where computation is treated as the evaluation of functions that avoid changing state or mutating data. For this reason, functional programming is ideal for distributed computing since fixed state and functional processes are required to ensure consistent coordination.

generalizable

In machine learning, a model is said to be generalizable if it can do a good job of making predictions based on unseen input data. If a model is underfit, then the model cannot generalize to a larger decision space. If it is overfit and has simply memorized the data, even in a local decision space it will be incorrect on unseen data.

generative model

Models that use joint probability distributions as opposed to conditional probability distributions (discriminative model) to determine how data was generated. For classifiers generative models answer the question of what class was most likely to generate the signal.

global interpreter lock (GIL)

A mechanism used in interpreted languages to synchronize the execution of threads such that only one executes at a time in order to protect memory that is not thread-safe. The GIL is a structural part of Python that gives Python no native concurrency; instead to achieve parallelism in Python, one must use multiple processes, each with their own GIL.

Google's BigTable architecture

Bigtable is a distributed storage system for managing structured data that is designed to scale to a very large size. It was discussed at length in Google's 2006 paper, "Bigtable: A Distributed Storage System for Structured Data" by Chang et al.

graph analysis

Analytics that assess a data structured as related vertices connected by edges. Both vertices and edges can contain data, and data sets structured in this form as opposed to a matrix form can be computed upon by traversal. Traversals are inherently parallelizable, and as such graph algorithms can be immediately applied in a big data context. Libraries like Spark GraphX provide graph analysis tools.

Hadoop Pipes

An internal MapReduce system that allows C++ code to access HDFS and to execute mappers and reducers. The Pipes approach is similar to the Streaming approach, splitting the Pipes code into a separate, application specific library.

However, unlike Streaming, Pipes allows typed byte serialization and a fuller API.

Hadoop Streaming

A utility to the MapReduce application that allows any executable to be used as a mapper or reducer. Hadoop Streaming is itself a MapReduce application that streams data to the executable via standard input, it then collects information from the executable via standard output and standard error. Hadoop Streaming allows Python and R developers the ability to write MapReduce code.

hashable

In Python, an object is hashable if it has a hash value which never changes during it's lifetime. Hashable objects are therefore immutable objects, or instances of classes that are hashed by their memory address. Anything that can be used as a key in a dictionary is hashable (e.g. not lists or other dictionaries).

HDFS

One of the two primary components of Hadoop: the Hadoop Distributed File System. HDFS provides distributed storage via the implementation of three types of services on a cluster: a NameNode, a Secondary NameNode, and DataNodes.

high-cardinality

Refers to columns or attributes of data whose values are very uncommon or unique (one value per record). Columns with high-cardinality are difficult to analyze or aggregate, and often automatic data type detection does not work on them.

Hive

A system that provides a SQL-like interface to data stored in HDFS. Hive allows data scientists the ability to treat Hadoop as a distributed data warehouse and perform OLAP operations in parallel in a structured fashion.

Hive CLI

The Hive Command-Line Interface, which comes packaged with Hue and provides an interactive shell for working with Hive and running HiveQL statements.

Hive metastore

A database that is used by Hive to store meta information about Hive tables and partitions on HDFS.

HiveQL

Hive Query Language, the Hive Data Definition Language (DDL) that is a subset of ANSI SQL.

hypothesis-driven development

An agile data product development methodology that replaces requirements with hypotheses and attempts to align the iterative agile development process with an iterative scientific method model of experiment, observe, and reformulate.

identity function

A function that always returns the same value that was used as its argument. In mathematics this appears as $f(x) = x$.

immutable

Unchanging over time or unable to be changed. In Python, immutable objects can not be modified during the runtime, such as tuples, strings, integers, or booleans. Immutable objects provide a number of beneficial properties such as safety (no accidental mutation as the object is passed to functions), compactness (requires less memory), and comparability via hashes.

indexing

A computation wherein a summary data structure is derived from a longer form of data such that individual records can quickly be looked up. Indices are used as a preprocessing step to speed up downstream computations.

ingestion

Data ingestion refers to the manual or automatic processes by which data is collected from an external source and managed in a local computing environment. In a Big Data context, ingestion typically means handling input streams of data in parallel so that data arrives in a timely fashion.

input/output

In programming, the input is data provided to a process or function to be computed upon, the results of which are presented as output. Typically input/output (I/O) in this form refers to the process of gathering data from disk, sending it to the processor, then writing the results back to disk.

interactive analyses

A technique wherein the computational power of computers to handle many repetitive tasks on vast amounts of data is combined with human cognitive perception that is able to identify patterns and generalities on a more global level. Interactive analysis can come in the form of steering automatic model generation, or through the use of visualization to tune how models behave.

inverted index

A specialized index that maps content such as word, numbers, users, or important information to their locations in a database, in a file, or in a document or set of documents.

iterative computing

Repetitive computing where a single block of computation is defined as an iteration, and each iteration is repeated such that the output of the previous iteration is used as the input to the next. Iteration and recursion are the basic building blocks of computer algorithms.

iterative data processing

A form of iterative computing where an algorithm makes multiple passes over the same data, passing the results of each iteration to the next iteration, but not changing the data. Optimization is an example of iterative data processing, where a single pass over the data is used to compute error, the parameters are modified for the next iteration to reduce error, and the algorithm continues iterating until the error falls below some small threshold.

Java Database Connectivity (JDBC)

The Java-based interface that allows clients to access JDBC-supported databases by using a compatible adapter. Sqoop uses JDBC connectors to integrate with third-party databases.

job

In distributed computing, a job refers to the complete computation, and is made up of many individual tasks which can be run in parallel.

job chaining

A technique used in MapReduce applications to build more complex algorithms by chaining together one or more MapReduce jobs by applying the output(s) from the previous jobs as the input to the next.

job client

The client is the issuer of the job, the party most concerned with the results. The client can either be connected for the duration of the job, or the job can be run on the cluster independently and the client can return to find the results at a later time.

job configuration

The parameters of the job that are used to define the scope, such as the number of mappers, reducers, or executors that should be used.

Jupyter Notebook

Formerly an iPython notebook, notebooks are documents that combine executable code and rich text. The are intended as a presentation format to demonstrate an analysis as well as their results. As such, they are widely used in analytics to show reproducible results.

Kerberos

A secure method for authenticating a request for a service. Kerberos can be used for the HDFS and YARN APIs as well as to secure the cluster.

key/value

A linked data item where the key is a unique identifier associated with a data value. Key/value pairs are used to distributed relations (defined by the keys) to multiple processors, then aggregate (reduce) their results.

keyspace

The domain of keys in the key/value pairs being computed on in a system. The keyspace defines how data is partitioned to reducers, and how they are grouped and compared.

lambda architecture

A design for systems that deal with high volume data that is constantly being ingested and requires a distributed computing framework such as MapReduce or Spark Streaming to handle the data in a timely fashion. The architecture uses a message queue frontier to buffer incoming data to potentially slower processing applications, which performs preliminary computations and stores them in a speed table and final computations in a batch table. Clients query the approximate speed table for timely results, but rely on the batch table for more accurate analyses.

lambda function

In Python, the lambda keyword is used to define an anonymous function that is not bound to an identifier. See also anonymous functions and closure.

lazy execution

A strategy which delays the evaluation of an expression until it is needed to minimize computation and repetitiveness. In Spark, transformation operations applied to an RDD are lazily executed by producing a lineage graph that is only executed when an action operation is applied to the RDD.

lexical diversity

The ratio of the number of words in a natural language corpus to the vocabulary, e.g. the average number of times a word is used in a corpus. Lexical diversity is used to monitor text data for abnormal change.

lineage

In Spark, each RDD stores the mechanism from which it was built from other data sets through the application of transformations. The lineage allows RDDs to rebuild themselves locally on failure, and provide the basic mechanism for fault-tolerance in Spark.

linear job chaining

A sequence of jobs where in the output from one previous job is applied as the input to the next job. See also job chaining.

log4j

An open source Java project that allows developers to control the granularity of the output of log messages. Modifying the log4j settings in both Spark or Map-Reduce can minimize the amount of console output and allow analysts to more easily understand their results.

machine learning

Techniques for discovering patterns in data then building models that leverage those patterns to make predictions or estimates about new data.

map

A functional programming technique in which a function is applied to each individual element of a collection, generating a new collection as the output of each map. Mapping is inherently parallelizable since the application of the map function to an element does not depend on any other application of the map.

master

A node in a cluster that implements one of the master daemons (processes that are used to manage storage and computation across the cluster). The master processes include the ResourceManager, the NameNode, and the Secondary NameNode.

maximum

In descriptive statistics, the largest value in a data set.

mean

In descriptive statistics, a value that describes the central tendency of data by computing the sum of the values divided by the number of values in the data set.

median

In descriptive statistics, the middle value in a list of ordered data.

micro-framework

A term to refer to minimalistic application frameworks. In this book we have constructed a micro-framework for Map-Reduce using Python and Hadoop Streaming.

minimum

In descriptive statistics, the smallest value in a data set.

mode

In descriptive statistics, the value that occurs most often in a data set.

model family

In machine learning, a model family describes at a high level the connection between variables of interest that lead to prediction. For example a linear model describes the prediction of a continuous target value, Y, based on the linear combination of a vector of coefficients with a vector of dependent variables.

model form

A specification of a model outline before it's fitted, particularly defining the hyper-parameters, and the feature space the model will be fit to. For example, given a support vector machine model family, a model form might be an SVM with a RBF kernel function, a gamma of 0.001 and a slack variable of 1.

munging

Originally from the MIT model train club, munging refers to the art of the potentially destructive mashing together of data into a unified or normalized whole.

NameNode

The HDFS master node responsible for the central coordination of cluster DataNodes. The NameNode allocates storage resources and chunks large files into blocks to be replicated across the cluster. The NameNode also connects clients directly to the DataNodes they want to access data from.

node

A single machine participating in a cluster by implementing services, particularly daemon services like the NodeManager and the DataNode.

NodeManager

In YARN, a process or agent that runs on every single node in the cluster. The NodeManager is responsible for tracking and monitoring the CPU and memory of individual executors (containers) as well as the node's health and reporting back to the ResourceManager. The NodeManager also executes framework jobs on behalf of the ApplicationMaster by scheduling executors (containers) to do work locally.

NoSQL

"Not only SQL" or "Not relational", a term originating from a hashtag used at a meetup that discussed database technologies such as Cassandra, HBase, and MongoDB. NoSQL now refers to a class of database that doesn't fit the more traditional definition of a relational database management system and usually exposes a domain specific data model (like graphs or columns) along with some distributed functionality.

operating system for big data

Hadoop has become the operating system for big data by becoming a platform for cluster computing through it's two pillar services: distributed data storage with HDFS and cluster computing resource management via YARN.

operational phase

In machine learning, the operational phase follows the build phase, when a fitted model is used to perform predictions (make continuous value estimates for a regression, assign a category for a classifier, or determine membership for clustering).

operationalization

Using a fitted model in a data product. See "operational phase".

pairs and stripes

Two approaches to performing distributed computations on a matrix (for example a word co-occurrence matrix). In the pairs approach, each cell for row i and column j in the matrix is mapped individually as in (i,j)/value. In the stripes approach, each row i is mapped as a complete value, usually as an associative array of the j columns.

Pandas

An open source library that provides an easy-to-use data structures such as Series and DataFrames upon which a number of data analysis tools can be applied.

parallel

Two computations running concurrently are said to run in parallel.

parallelizable

An algorithm is said to be parallelizable if it can be broken into discrete tasks that can be run concurrently. Parallelizable algorithms have the property that the more tasks that can be run in parallel, the faster the algorithm will complete.

parallelization

The conversion of an algorithm to a parallelizable form.

peer-to-peer cluster

As opposed to a centrally managed cluster, a peer-to-peer cluster is fully decentralized with no one source of control. Algorithms that enforce peer-to-peer coordination can not rely on a central authority. Whereas Hadoop and Spark are centrally managed clusters, applications like Bitcoin are fully decentralized and are referred to as peer-to-peer distributed computing.

Pig

Pig is a framework for big data that is composed of Pig Latin, a high level language for expressing data analysis programs, and a compiler that translates Pig Latin into a sequence of MapReduce jobs that can be executed on Hadoop.

Posix

The "Portable Operating System Interface" is a family of standards created by the IEEE Computer Society to improve compatibility between operating systems.

predictive model

A statistical tool that uses inferential techniques to describe behaviors that may happen in the future.

procedural language

As opposed to declarative languages, procedural languages define an ordered set of commands that must be executed one after the other. Python can be written in a procedural style, as well as in a functional or object-oriented style.

process

A process is an instance of a computer program that is being executed and includes a complete computing environment and resources. Processes can be made up of multiple threads of execution that run concurrently, but generally speaking when we discuss a process in a distributed context, we mean one independent program that must communicate with other programs over a network.

product impressions

An online marketing term referring to a single user having the opportunity to view a particular product, usually one associated with a hyperlink. Data ingestion techniques allow us to monitor the success of such impressions by comparing the web logs generating impressions and their associated clickthrough rate.

projection

A projection is an operation on a relation (a table) that is defined by a set of attributes. The projection outputs a new relation discarding or excluding an attributes from the original relation that were not in the projection. Said another way, a projection removes columns in a table.

PySpark

The interactive Python Spark shell, which is implemented as a command-line REPL (read, evaluate, print loop) and started by the pyspark command.

Python Spark application

An application written in the Python programming language and using the Python Spark API run on Spark using spark-submit.

random access

Refers to the ability to access a specific item of data at any given memory address within a population of addressable elements. This is in contrast to sequential access, which reads data elements in the order it is in on disk.

recommendation systems

An information system whose goal is to predict the rating or preference of a user to some item. Recommendation systems are typically implemented as collaborative filtering algorithms, where the entire space of items is filtered based on similar user preferences. Machine learning techniques such as non-negative matrix factorization and regression models are then used to make predictions about the ratings.

recoverability

A property of a distributed system such that in the event of failure, no data should be lost.

relation

A relation is a set of tuples where each element of the tuple is a member of a data domain (or data type). Usually in a database system we refer to a relation as a table of rows who have typed columns.

relational database management system (RDBMS)

A database system that organizes data according to relational modeling principles of databases, tables, columns, and relations. Query operations in RDBMSs typically utilize some variant of the SQL query language.

reservoir sampling

A family of randomized algorithms for randomly choosing k samples from a list of n items, where n is either a very large or unknown number.

resilient distributed datasets (RDD)

The basic abstraction in Spark which represents an immutable, partitioned collection of elements that can be operated on in parallel.

ResourceManager

In YARN, a master process that schedules computing work on the cluster by allocating resources, free NodeManager executer instances, to ApplicationMasters on demand. The ResourceManager attempts to optimize cluster utilization (keeping as many nodes as busy as possible) with capacity guarantees, fairness, or service-level agreements based on preconfigured policies.

ridge regression

A regularized model form in the linear regression model family that penalizes model complexity (and thus reduces the bias of the model) by regularizing the error minimization function with the L2 norm of the coefficients. The use of the L2 norm causes the weights to be smoothed together, reducing the effects of variance due to multicollinearity.

row key

In HBase, rows are accessed and sorted by their unique row key. The row key itself is just a byte array, but good row key design is the most important consideration in designing robust data access patterns for an HBase database.

scalability

The property of a distributed system such that adding load (more data, more computation) leads to decline of performance, not failure; increasing resources should result in a proportional increase in capacity.

Secondary NameNode

The secondary name-node performs periodic checkpoints of HDFS by copying the edit logs of the primary name-node image at regular intervals. It is not a replacement or backup for the primary name-node, but enables faster recovery on restart.

self-adapting

A property of some machine learning models that can be incrementally updated with new information. Data products themselves should be self-adapting, but without the incremental updates, complete retraining of the model is required.

separable

A property of data such that in feature space classes can be divided or separated using hyperplanes, with some slack. Separability means that models like support vector machines and random forests will be unreasonably effective.

serialization

In the context of data storage, serialization is the process of translating data structures or object state into a format that can be stored (for example, in a file or memory buffer, or transmitted across a network connection link) and reconstructed later in the same or another computer environment.

shebang

The character sequence consisting of the characters number sign and exclamation mark #! at the beginning of a script.

single node setup

In Hadoop, a single node setup installs all processes (including YARN, HDFS, Job History Server, etc) on a single machine. Also referred to as a pseudo-distributed setup.

sink

A recipient or target of incoming data in a data flow.

source

A database, data storage device, or process that emits outgoing data that feeds into a data flow for further processing or transfer to a data sink.

spam

Unsolicited and undesired messages or email.

Spark Core

The components, services, and APIs that comprise the fundamental Spark programming internals and abstractions, including the RDD APIs.

Spark Python API

The application programming interface that Spark exposes in Python to create Spark applications. In particular, it provides access to the PythonRDD and the many library tools and code inside of Spark.

sparse

Describes data that in which a relatively high percentage values or cells do not contain actual data or are "null".

speculative execution

A technique for minimizing the effect of latency or failed jobs, wherein if a slow task is detected, a new task is immediately allocated upon the same data; whichever task completes first is the winner.

splitting

The process of dividing a data set into multiple subsets based on some criteria.

staging

The process of transferring data to an intermediary data target or checkpoint for further processing.

standalone mode

In Spark, this mode can be used to run Spark on the local machine within a single process.

streaming data

Uninterrupted or unbounded flow of data that is transferred and processed as a steady and continuous sequence.

stripes and pairs

See "pairs and stripes".

subject matter expert

A critical part of data teams, subject matter experts are data scientists who contribute domain-specific knowledge to data problems and models. See also domain expert.

supervised

As opposed to unsupervised, supervised machine learning fits models to data sets where the correct answers are known in advance. Classification and regression are two examples of supervised machine learning.

task

A unit of work within a single YARN job. In MapReduce, a task refers to a single execution of a map or reduce operation.

task parallelism

A form of parallelization wherein the simultaneous execution of multiple functions on the same or different data sets leads to a performance gain. This is in contrast to data parallelism where the same function is applied to different elements of a data set. Generally speaking, mapping is data parallelism and reduction is task parallelism.

three Vs of big data

The three defining properties of big data: volume, velocity, and variety. See also volume, velocity, and variety.

transformations and actions

Refers to the two primary types of Spark operations, where transformations take an RDD as input and produce a reformatted RDD as output, and actions perform computations on an RDD to produce a value back to the Spark Driver.

tuple

A finite and immutable set of ordered elements.

unsupervised

As opposed to supervised, unsupervised machine learning fits models based on patterns via similarity or distance between instances. These model families are said to be unsupervised because there is no "correct" answer with which to judge the results of the fitted model or to minimize error with. Clustering is an example of unsupervised learning.

variance

In machine learning, variance refers to the variability of a model's prediction given a specific data point (e.g., a low variance might indicate a confidence in the amount of error for the prediction). As variance decreases, bias increases. See also bias.

variety

The growing range of structured (CSV, Excel, database, etc) and unstructured formats (images, sensor data, video, etc) of data.

velocity

The speed or rate at which data must be processed.

vocabulary

The set of unique tokens (or words) in a text corpus.

volume

The amount of data to be processed and stored.

worker

A node that implements worker daemons, usually both the NodeManager and the DataNode services.

workflow management

The process of building repeatable data processing jobs that can be triggered, parameterized, scheduled and automated.

wrangling

The process of converting or mapping data from one format (typically a "raw" unprocessed format) into another format that can be easily consumed by downstream processes for analysis.

YARN

An acronym for "Yet Another Resource Negotiator", and a generalized cluster management framework for distributed computation engines including MapReduce and Spark. Handles resource management and job scheduling for jobs submitted to a cluster.

Index

Flume agent, 166-169
FOREACH…GENERATE operation, 179

G

generalized linear models (GLM), 123
get command, 25
getmerge command, 25
global interpreter lock, 194
GlusterFS, 217
GraphX, 71
grouping, Pig, 180

H

Hadoop ecosystem, 11
    basic installation/configuration steps, 238
    Hadoop Streaming and, 42
    HBase-specific configurations, 242-244
    Hive-specific configurations, 240-242
    packaged distributions, 237
    product installation, 237-246
    self-installation of products, 237-246
    Spark installation, 244-246
    Sqoop-specific configurations, 240
hadoop jar command, 39
Hadoop Pipes, 41
Hadoop Streaming, 41-66
    about, 42-45
    advanced MapReduce topics, 60-65
    computing on CSV data with, 45-50
    counting bigrams with, 57-60
    executing jobs with, 50-52
    framework for MapReduce with Python, 52-60
    word counts with, 55-60
Hadoop, evolution of, vii
hashable types, 93
HBase, 144-156
    configurations specific to, 242-244
    data insertion with put, 150
    filters, 154
    for computational data stores, 221
    get command, 151
    importing data from MySQL, 163
    namespaces, tables, and column families, 149
    NoSQL and column-oriented databases, 145-148
    realtime analytics with, 148-155
    row keys, 150

scan operation, 153
schema generation, 149
starting, 243
HDFS (Hadoop Distributed File System)
    about, 20
    and NameNode formatting, 234
    basic operations, 23-25
    basics, 15-16
    blocks, 20
    data management, 21
    file permissions in, 25
    for data lakes, 217
    Hive warehouse directory configuration, 240
    implementation, 17
    importing data from MySQL, 159-161
    master and worker services, 17
    site configuration editing, 233
    various interfaces, 26
Hive
    aggregations and joins, 141-144
    and HQL, 134-139
    CLI, 133
    configurations specific to, 240-242
    data analysis with, 139-144
    database creation, 134
    for computational data stores, 220
    grouping, 139
    importing data from MySQL, 161
    loading data into, 137
    metastore database configuration, 241
    structured data queries with, 132-144
    table creation, 134-137
    verifying configuration, 241
    warehouse directory configuration, 240
HiveQL (HQL), 132, 134-139
Hortonworks, 227

I

identity function, 100
indexing, 110-117
    inverted index, 110
    TF-IDF, 112-117
ingestion stage (see data ingestion)
INPATH command, 138
input, 105
inverted index, 110
IPv6, disabling, 230
Isilon OneFS, 217

About the Authors

Benjamin Bengfort is a data scientist who lives inside the Beltway but ignores politics (the normal business of DC), favoring technology instead. He is currently working to finish his PhD at the University of Maryland where he studies machine learning and distributed computing. His lab does have robots (though this field of study is not one he favors) and much to his chagrin, they seem to constantly arm said robots with knives and tools—presumably to pursue culinary accolades. Having seen a robot attempt to slice a tomato, Benjamin prefers his own adventures in the kitchen where he specializes in fusion French and Guyanese cuisine as well as BBQ of all types. A professional programmer by trade and a data scientist by vocation, Benjamin's writing pursues a diverse range of subjects from natural language processing, to data science with Python to analytics with Hadoop and Spark.

Jenny Kim is an experienced big data engineer who works in both commercial software efforts as well as in academia. She has significant experience working with large scale data, machine learning, and Hadoop implementations in production and research environments. Jenny (with Benjamin Bengfort) previously built a large scale recommender system that used a web crawler to gather ontological information about apparel products and produce recommendations from transactions. Currently, she is working with the Hue team at Cloudera to help build intuitive interfaces for analyzing big data with Hadoop.

Colophon

The animal on the cover of *Data Analytics with Hadoop* is a cattle egret (*Bubulcus ibis*), a cosmopolitan species of heron. Originally native to parts of Asia, Africa, and Europe, it has colonized much of the rest of the world in the last century—undergoing one of the most rapid and wide-reaching natural expansions of any bird species. It is mostly found in the tropics, subtropics, and warm temperate zones. They often follow cattle or other large mammals around, feeding on insects or small vertebrate prey that the large animals stir up, hence its name.

The cattle egret is a white bird with orange-buff plumes on the back, breast, and crown in breeding season. Its bill, legs, and irises briefly turn bright red during breeding season, right before pairing with a mate. Nonbreeding adults have mainly white plumage, yellow bills, and grey-yellow legs. It's a stocky bird with a 35–38 inch wingspan; it measures up to 18–22 inches long and weighs around 10–18 ounces. It nests in colonies on a platform of sticks in trees and shrubs often near bodies of water.

Because of its relationship to cattle, this egret is a popular bird with cattle ranchers and is perceived as a biocontrol of cattle parasites. On the other hand, cattle egrets can present a safety hazard to aircraft when they feed in large groups in the grassy verges of airports. It's also been implicated in the spread of animal infections such as heartwater, infectious bursal disease, and possibly Newcastle disease.

Many of the animals on O'Reilly covers are endangered; all of them are important to the world. To learn more about how you can help, go to *animals.oreilly.com*.

The cover image is from *Lydekker's Royal Natural History*. The cover fonts are URW Typewriter and Guardian Sans. The text font is Adobe Minion Pro; the heading font is Adobe Myriad Condensed; and the code font is Dalton Maag's Ubuntu Mono.

Get even more for your money.

Join the O'Reilly Community, and register the O'Reilly books you own. It's free, and you'll get:

- $4.99 ebook upgrade offer
- 40% upgrade offer on O'Reilly print books
- Membership discounts on books and events
- Free lifetime updates to ebooks and videos
- Multiple ebook formats, DRM FREE
- Participation in the O'Reilly community
- Newsletters
- Account management
- 100% Satisfaction Guarantee

Signing up is easy:

1. Go to: oreilly.com/go/register
2. Create an O'Reilly login.
3. Provide your address.
4. Register your books.

Note: English-language books only

To order books online:
oreilly.com/store

For questions about products or an order:
orders@oreilly.com

To sign up to get topic-specific email announcements and/or news about upcoming books, conferences, special offers, and new technologies:
elists@oreilly.com

For technical questions about book content:
booktech@oreilly.com

To submit new book proposals to our editors:
proposals@oreilly.com

O'Reilly books are available in multiple DRM-free ebook formats. For more information:
oreilly.com/ebooks

CPSIA information can be obtained at www.ICGtesting.com
Printed in the USA
BVOW04s0522250816

460029BV00009B/32/P